PRAISE FOR
CON JOB

"If you believe that 'Black Lives Matter,' why do you keep voting for Democrats? The bold and brave Crystal Wright destroys the stubborn mythology that the Left has the best interests of black families, black business owners, and black voters at heart. This is an especially searing indictment of how race-hustling, abortion profiteers, and liberal crime policies endanger black America—and all of America."

> —Michelle Malkin, author of *Culture of Corruption: Obama and His Team of Tax Cheats, Crooks, and Cronies* and *Invasion: How America Still Welcomes Terrorists, Criminals, and Other Foreign Menaces to Our Shores*

"In 1965 Democrat President Lyndon B. Johnson embarked America upon a grand endeavor called 'The Great Society'; at its core was the infamous War on Poverty. Today, right at fifty years later, we have more Americans in poverty, more Americans on food stamps, decimated inner cities, an out-of-wedlock birthrate in the black community that is disconcerting, and a black abortion rate that is genocidal. And that is why conservative commentator Crystal Wright's *Con Job: How Democrats Gave Us Crime, Sanctuary Cities, Abortion Profiteering, and Racial Division* sounds an important clarion call for our nation. Having grown up in inner-city Atlanta, Georgia, I can attest that today's Democrat Party, dominated by progressive socialist ideology, is not the same party my parents supported. Crystal's book is a must-read in this coming election cycle, if we are to reject the con job."

> —Lieutenant Colonel Allen B. West (U.S. Army, ret.), president and CEO of the National Center for Policy Analysis and member, 112th U.S. Congress

"The first time I booked Crystal on my program I knew I had put someone on the air who was intellectual and fearless. She lays waste to myths, nonsense, and phony PC narratives with clarity and conviction. With *Con Job: How Democrats Gave Us Crime, Sanctuary Cities, Abortion Profiteering, and Racial Division*, Crystal will continue to dismantle the stranglehold the progressive Left has over the majority of the black vote. That is not to say that this book is only for a black audience, because it's not. Just as Crystal's contributions to political discourse have been worthy of consideration by all, so too will be the content of *Con Job*."

—Andrew Wilkow, host of *The Wilkow Majority* on SiriusXM Patriot

"In *Con Job*, Crystal Wright brilliantly exposes the failures of liberal ideology and explodes the lies being used to keep voters uninformed, unemployed, and unenthusiastic about America's future and its potential for greatness. Crystal Wright is one of the greatest voices for freedom in America today. As a black woman who studies the facts and comes to her own conclusions, she is a threat to the heart of liberalism itself. In the battle of ideas, she is a combat-tested gladiator who takes slings and arrows 24/7 and never retreats from the fight. If liberty is important to you, buy this book! In fact, buy two and give the other copy to someone who needs to hear Crystal's message: America's best days are in front of it, as long as it puts liberalism behind it."

—Brad Thor, *New York Times* bestselling author of *Code of Conduct, Hidden Order,* and *Act of War*

Con Job

CON JOB

HOW DEMOCRATS GAVE US CRIME, SANCTUARY CITIES, ABORTION PROFITEERING, AND RACIAL DIVISION

CRYSTAL WRIGHT

CONSERVATIVEBLACKCHICK.COM

REGNERY
PUBLISHING
A Division of Salem Media Group

Regnery® is a registered trademark of Salem Communications Holding Corporation

Library of Congress Cataloging-in-Publication Data

Names: Wright, Crystal, author.
Title: Con job : how Democrats gave us crime, sanctuary cities, abortion profiteering, and racial division / Crystal Wright.
Description: Washington, DC : Regnery Publishing, 2016.
Identifiers: LCCN 2015044490 (print) | LCCN 2015046495 (ebook) | ISBN 9781621574293 (hardback) | ISBN 9781621574392 (ebook)
Subjects: LCSH: Democratic Party (U.S.) | African Americans--Politics and government--20th century. | African Americans--Politics and government--21st century. | Party affiliation--United States. | United States--Race relations--Political aspects. | United States--Politics and government--20th century. | United States--Politics and government--21st century. | BISAC: POLITICAL SCIENCE / Political Ideologies / Conservatism & Liberalism.
Classification: LCC JK2316 .W75 2016 (print) | LCC JK2316 (ebook) | DDC 324.2736--dc23
LC record available at http://lccn.loc.gov/2015044490

Published in the United States by
Regnery Publishing
A Division of Salem Media Group
300 New Jersey Ave NW
Washington, DC 20001
www.Regnery.com

Manufactured in the United States of America

10 9 8 7 6 5 4 3 2 1

Books are available in quantity for promotional or premium use. For information on discounts and terms, please visit our website: www. Regnery.com.

Distributed to the trade by
Perseus Distribution
250 West 57th Street
New York, NY 10107

To my mother,
Barbara Baker Wright,
for her courage

CONTENTS

INTRODUCTION

What if I told you to vote for a political party that supports crime, infanticide, racism, and lawlessness? If I asked you to join this party or vote for its candidates, you—like most rational people—would tell me, "Go to hell." You would guess I was talking about the Nazi Party. But the political party I've just described is today's Democrat Party.

The Democrats have become the party of moral turpitude. And yet this destructive party, which feeds off of and exacerbates the very worst things in America, still has broad appeal.

Seriously, think about it for a minute. Twenty-first-century Democrats and the interest groups they're in bed with gain political power and profit from aiding, abetting, and promoting crime, abortion, and racial hatred—among other deviant behaviors.

Yes, *deviant*. That's what old-style liberal Senator Daniel Patrick Moynihan—a prominent Democrat from the era back before his party ran completely off the rails—called the kind of behavior that today's

Democrats are gleefully enabling for their own political profit. I had
the good fortune to meet and interview Moynihan back in the 1990s
when I first moved to Washington and was working as a very green
off-air reporter for ABC News. I was smitten with his no-nonsense,
commonsense approach.

The senator was one of the breed of old-style liberals who actually
endeavored to improve the lives of their less fortunate constituents—
instead of encouraging widespread dysfunction and then callously
exploiting it for electoral gain.

In a 1993 article, "Defining Deviancy Down," published in the
American Scholar, Moynihan revealed the dynamic that explains the
modern Democrat Party's wrecking ball agenda:

> A growth in deviancy makes possible a transfer of resources,
> including prestige, to those who control the deviant popula-
> tion. This control would be jeopardized if any serious effort
> were made to reduce the deviancy in question. This leads to
> assorted strategies for re-defining the behavior in question as
> not all that deviant, really....
>
> ... What is going on here is simply that a large increase
> in what once was seen as deviancy has provided opportunity
> to a wide spectrum of interest groups that benefit from re-
> defining the problem as essentially normal and doing little to
> reduce it.[1]

No wonder the Democrats today rush to defend criminals, illegal
aliens, race hustlers, and even abortion clinic executives caught on
video joking about selling baby parts so they can afford luxury cars.
The "wide spectrum of interest groups" that benefit from redefining
formally abnormal behavior as normal is a laundry list of Democrat
campaign donors and activists, starting with Planned Parenthood, Al
Sharpton's National Action Network, the National Council of La Raza,

the American Federation of Teachers, the National Association for the Advancement of Colored People (NAACP), the Urban League, GLAAD, and a host of others who have done nothing to fix the problems they exist to combat but have amassed a lot of power and money perpetuating them.

Over the past three years, every Democrat from President Barack Obama on down to Baltimore mayor Stephanie Rawlings-Blake has stood up for thugs and told police officers to stand down to criminals. When black Baltimoreans were pillaging and looting in the spring of 2015 after the death of Freddie Gray, a black drug dealer and addict who died in police custody, Blake said, "It's a very delicate balancing act, because while we tried to make sure that they were protected from the cars and the other things that were going on, we also gave to those who wished to destroy space to do that as well."[2]

It's no wonder crime is up.

Fifty-five homicides took place in Baltimore in the six weeks beginning May 1, 2015 (the week after the mayor's remarks giving cart blanche to the rioters)—"the highest pace since the early 1970s."[3]

Meanwhile, from the White House to the streets of San Francisco, Philadelphia, and New York City, these same Democrats have given refuge to millions of illegal immigrants in "sanctuary cities"—where they kill Americans.

While Democrats may tell blacks that #BlackLivesMatter to them, the opposite is true. Proportionally more black babies are aborted than any other race.[4] Nearly 80 percent of Planned Parenthood abortion clinics are located near minority neighborhoods.[5]

Time and time again, Democrats have come to the defense of the abortion industry, fighting for even the most gruesome late-term abortions. Texas state senator Wendy Davis literally became an overnight sensation in the Democrat Party in 2013 when she filibustered a bill updating regulations on abortion clinics and banning abortion after twenty weeks—though babies born at only twenty-two weeks can live outside the womb.

Democrats were so proud of Davis's fight for a woman's right to kill her baby that they nominated her to run for governor of Texas in 2014. A race she lost.[6]

Not to be outdone by little Wendy, new grandmother and heir apparent to the Democrat throne Hillary Clinton stood by Planned Parenthood when it was exposed harvesting aborted fetal organs and selling them to medical research firms for profit. While Clinton admitted that the practice was "disturbing," she vowed to "defend Planned Parenthood," which she claimed "for more than a century has done a lot of really good work for women...."[7] In the 2013–14 fiscal year, Planned Parenthood had revenue of over a billion dollars, performing more than three hundred thousand abortions.[8]

And Hillary doesn't just cheerlead for Planned Parenthood's baby chop shop. The Bill, Hillary & Chelsea Clinton Foundation gives money to groups providing abortion services and supplies. According to its 2013 annual report, the Clinton Foundation helped fund four thousand abortions.[9]

As a black woman, I'm outraged that the political party that regularly gets over 80 percent of the black vote is in the tank for the abortionists preying on vulnerable black women—and for the government programs and "alternative family" values that have destroyed the black family. In 1993 Senator Moynihan pointed out that out-of-wedlock births had soared to one in five for whites and two in three for blacks. As he had already warned in the 1960s:

> From the wild Irish slums of the 19th century Eastern seaboard to the riot-torn suburbs of Los Angeles, there is one unmistakable lesson in American history: a community that allows a large number of young men to grow up in broken families, dominated by women, never acquiring any stable relationship to male authority, never acquiring any set of rational expectations about the future—that community asks

for and gets chaos. Crime, violence, unrest, unrestrained lash-
ing out at the whole social structure—that is not only to be
expected; it is very near to inevitable.[10]

The past five decades have proved Moynihan right. Remind me,
which party insisted on redefining the single-parent family as a normal
"alternative family"? The Democrats strike again.

Voila! A black family and crime epidemic, thanks to decades of
Democrats encouraging rampant out-of-wedlock births among blacks
as normal, something they're just going to do. Today more black babies
are born out of wedlock than to married couples—over 70 percent.

This Democrat-bred pathology has led to more blacks killing each other
with guns and being killed by guns than *ANY OTHER RACE IN
AMERICA*. And yet bizarrely, exterminating blacks on the street and in the
womb and keeping them in underclass status translates into the Democrats'
owning the black vote. Black lives don't matter as much as black votes.

"The inevitable, as we now know, has come to pass, here again our
response is curiously passive," noted Moynihan.[11] Instead of actually
doing something to fix the worst problems in our society, Democrats
perpetuate them for political gain.

The Democrat Party never lets an opportunity to race bait pass it
by—because racial strife is the party's bread and butter. When a few
white men killed a handful of young "unarmed" black men over the past
three years, their deaths made headlines. The liberal news media and
every Democrat under the sun—from politicians to race hustlers like Al
Sharpton, and including most notably our first black president—fanned
the flames of racial strife, sparking widespread violence, looting, and the
wholesale destruction of black neighborhoods.

When a white person harms a black person, regardless of the
circumstances, Democrats of all complexions unleash rage, marches,
protests, and riots. You'll see none of this in cities like Chicago or Baltimore when blacks are killed daily...by each other.

The running narrative is that white police officers have declared open killing season on the black man—despite the reality that statistics and facts don't support this argument. Any white person in America who doesn't buy into this lie is called "racist."

So it's no surprise that six in ten Americans think race relations in this country are bad and getting worse, according to a July 2015 CBS News/*New York Times* poll. Some 68 percent of blacks felt race relations were bad. That was an increase from the 60 percent of blacks who thought things were bad in 2008, back before Obama was elected, when he was campaigning as the candidate whose election would bring America racial healing.[12] Why did we believe him? The Democrats have never been the party of racial harmony.

From the days of Thomas Jefferson through the Civil War and civil rights movement, racism has been the foundation upon which the Democrat Party is built. Democrats have a history of fighting for slavery, imposing segregation, and profiting off of racial division.

The Democrats pose as the champions of blacks, of women, of victims, of the underprivileged and the downtrodden and the oppressed—but it's all a con job. In reality, they profit from the misery and oppression they complain about, and it pays them—in money and votes—to keep making all the worst problems in America worse.

This book will demonstrate in alarming detail the sinister dynamic at work between the Democrat Party and its constituents. One is selling dysfunction, the other gobbling it up without pause, as their cup of salvation. In the meantime, as Moynihan put it with his characteristic understatement, Americans "are getting used to a lot of behavior that is not good for us."[13] You decide which political party is the party of evil!

CHAPTER ONE

THE PARTY OF CRIME

At about 6:30 p.m. on Friday, January 23, 2014, I was shopping in the Neiman Marcus department store in Washington, D.C. As I browsed the cosmetics, all of a sudden I heard women screaming. One female salesperson yelled, "He's hitting him! Stop him!" Startled, I looked to my left. About twenty feet away, I saw a young black man who appeared to be about eighteen years old holding a Chanel handbag with the store security chain and sensor attached and hitting a tall white male sales associate. Within seconds, two security guards and the salesperson wrestled the criminal to the floor and attempted to place him in handcuffs. He resisted, trying to play the victim, murmuring something to the security guards that prompted them to ask him if he was all right. After about two minutes, the three were able to get the young man in handcuffs.

Later, the sales associates confirmed that the black man had been trying to steal the handbag. He had committed a crime but immediately turned around and wanted to be treated like a victim. But what gave this young thug the idea that he could steal a valuable item, physically attack a store employee, and then pose as the injured party?

Short answer: the Democrats.

Democrat politicians and their allies have given criminals a license to play the victim—thus enabling more crime. Democrats all the way up to the president of the United States treat criminals with sympathy, and the police with suspicion. Remember in the first year of Barack Obama's presidency, when he saw fit to opine on the arrest of black Harvard professor Henry Louis Gates, saying that "the Cambridge police acted stupidly" and bringing up the "long history in this country of African Americans and Latinos being stopped by law enforcement disproportionately"? Remember when Democrat New York mayor Bill de Blasio explained how he warns his biracial son against the police? The myth—perpetuated by Democrats in office and their race-hustling sidekicks like de Blasio buddy Al Sharpton, and sold to the public by their willing allies in the media—is that law enforcement is waging a war on young black men in this country, resorting to unjustified "racial profiling," and putting innocent "unarmed black men" in constant jeopardy of being shot by the police.

But this is just a convenient fiction—convenient to the Democrats who want to keep the black vote they've had for fifty years on lockdown by inflaming racial grievances. The reality is that young black men are "targeted" by the police for a simple reason—because, tragically, they commit more crime than their fellow citizens.

The District of Columbia police department's Twitter feed reflects this same reality. One glance at it reveals innumerable references to B/M (black male) suspects. While the Democrats would have Americans believe blacks are being singled out by racist police, @DCPoliceDept tells a very different story. Without exception, every day the D.C. police department's Twitter feed is mostly populated with descriptions of black male suspects wanted for shootings and robberies. Here is a sample of the department's tweets:[1]

DC Police Department @DCPoliceDept · Feb 14
Robbery Gun, 2137 hrs, 1100 Chaplin St SE. LOF 2 Juvenile B/M's wearing mask last seen toward Hillside Rd. SE.//2237   *B/M = Black Male*

DC Police Department @DCPoliceDept · Feb 15
Robbery(Gun)_2000hrs_3800 blk 26th St NE. LOF: B/M, 20-25yrs, 5'8-5'9, 160-180, red jkt, blk hat, blk skullcap, blk jeans, clean shaven

DC Police Department @DCPoliceDept · Feb 15
Alert: Robbery Hold up Gun. in the 300 block of Southern Ave, SE LOF: 4 B/M, 2 suspect wearing HH jump suit. Suspect (1) is light completion

DC Police Department @DCPoliceDept · Feb 16
Robbery (Gun), 1854, 500 blk of Tennessee Ave NE. LOF: B/M, 20 yoa, 5'5, slim, blk jacket, pants, hoody, blk hand gun

DC Police Department @DCPoliceDept · Feb 16
Attempt Robbery F/V, 1354,100 blk 6th St. SE. LOF: B/M, 5'10, light skin, grn/brown strpd shirt, blk SUV occ. 3 times

DC Police Department @DCPoliceDept · Feb 16
6D stabbing_2356 hrs_700 Blk 31st St. SE. LOF B/M..30'S/armed w/knife wearing blk ski mask, dk clothing

If black males weren't the ones committing so much crime in D.C. and other cities across the nation, perhaps police officers and citizens wouldn't view them with as much suspicion. It is really that simple. The eyewitness descriptions of suspects included in the above D.C.

police department tweets indicate the suspects are black males. Why should D.C. police officers go looking for white males who don't fit the description? They shouldn't because that would be STUPID.

But Democrats approach violent crime in America by making excuses for the criminals rather than doing anything to stop them. Democrats love themselves some criminals! In Democrats' minds, the thug is always right even when he's wrong. They will do anything and everything to take the side of the thug over law enforcement or the victim.

And that includes black victims. As a matter of fact, the Democrats' loyal black voters suffer more than white Americans do from the criminals the Democrats have enabled to terrorize our nation's cities. This demonstrates that black lives really don't matter to Democrats. Blacks aren't as scared of white people harming or killing them as they are scared of other blacks. During the summer of 2013, when the trial for the shooting death of Trayvon Martin took place in Sanford, Florida, I provided commentary for HLN's *Dr. Drew on Call* and some CNN programs. One evening after my appearance on *Dr. Drew on Call*, a black security guard working in CNN's D.C. bureau walked me to my car. We chatted about the case, as we sometimes did after my appearances, and he told me, "When I get off of work and walk out here at night, who do you think I'm afraid of on the streets? It's not the white guys walking around, it's the black guys because they're the ones committing the crimes." He's right. Go to any predominantly black inner-city neighborhood in America and you will find black males not working, hanging out during the day, and committing crimes. You will also find other blacks (everybody else in the neighborhood) living in fear of them. Today, though blacks are only 13 percent of the population, they actually make up a larger percentage of federal and state prisoners (38 percent) than whites (34 percent). That's because black males are responsible for more crimes than any other racial group, and thus they are 6.4 times more likely than white men to be incarcerated. The incarceration rate for blacks hasn't improved since 1960, when blacks accounted for 37 percent of all federal and state prisoners.[2] Black men perpetrate criminal offenses including robbery, aggravated assault, and property crimes at a rate that's typically two to three times their representation in the population.[3]

THE BLACK VICTIMS OF DEMOCRAT-ENABLED CRIME

The Democrats would have you believe that white-on-black crime—and particularly shootings of "unarmed black men" by racist cops—is out of control. In fact, black crime victims are overwhelmingly suffering violence at the hands of the black criminals the Democrats are giving a pass to. As former New York City mayor Rudy Giuliani famously pointed out on *Meet the Press*, 93 percent of homicides of black victims are committed by other blacks.[4] "Murders with guns are the No. 1 cause of death for African-American men between the ages of 15 and 34," wrote journalist Juan Williams in the *Wall Street Journal*,[5] citing disturbing data from the Children's Defense Fund: "The 44,038 black children killed by guns since 1979 (when national data on the age of gun violence victims was first collected) is 'nearly 13 times more' than all the black people killed by lynching in the 86-year period of 1882 to 1968."[6] Characterizing the murder rate for black Americans as "a national crisis," the Violence Policy Center found the 2012 homicide victim rate for black males was nearly 10 times that of white males, at 32.78 for 100,000 blacks compared to 3.86 for 100,000 whites. Of the 6,565 black homicide victims that year, 87 percent were male.[7] So there actually is a disgraceful epidemic of murders of black men. But they're not being perpetrated by the police, racists, or white people in general. More than 90 percent of these homicides of black victims are committed by black criminals.

Yet in the face of these horrifying statistics, Democrats take great umbrage at police departments across America that engage in racial profiling of crime suspects. If blacks, specifically black males, are committing the bulk of crime in the country, why would police officers search for suspects who don't fit that description? As a black woman, do I enjoy being viewed with suspicion on occasion when I'm shopping in a store? No, but if a significant proportion of black people are going to behave like criminals and thugs, the police will treat us accordingly. And, as a black woman, I would definitely prefer a nasty look from a suspicious security guard to a punch in the head by a fleeing shoplifter.

Distracting attention from the real day-to-day criminal threats to black Americans' well-being—and our very lives—with hysteria about "profiling" is just part of the Democrats' con job. Black-on-black violence has persisted for decades, and for decades it has been completely ignored by the Democrats, who have claimed to be the political saviors of blacks for just as long. It's not like the Dems don't know the facts. More than fifty years ago, Daniel Patrick Moynihan, who was then assistant secretary of labor in Lyndon Johnson's administration, addressed black-on-black violence in his famous report on problems of the black community, *The Negro Family: The Case for National Action*: "The overwhelming number of offenses committed by Negroes are directed toward other Negroes: the cost of crime to the Negro is a combination of that to the criminal and the victim."[8] As was the case then, the black race today is still destroying itself with violence—having been abandoned to that fate by the Democrats, who are supposed to be our champions, but who simply take our votes and give us nothing in return but race-baiting excuses for the criminals who have turned black neighborhoods into nightmares.

I know something about this from firsthand experience. In 1970 my grandfather Arthur E. Baker was gunned down by two armed black teens in the dry cleaning business he owned, Baker's Dry Cleaners & Laundromat, in Richmond, Virginia. The young thugs walked in and demanded that my grandfather give them the money in the cash register. When he reached for the handgun he kept under the counter to defend himself, one of them shot him. On a recent trip home to visit my parents, I rummaged through a box of old papers that had belonged to my grandmother Pauline Sarah Baker and discovered a copy of my grand-father's death certificate. Neatly folded like a letter, the preserved, slightly yellowed document revealed after all the years what I had never known—the details of my grandfather's death. William Arthur E. Baker was "shot by an assailant" between 7:15 p.m. and 7:30 p.m. and died "from a gunshot wound of the chest" (homicide) on November 18, 1970. The certificate gives the time of death as 8:12 p.m. and clearly states that my grandfather was DOA, dead on arrival, when the police appeared at the scene. As I read the certificate for the first time, I wondered if he had died instantly or suffered in agony. My grandfather was sixty-three years old. Just as Moynihan had predicted in that same report on "the Negro fam-ily" five years earlier, the breakdown of the black family was leading to a rise in violent crime among black men in solidly black neighborhoods across the country.

At the time of my grandfather's death, the black middle-class neighborhood where the dry cleaner and my grandparents' home were located was changing, and my grandmother Pauline was worried some-thing bad could happen to my grandfather working late nights at the cleaners by himself. To make more money, my grandfather had installed a laundromat service. As my mother explained, his dry cleaning business was falling off a little because of the new popularity of polyester clothing, which didn't need to be dry cleaned as often as clothes made of natural fibers such as cotton or wool. To make money from the laundromat, he had to keep the cleaners open late in the evening so people could do their laundry after coming home from work. The day I found his death cer-tificate, I also came across a crumpled-up black-and-white eight-by-ten photo of my grandfather standing with his left hand resting on one of the newly installed washing machines and smiling proudly. It's one of the few photos we have of him, and when I showed it to my mother, she said, "That's my daddy," and beamed like she was a little girl again.

Ironically, the thing my grandfather did to make more money was the very thing that led to his tragic death. Those two armed black teens knew the dry cleaner would make a good target for a robbery because it was open late, my grandfather was the only person working, and there would be cash on hand.

I have only faint memories of my grandfather, like the smell of his pipe. What I know about him mostly comes from my mother telling me how wonderful he was, how he used to bring me candy and soda on his visits to our home, and how much he loved me and my little brother Trey (Thomas Wright III). His horrific murder still profoundly saddens my mother, his only daughter, who gave him three grandchildren—one, Arthur Baker Wright, his namesake whom he would never meet in this life. Those two black thugs served some time in prison and then were released. They were given their lives back after taking away my grandfather's, which is wrong.

"UNARMED BLACK TEEN" KILLED BY "WHITE HISPANIC"

When confronted with decades of homicides committed by black men, the Democrats and their allies in the news media have become apologists for the worst black people—those who are terrorizing law-abiding Americans, both black and white. When Republicans, conservatives, or simply people in law enforcement warn the public about the epidemic of black violence in America, the Democrats cry "racist!" That's exactly what happened in the case of Trayvon Martin, the "unarmed black teen" who was shot and killed by "white Hispanic" neighborhood-watch volunteer George Zimmerman on February 26, 2012. Those phrases were used to deflect attention from the criminality that the Democrats are enabling by falsely suggesting that racist "white" law-and-order types are killing off the black race. Al Sharpton descended on Sanford, Florida, where the shooting had taken place, like a fly to the flesh of a rotting animal, breeding protests and violence. So-called "civil rights leaders" went so far as to use the rare case of a "white"-on-black shooting to suggest that white racists are going on killing rampages of black men as they did in the Jim Crow South.

The Sanford, Florida, police had no intention of filing charges against George Zimmerman for shooting the seventeen-year-old Martin. The police chief found no evidence that Zimmerman shot Martin in cold blood; in fact there was evidence—including injuries to Zimmerman's face that could have resulted from Martin's repeatedly smashing Zimmerman's head into a concrete sidewalk, as Zimmerman claimed—that the neighborhood watchman had been acting in self-defense. Nevertheless, Sharpton's racist circus was successful not only in pressuring the Florida state attorney to charge Zimmerman with murder but also in getting the FBI to investigate the case. When asked about the shooting, even before any charges were brought against Zimmerman, President Obama weighed in on what then–White House press secretary Jay Carney agreed had become a "major news story." Naturally, the Democrat president chose to identify with Trayvon Martin:

Q: Mr. President, may I ask you about this current case in Florida, very controversial, allegations of lingering racism within our society—the so-called do not—I'm sorry—Stand Your Ground law and the justice in that? Can you comment on the Trayvon Martin case, sir?

The President: Well, I'm the head of the executive branch, and the Attorney General reports to me so I've got to be careful about my statements to make sure that we're not impairing any investigation that's taking place right now.

But obviously, this is a tragedy. I can only imagine what these parents are going through. And when I think about this boy, I think about my own kids. And I think every parent in America should be able to understand why it is absolutely imperative that we investigate every aspect of this, and that everybody pulls together—federal, state and local—to figure out exactly how this tragedy happened.

So I'm glad that not only is the Justice Department looking into it, I understand now that the governor of the state of Florida has formed a task force to investigate what's taking place. I think all of us have to do some soul searching to figure out how does something like this happen. And that means that we examine the laws and the context for what happened, as well as the specifics of the incident.

But my main message is to the parents of Trayvon Martin. If I had a son, he'd look like Trayvon. And I think they are right to expect that all of us as Americans are going to take this with the seriousness it deserves, and that we're going to get to the bottom of exactly what happened.[9]

Obama, as the nation's first black president, felt it was "imperative" "to investigate every aspect" of this one case. Yet when did he express any urgency about investigating the thousands of black men killing and being killed in America every year?

In the end, none of this posturing by the Democrats or their allies in the media and the "black leadership" (a.k.a. Al Sharpton and associated race-mongers) prevailed. In July 2013 the jury found Zimmerman not guilty. One juror commented that she felt the case never should have been brought to trial because there wasn't enough evidence to support the prosecution's (or the Democrats') claim that Martin was a victim. Witness after witness, including the case's lead detectives and Zimmerman's neighbors, testified that the volunteer neighborhood watchman didn't hate blacks, but wanted to do something to stop the burglaries in his neighborhood (there had been eight of them)—the reason he volunteered to be a neighborhood watchman in the first place. In response to the verdict, I wrote the following in a blog post entitled "Zimmerman, the Media and Black Leaders Pimping of Blacks": "The prosecution left unanswered too many questions on a mountain of reasonable doubt. After returning from the 7-Eleven, why didn't Martin go back to his Dad's house or call 911 if he was scared Zimmerman was following him? Why did Zimmerman have scratches on his head, a broken nose and bruised eyes, evidence of a fight with Martin? Testimony by renowned forensic pathologist Dr. Vincent Di Maio revealed Martin's bullet wound was consistent with Zimmerman's account that there was a fight and Martin was on top of him, beating him."[10]

Plain and simple, the Democrats and their allies ignored the facts that night and continued to spin the lie that black men are victims of racial profiling. Obama was still making the same argument in a 2013 press conference: "You know, when Trayvon Martin was first shot I said that this could have been my son. Another way of saying that is Trayvon Martin could have been me 35 years ago. And when you think about why, in the African American community at least, there's a lot of pain around what happened here, I think it's important to recognize that the African American community is looking at this issue through a set of experiences and a history that doesn't go away."[11]

Our Democrat president demonstrates blatant dishonesty here. First, the chances of Obama being shot as a teen approached zero. He was raised by a mother and grandparents devoted to his upbringing who would never have allowed him to behave the way Martin did. Martin was suspended from school three times. He posted pictures on Facebook and other social media channels asking how to make a drink called "lean" to get high. Evidence that was gathered by Zimmerman's defense team but not introduced in the case suggests Martin went to the 7-Eleven that night to buy ingredients to make lean. Skittles and a bottle of Arizona Fruit Punch were found on Martin. Lean, an intoxicant popularized by hip-hop musicians, is made with cough syrup, Skittles, and fruit punch.

Democrats like Obama love to complain about police profiling of blacks. But the reason blacks are stopped and frisked more by police is that blacks are committing more crimes than whites. One of the most controversial crime-prevention programs in the country has been the stop-and-frisk program run by the NYPD. Critics say the program unfairly targets blacks. But the numbers don't lie. The New York City Crime and Enforcement report for 2013 found that blacks accounted for 62.9 percent of murder victims, 55 percent of suspects, and 54 percent of arrests. Whites, meanwhile, accounted for 7.2 percent of victims, 5.8 percent of suspects, and 6.5 percent of arrests.[12] The numbers demonstrate why there shouldn't be anything "controversial" about the stop-and-frisk program's "targeting" of blacks—it's because of the higher frequency with which they commit crimes. Likewise, Zimmerman wasn't engaging in "racial profiling"; he was defending himself against a hoodie-wearing teen he had seen peering through windows of homes as if he were casing them for a robbery.

Democrats at every level—from the president of the United States to the mayor of New York City down to the sleazy race-mongers who claim the "black leadership" mantle—show solidarity with criminal thugs and portray law enforcement as violent racists. Is it any surprise that America now finds itself in the middle of crime wave? "We have not seen what we're seeing right now in decades," observed a dismayed D.C. police chief Cathy L. Lanier at a recent summit on violent crime hosted by the Major Cities Chiefs Association (MCCA) in Washington, D.C., and including law enforcement officials from D.C., St. Louis, Chicago, Houston, and Philadelphia. As of August 2015, D.C.'s homicides for the year were already at 105—equal to the *total* number for the entire year of 2014[13]—with four months still to go. After conducting a survey of its members, MCCA found that 40 percent of cities were reporting an increase in guns and shootings. Conference attendees concluded the solution was more gun control, even though the guns causing the violence are already illegal. In Chicago, with some of the strictest gun laws in the nation, the police department confiscated 3,400 illegal firearms in 2015, and the killings continue—as they do in other high-crime, Democrat-governed cities.[14]

Guns aren't the problem in these Democrat-run ghettos. The criminals are. This is what happens when Democrats like Baltimore mayor Stephanie Rawlings-Blake tell cops to stand down and criminals to stand up. It's called "the Ferguson effect." It's named after the shooting of Mike Brown in Ferguson, Missouri—which we'll look at in detail in the next chapter, along with the Baltimore riots after Freddie Gray's death. In August of 2015, a police detective who was "pistol-whipped unconscious" by a criminal explained that he had "hesitated to use force because he didn't want to be accused of needlessly killing an unarmed man."[15] As a result of the Obama administration's pro-thug and anti-cop rhetoric, Manhattan Institute senior fellow Heather Mac Donald found crime rising in America. Police are not doing their jobs of maintaining law and order for fear of being called racist, fired, or—worse—indicted! As of May 2015, arrests in Baltimore had declined 56 percent compared to the same period in 2014.[16] Consequently, it's no surprise that when police stopped arresting the bad guys in July 2015, Baltimore recorded its deadliest month of homicides (forty-five) since 1972.[17]

Obama and Democrats defend criminals on the pretense of defending blacks, who suffer more as a result—because they are disproportionately the victims of violent crime, not just the perpetrators. According to Justice Department data from 1980 to 2008, blacks are six times more likely to commit a homicide than whites and seven times more likely to be a homicide victim.[18] Thanks to the Democrats enabling criminals and intimidating the police, those homicides are going up.

Below is a sampling of Mac Donald's findings for crime rates in cities across the country in 2015 compared to 2014:

Atlanta: Murders increased 32 percent.

Baltimore: Gun violence jumped 60 percent in 2015 compared to 2014. In a city whose population is over 60 percent black, the people who are harmed most are blacks.

Chicago: Shootings increased 24 percent while homicides jumped by 17 percent.

Los Angeles: Shootings and other violent crime increased 25 percent.

Milwaukee: Homicides increased by 180 percent.

New York: Shootings soared 500 percent in East Harlem. Murders in the city increased by 13 percent, and gun violence by 7 percent.

St. Louis: Shootings increased 39 percent; robberies jumped 43 percent, and homicides 29 percent.

It bears repeating that a Democrat mayor governs every single one of these cities. You can vividly see whose side they're on. When Democrat politicians become proponents of black criminality instead of holding criminals accountable, blacks suffer. In fact, all law-abiding citizens suffer from the wave of criminality the Democrats have unleashed across America.

Maybe black America should remove the collective hoodie blinding us to reality and see who's really holding the black man down. It's not the racist Republican Party, racist white people, or racist cops, it's the Democrat Party—a criminal menace to the whole country.

CHAPTER TWO

THE PARTY OF MOB VIOLENCE

After the not-guilty verdict in the Zimmerman trial, celebrities, "black leaders," and other Democrats wore hoodies to protest the verdict and show solidarity with Trayvon Martin. But the hoodie brigade didn't do anything to stop blacks from being killed. Wearing hoodies only encouraged black men to believe that they could engage in violence and not be held responsible for their actions. In fact, I believe the Democrats' exploitation of Trayvon Martin's death only contributed to eighteen-year-old Michael Brown's getting himself killed two years later.

Brown was shot by white police officer Darren Wilson in Ferguson, Missouri, on a hot August afternoon in 2014. Again Al Sharpton reprised his role as race agitator, descending upon this mostly black town—nearly 70 percent of Ferguson residents are black. Throughout the summer and continuing up to November 2014, when a St. Louis grand jury decided not to indict Wilson, Sharpton's presence instigated violence that harmed, not helped, black people—especially the black owners of businesses torched during the riots. In true politically correct fashion, liberal news reporters referred to the mostly black looters caught on video and in photographs as peaceful protestors. If these people were white, the media would have called them what they were—criminals. The media not only jumped on the "unarmed teen" bandwagon again, they also frequently referred to the hulking Brown, who stood at six foot four and weighed over two hundred pounds, as a "gentle giant." He was anything but. Moments before Officer Wilson encountered him in a street, a surveillance video shows, Brown was stealing cigars from a convenience store, then roughing up the store clerk who confronted him. Autopsy reports found marijuana in Brown's system.

Following the robbery that was caught on the surveillance tape, Wilson saw Brown walking in the street with his friend Dorian Johnson and noticed that Brown matched the profile of the suspect who had robbed the convenience store. Wilson asked Brown to move out of the street onto the sidewalk, but he refused. This is when Brown confronted Wilson, reaching inside his police car to grab his gun. (Investigators found Brown's DNA inside the car, a fact that supports Wilson's testimony.) Brown then walked away from the vehicle. But then, according to Wilson, Brown turned around and started coming back toward him—at which point Wilson shot him in self-defense. A grand jury of nine white jurors and three black jurors found the evidence didn't support an indictment of Officer Wilson. The Associated Press reviewed a thousand pages of transcript from the grand jury's deliberations and found that of the more than sixty witnesses, many gave "inconsistent, fabricated and provably wrong testimony."[1] Some admitted they had outright lied about seeing Wilson shoot and kill Brown that night—shaping their stories to fit news accounts. Others admitted they had ignored facts and twisted their testimonies to convict Officer Wilson only because he is white.[2]

Perhaps Brown, who was headed to college, thought engaging in criminal behavior was something an "unarmed black teen" could get away with. After all, Brown may very well have watched the president's remarks about Trayvon Martin a year earlier, painting young black men as victims never responsible for their actions.

After Brown's shooting death, Democrat Eric Holder, America's first black U.S. attorney general, traveled to Ferguson and announced that the Justice Department would conduct its own investigation to determine if Brown's civil rights had been violated. "The shooting incident in Ferguson, Missouri this weekend deserves a fulsome review.... At every step, we will work with the local investigators, who should be prepared to complete a thorough, fair investigation in their own right," said Holder in a statement issued from Ferguson.[3]

Why did Brown's death deserve a "fulsome review"? (The murders of hundreds of black teens killed in Chicago each year by other blacks never got such a review from the Justice Department. But black lives only matter when a white person kills a black person.) Why would Holder suggest that local investigators wouldn't conduct a fair investigation of the shooting? The answer to both questions: the assailant was white and Ferguson's fifty-three-person police force is comprised largely of white officers, with only three being black. Holder didn't bother to hide his prejudice in the case, publicly implying that the whole police force—and one of its officers in particular, Wilson—were racist. Holder's mere presence in Ferguson was intended to send a message to the grand jury to bring back an indictment against Wilson, regardless of what the facts showed.

Just as the Justice Department had concluded in its investigation into George Zimmerman's shooting of Trayvon Martin, it found that Wilson hadn't violated Brown's civil rights. But that conclusion came seven months after Brown's death—after Holder's initial grandstanding had contributed to the atmosphere of racial recrimination and the resulting mob violence in Ferguson. "This morning, the Justice Department announced the conclusion of our investigation and released a comprehensive, 87-page report documenting our findings and conclusions that the facts do not support the filing of criminal charges against Officer

Darren Wilson in this case. Michael Brown's death, though a tragedy, did not involve prosecutable conduct on the part of Officer Wilson," Holder explained in remarks on March 4, 2015.

Any person willing to open his eyes to the facts in the case rather than buy into the trumped-up racist fiction wasn't surprised by the Justice Department's findings. But despite having to admit to the facts of the case, the Democrats in the administration weren't finished with the race baiting. During that same press conference, Holder announced the findings of another "searing report"—a second investigation into the Ferguson Police Department. Describing black residents in Ferguson as living "under siege by those charged to serve and protect them," Holder said the police department and court system "disproportionately harmed African Americans."[4]

The report concluded, for example, that blacks were harmed by the department's use of ticketing not as a law enforcement tool but as a revenue-generating tool for the city. "Along with taxes and other revenue streams, in 2010, the city collected over $1.3 million in fines and fees collected by the court."[5] This isn't racism; it's a money grab. After all, Washington, D.C., a city where a majority-black population (like in Ferguson) is served by a majority-black police force[6] (unlike Ferguson), is notorious for issuing parking fines, red-light camera citations, and speeding tickets not for public safety but to make money. D.C., where former attorney general Eric Holder has lived and worked for years, raked in $179 million in fines in 2013, but I didn't see his Justice Department conducting an investigation into the D.C. police department's abuses against blacks.[7]

Some other findings in the Justice Department's report are troubling and would bear further investigation. The report found, for example, that the Ferguson police violated blacks' First Amendment rights, conducted searches of blacks without reasonable suspicion, and used excessive force against blacks at a greater rate than against other races. "And the use of dogs by Ferguson police appears to have been exclusively reserved for African Americans; in every case in which Ferguson police records recorded the race of a person bit by a police dog, that person was African American." If these findings reflect real discrimination against blacks by police, rather than the demographics of the town and of its criminals, police need to be punished and their conduct reformed. Without question the racist e-mails sent by two officers (of the fifty-three-person police force), including one comparing Obama to a chimpanzee and another showing a picture of topless African women with the caption "Michelle Obama's high school reunion," were wrong, and the officers deserve to be reprimanded.[8]

But the fact that from October 2012 to October 2014, blacks, who make up 67 percent of Ferguson's population, accounted for 85 percent of traffic stops and 85 percent of charges brought by the Ferguson Police Department doesn't necessarily prove a racial bias. Blacks are the majority in the town, and they could easily be committing proportionately more traffic violations than others. In a nation where statistics show blacks are generally committing more crime than whites, it's not impossible to believe that blacks are committing more crime in Ferguson than any other race, which would explain why blacks are charged more and why they are more frequently on the receiving end of other unwelcome and even abusive attention from the police.

The racist e-mails sent by the two officers are inexcusable, and so is any unreasonable search or use of excessive force. But it still doesn't change the fact that in Ferguson, as in other predominately black cities across the country, blacks are the ones committing most of the crime. An all-black Ferguson Police Department isn't going to change that. Black officers make up nearly 60 percent of D.C.'s police department, and blacks are still committing most of the crime in D.C., where black residents outnumber other races.[9] Despite the obvious counterexamples, liberals assume that if there were more black police officers working in predominantly black cities like Ferguson there would be fewer blacks killed by police officers. In fact, black officers made up 12 percent of the nation's 477,000 local police officers in 2013, according to the Bureau of Justice Statistics' *Local Police Departments, 2013: Personnel, Policies, and Practices* survey.[10] That's almost exactly the same percentage as the number of blacks in the U.S. population as a whole. But still there are calls to boost the number of blacks in law enforcement—on the unproved theory that more black police will make blacks safer, which itself is based on the erroneous assumption that racist white police, not black criminals, are the chief danger to "unarmed black men."

"Experts" cited by the *Wall Street Journal* allege that larger numbers of blacks can't become police officers since so many of them are unable to clear rigorous background checks because they have criminal records or can't pass written tests that are "not culturally neutral."[11] Since when did anyone want a person with a criminal record becoming a police officer? The solution to getting more blacks to become cops isn't lowering qualification standards but rather persuading young blacks not to commit crimes so they won't have to worry about passing "extensive background checks." As for written tests being racist, whites and many blacks are passing the same knowledge tests because they're studying for them. Holder talked about the need for "police accountability" in his Ferguson remarks, but he never talked about the need for "black accountability." The best way to improve the relationship between law enforcement and blacks is for blacks to be held accountable, like other American citizens, for our actions across all aspects of society, whether we're talking about crime or responsible parenting or studying to pass police department exams. But it makes for better politics—for Democrats, that is—to make excuses for criminals and incompetents.

BALTIMORE BURNING

When a black man is killed by a white man, Democrats are immediately on the spot turning that single act of violence into an excuse for mob violence. Isn't violence against blacks supposed to be the very thing at which they're outraged? And yet the interventions of Democrats and their reliable allies—from President Obama and the officials in his Department of Justice (DOJ) down to the bottom-feeding Al Sharpton—inevitably offer excuses for crime, inflame racial resentments, and end in more black citizens' being hurt in the ensuing riots and looting. The death of twenty-five-year-old Freddie Gray at the hands of Baltimore police officers was the next opportunity for the Democrat racial-grievance machine to descend on another American city to provide the mob with inspiration to loot and riot.

Gray, who had had numerous previous run-ins with the law and had served prison time, was arrested by Baltimore police officers on April 12, 2015, after he made eye contact with an officer and took off running. Gray turned out to have a switchblade on him, and the officers arrested him and put him in a police van. While in their custody, Gray suffered fatal injuries of a nearly severed spine and three broken vertebrae, then fell into a coma and died a week later. Six police officers were initially suspended from the Baltimore Police Department on account of Gray's death and then indicted by Baltimore's state's attorney Marilyn Mosby. In a press conference, Mosby recounted how officers threw Gray into a police van handcuffed and with his ankles shackled and never secured him in a seat belt. Mosby said officers had five different opportunities to buckle Gray in the van but never did during the time that they made several stops and he was tossed around inside. When the van finally arrived at the police station, Gray wasn't breathing and was rushed to the University of Maryland Shock Trauma Center. Most Americans agreed that Gray's death appeared to have been caused by the police. But many legal experts believed that Mosby, a Democrat, had rushed to file charges against the officers without weighing all the evidence, just to quiet the angry mob. It will be a challenge for the prosecution to win convictions, yet Baltimore likely will see more unrest if the jury doesn't render the justice the mob seeks. Three of the six officers charged were black, but the liberal news media didn't lead with the race of the police officers involved, as they did in the Brown or Martin cases, when the guys on the side of law and order were white.

Before the charges were brought against the officers, rioters had already brought Baltimore to her knees. Hundreds of "unarmed black men" used Gray's tragic death as an excuse to embark on several days of terrorizing the city. Images of rioters burning police vehicles and other cars, torching and looting businesses, and hurling bottles, rocks, and bricks at police officers blanketed the news. And the Democrats just continued to pour gasoline on the flames. Al Sharpton descended on Baltimore, as he had on Sanford, Florida, and Ferguson, Missouri. But in Baltimore he was given an even bigger platform—welcomed with open arms by the Democrat mayor, Stephanie Rawlings-Blake, who herself spoke in front of Sharpton's National Action Network "No Justice No Peace" backdrop.[12] And Eric Holder's replacement, the new Obama administration attorney general Loretta Lynch, announced that the Justice Department would be investigating the entire Baltimore Police Department.[13]

Even before the DOJ probe was announced, the Baltimore police were already intimidated from doing their job. In the wake of the Martin and Brown cases, the police in Baltimore seemed to bow to the Democrat narrative that law enforcement was the problem, initially watching on the sidelines while the angry mob wreaked destruction. "They just stood there," a citizen named Alan Hastings told the *Washington Post*.[14] Apparently, both the Baltimore Police Department and the rioters were taking marching orders from Baltimore's Democrat mayor—the rioters to express their rage, and the police to stand down and let them riot. Mayor Rawlings-Blake had held a press conference on Saturday, April 25, extending an open invitation to rioters. "I made it very clear that I work with the police and instructed them to do everything that they could to make sure that the protesters were able to exercise their right to free speech," she said. "It's a very delicate balancing act. Because while we try to make sure that they were protected from the cars and other things that were going on, we also gave those who wished to destroy space to do that as well."[15]

In true Democrat denial fashion, instead of unequivocally denouncing the violence as it began, Maryland congressman Elijah Cummings praised Baltimore residents in an interview on CBS's *Face the Nation* the day after the mayor's press conference, blaming the violence on "protestors from out of town."[16] But most of the photos showed young men who seemed right at home in Baltimore tearing the city down, and in fact the Maryland prison system confirmed that of the thirty-five protestors arrested on the day of the Rawlings-Blake's remarks, most were from Baltimore.[17] A reporter with RT shot video of a crowd of about eight "unarmed black teens" holding up their middle fingers, yelling, "Fuck the police" and "They ain't doing shit but killing us." On the video, one of the teens steals the female reporter's purse and she can be heard yelling, "Give me back my bag," as police officers appear.[18] On Monday, April 27, the day after Cummings's appearance and the day Freddie Gray was buried, police confirmed that twenty-seven people were arrested and between seventy-five and a hundred school-aged children had participated in the violence.[19]

Rioters heard the Democrats' message loud and clear. By Monday night Baltimore had descended into riotous chaos. Republican Maryland governor Larry Hogan had to declare a state of emergency and call in the National Guard to restore law and order to the mess the Democrat mayor had helped make.[20]

But the Democrats' loyal allies in the media didn't see things that way. CNN contributor Marc Lamont Hill wouldn't even call the riots "riots." Appearing on the network's coverage of the riots, Hill explained, "I'm calling these uprisings and I think it's an important distinction to make." Hill added that violent black protestors had every right to engage in "uprisings," and presumably destroy property and loot, because of "the decades and centuries of police terrorism" that blacks have endured. Calling the riots "uprisings" was meant to dignify them by putting them in the same class as historical revolts organized by groups of people to bring about a positive change, and even in the same class as the nonviolent protests of Martin Luther King Jr. and millions of other blacks during the civil rights movement. But "uprisings" are not orchestrated as an excuse for theft and destruction. "This city is burning because police killed Freddie Gray," Hill continued with righteous indignation.[21] No, Baltimore burned because rioters burned it down. What's most offensive about Hill's comments is the fact that he is given a paid national platform to act as an apologist for his fellow blacks who are behaving badly. Many black men watch Hill on television and interpret his false rhetoric as a license to commit carnage, harming other blacks in the process. Thanks to these "uprisings," over two hundred businesses, mostly minority owned, were destroyed. In the predominately black city of Baltimore, many blacks couldn't work to earn money for a week because businesses were either destroyed or closed for safety reasons, as were the schools. Nearly 500 people were arrested and 113 police officers were injured.[22]

In his interview on *Face the Nation* as the riots unfolded in Baltimore, Representative Cummings commented that "this whole police-community relations situation is the civil rights cause of this generation."[23] Contrary to the tall tales Cummings and other Democrats want to peddle, the biggest civil rights issue of this generation, and frankly of our time, is the persistent generational problem of young black men turning to lives of violence rather than work—egged on by Democrats' lies.

Throughout the weeklong media coverage of the riots, Democrat politicians, commentators, professors, and the like parroted the same meme: that blacks were engaging in violence because they had no opportunity in inner cities like Baltimore across the nation. Should rational adults in post–civil rights America be condoning wholesale black violence like this? When white males engage in mass murders or school shootings, which they have done on numerous occasions, Democrats don't say whites have no other options but to kill people—because that is a preposterous, illogical argument. It makes no more sense applied to blacks than it would applied to whites.

"The deeper problem is that much of Baltimore is a disaster even when no one is rioting," observed Rich Lowry.[24] And he's right. Baltimore, with a black population over 63 percent,[25] like many Democrat-controlled cities across the country, is deteriorating under one of the worst crime and unemployment rates in the nation. In 2013 Baltimore ranked fifth in the nation for murders "behind Detroit, New Orleans, Newark and St. Louis," respectively.[26] Equally grim, the unemployment rate in 2013 for young black men ages twenty to twenty-four in Baltimore was 37 percent, according to data from the U.S. Census.[27] Most urban areas in the United States like Baltimore, where crime and unemployment rates are high, have been governed by Democrats for decades. Baltimore hasn't had a Republican mayor since Theodore Roosevelt McKeldin in 1967. During those decades of so many American cities' being run into the ground by Democrats, blacks have become poorer, more violent, and further banished to ghettos thanks to their undying loyalty to the Democrat Party at the ballot box. In 2015 Baltimore's mayor, city council president, and prosecutor were all Democrats.

Addressing the mayhem in Baltimore, President Obama said, "What I'd say is this has been a slow-rolling crisis. This has been going on for a long time. This is not new, and we shouldn't pretend that it's new.... But if we really want to solve the problem, if our society really wanted to solve the problem, we could." Our Democrat president blamed the crisis in Baltimore on the lack of government funding and those stingy Republicans who won control of Congress in 2014.[28] But the last thing Baltimore needs is more federal funding. Under the 2009 stimulus, the American Recovery and Reinvestment Act (ARRA), passed by a Democrat-controlled Congress and signed into law by Obama, Baltimore received $1.8 billion for education, job creation, and crime prevention.[29] Days of riots and looting in Baltimore proved what a waste of money that was. In thirty days, "from mid-April 2015 to mid-May, about 31 people were killed in Baltimore and another 39 injured by guns."[30]

BLACK LIVES DON'T MATTER TO THE DEMOCRATS

Democrats are spreading the big lie that "unarmed black teens" are victims, playing no role in their deaths as they get gunned down by racist police at an epidemic rate. The truth is, you can be unarmed, as both Trayvon Martin and Michael Brown were, and have intent to harm. In both the Martin and Brown cases, evidence showed the seventeen-year-old and eighteen-year-old boys, respectively, were the aggressors. Did they deserve to die? No. Did they contribute to their deaths by making bad decisions? Yes. And so did Freddie Gray.

When was the last time Al Sharpton or Jesse Jackson protested the horror of black-on-black crime? Did Sharpton and his race-baiting crew hold a protest when fifteen-year-old Chicago native Hadiya Pendleton was murdered by two black male teens in January 2013 in Chicago, just a week after she had performed at events for Obama's second inauguration?[31] Of course not. The raging violence in Chicago is mostly black-on-black crime, and Sharpton doesn't have any interest in protesting that because there is no media attention or money in it for him. One of George Zimmerman's attorneys, Mark O'Mara, was exactly right when he said following the trial that the case "certainly wouldn't have happened if [Zimmerman] was black."[32] No, there would not have been any outrage from Sharpton and his race-baiting allies demanding charges be brought against Zimmerman, any presidential comments, or any wall-to-wall media coverage.

Why didn't Sharpton, the professional protestor, call for marches when sixty-two people were injured by gun violence and twelve others killed in Chicago the weekend of July 4, 2013? The youngest victim that weekend was Jaden Donald, a five-year-old black boy.[33] The answer is simple: Sharpton and opportunists like Benjamin Crump—the attorney serially representing black families whose sons are killed by white police officers—aren't interested in justice or peace. And Democrat politicians are happy to take political advantage of the false narrative these charlatans peddle. They all want to perpetuate the lie of the "unarmed black teen" because it means more money for the likes of Sharpton and his National Action Network, more clients for Crump, and more votes for the Democrat Party.

It's to the Democrats' electoral benefit to side with the thugs. Their narrative blaming everything on racist police lets them off the hook for wrecking America's cities and black voters' lives. And it stokes blacks' suspicions about the Republican Party—in fact, about anyone who proposes policies that might actually get crime under control. Apparently black lives don't matter when they're taken by other blacks—at least not to the Democrats.

The #BlackLivesMatter campaign began after the acquittal of George Zimmerman and took off after the St. Louis grand jury decision against charging white Ferguson police officer Darren Wilson for shooting Michael Brown in self-defense. There were tweets, marches, and die-ins where protestors blocked traffic by lying down in streets. But this angry mob should have clarified that black lives matter only when they're killed by white people—which we know happens very rarely compared to how often blacks are killed by black criminals. By protesting the isolated cases of Martin, Brown, and Gray, the Democrats send the message that the black-on-black genocide permeating cities across the nation—cities governed by Democrats—is perfectly acceptable.

Again, in August of 2015, St. Louis witnessed protests after a black teen was shot and killed by white officers. This teen was armed, but that didn't matter to the protesters. The officers had entered a home with a search warrant to look for criminal activity. Mansur Ball-Bey, an eighteen-year-old armed teen, ran out the back door along with another suspect. Police shot Ball-Bey because he pointed a gun at them. Four guns were found in the house, and Ball-Bey also was in possession of crack cocaine. Not the MO of an innocent teen. But none of that mattered to the 150 protesters, who—encouraged by the Democrats' sympathy for black criminals and condemnations of the police—apparently believe that blacks have the right to commit crimes without facing retribution.[34]

That's essentially what Everett D. Mitchell, director of community relations at the University of Madison–Wisconsin, said during a community panel on "Best Policing Practices" the very month Ball-Bey was shot: "I just don't think they should be prosecuting cases for people who steal from Wal-Mart. I don't think that. I don't think that Target, and all them other places—the big boxes that have insurance—they should be using the people that steal from there as justification to start engaging in aggressive police behavior."

Apparently, when it comes to blacks and crime, Mitchell believes that *no* policing is the best policy. Marie Antoinette told the poor, starving French, "Let them eat cake." Democrats tell police, "Let blacks steal."[35]

As Fox News radio host John Gibson has pointed out, this is "a deadly concept." He astutely observes, "It will mean more young black people arrested and jailed. It will mean more young black people deciding they can challenge the police, even with a weapon, and they will be shot and killed." This lunacy shows that pandering to black voters is more important to Democrats than saving black lives.[36] Thanks to the Democrats, blacks are being encouraged to kill, steal, and destroy, all in the name of their race.

Thanks to the Democrats' making excuses for blacks and stoking racial hatred, black Americans have been taught that black lives matter more than any others. It's come to the point where the general Democrat sentiment is blacks should literally be allowed to get away with murder.

"OPEN SEASON" ON POLICE

"I said last December that war had been declared against the American police officer, led by some high-profile people. One of them coming out of the White House, another one coming out of the U.S.

Department of Justice. And it's open season right now, no doubt about it," commented Sheriff David Clarke on the uptick in violence that has erupted in America.[37]

Since 2002, Clarke, an outspoken critic of Obama's crime policy, has been the sheriff of Milwaukee, one of the nation's most violent cities. After the deaths of Martin and Brown, Obama become a defender of thugs and portrayed police officers as the enemies of black citizens. Now anyone wearing a badge is a marked man.

On August 28, 2015, Deputy Darren Goforth was gunned down "execution style" by Shannon Miles at a Chevron gas station near Houston, Texas. After shooting Goforth in the head, Miles wasn't finished.[38] As the deputy lay face down, dying, the thirty-year-old Miles unloaded the rest of his magazine, fourteen bullets, into Goforth's back. Goforth was a forty-seven-year-old father of two.[39]

Goforth was white and Miles is black. Investigators believe the murder of Goforth was a hate crime fueled by the Black Lives Matter movement declaring every cop is a racist out to get blacks. Days before Deputy Goforth was killed, Carol Sullivan hosted a blog radio show in Texas, encouraging blacks to kill and lynch whites. Here's a sample of what callers said on the episode of her *Sunshine's Fucking Opinion Radio Show* that aired August 25, 2015:

> Cause we already roll up in gangs anyway. There should be six or seven black mother fuckers, see that white person, and then lynch their ass. Let's turn the tables. I think if we start turning tables and cops, cops start losing people. This will be a whole different story. Then there will be a state of emergency.

And:

> Find a mother fucker that is alone. Snap his ass, and then fuckin hang him from a damn tree. Take a picture of it and then send it to the mother fuckers.[40]

Sullivan is the founder of #FukYoFlag, a radical outgrowth of the Black Lives Matter movement. "We, the people, are psychologically and physically breaking free of the imperialist, colonialist, and racist empires by burning representations starting on September 11th 2015," is how the group describes itself. According to its website, the group also planned to burn "American flags, confederate flags, police uniforms, and ALL representations of organized evil and oppressive nations."[41] This is some truly sick, twisted stuff.

Missing from the Goforth case was any press conference from Obama lamenting the senseless murder of this innocent white life and extending prayers to the victim's family. Nor is Obama's Justice Department investigating the case as a hate crime, as it did in both the Martin and Brown cases.

Time and again when blacks kill whites, there's nothing but silence from the first black president of the United States. Obama has single-handedly taken American race relations back to the violent times of the 1960s. All in the name of perpetuating a fallacy that black men are the ones being gunned down by whites, when in reality the statistics show black men are America's most wanted! Whatever it takes for Democrats to keep the black votes coming they will do, even at the expense of body bags.

Instead of doing anything to stop the violence, the Democrat Party champions the plight of the criminals who are perpetrating it. Young men like Trayvon Martin, Michael Brown, Freddie Gray, and Mansur Ball-Bey who buy into this detrimental lie are given another reason to continue their destructive behavior and not take personal responsibility for their actions. The #BlackLivesMatter campaign has become nothing more than an excuse for young black men to get confrontational with police, particularly white officers, across the country; to jeopardize their own lives; and to provide the Democrats and their race-charlatan allies with another incident they will leverage into more rioting, looting—and votes for candidates with "D" after their names. This certainly isn't justice, and it won't bring any peace. Frankly, Democrats' irresponsible rhetoric is getting young black men killed.

WE WERE WARNED

For more than twenty-five years, renowned scholar and famous black conservative Thomas Sowell has been warning about the real dangers of racial preferences and the race-baiters whose careers are built on demanding special treatment for minority groups. As his exhaustive research has demonstrated, affirmative action inevitably makes racial divisions and hatred worse wherever it is tried, often leading to racial violence. In numerous countries around the world—Sowell cites examples ranging from India to Sri Lanka to Malaysia to Nigeria—the same policies that the Democrats have been pushing for decades to "help" blacks in the United States have failed in their supposed purpose, and succeeded only in incubating a class of race-charlatan "activists" who thrive on inflaming racial resentments. The ultimate result can be race riots, even a race war.[42]

Now, that racial violence has come to America. The riots in Ferguson and Baltimore were telltale signs of how the racial resentment that the Democrats have fostered for their own political advantage is blossoming in bloodshed. So were the excuses made for the violence by the Dems' pet race-monger "activists."

And so were the horrific crimes of two mentally unstable individuals, one white and one black. On June 17, 2015, Dylann Roof opened fire and slaughtered nine innocent black people at a Bible study at Emanuel African Methodist Episcopal Church in Charleston, South Carolina. The murderer turned out to be a white racist who was "obsessed" with the George Zimmerman–Trayvon Martin case, believed that "blacks were taking over the world," thought that "someone needed" to rescue the white race from black crime, and "wanted to start a civil war."[43] Two days later, black TV reporter Vester Flanagan (known as "Bryce Williams" on the air), who would claim that the Charleston shooting "sent me over the top," made a deposit on a gun purchase. Two months later, he used that gun to murder a white reporter and cameraman during a live interview. Then he sent ABC News a manifesto explaining his motives. Addressing Dylann Roof, Flanagan wrote, "You want a race war?…BRING IT THEN…."[44]

Obviously—and thankfully—Roof and Flanagan are outliers, violent and likely mentally ill individuals. Flanagan believed that "Jehovah" was telling him to commit his heinous crime.[45] But these two men are also signs of the times, times shaped by the racial resentment and violence that has been stoked by the Democrats and their race-baiting allies. Will it take a real race war before we clue in to the horrific damage the Democrat Party is doing to blacks and, for that matter, our country?

CHAPTER THREE

THE PARTY OF HOPELESS SLUMS

When black Republicans like me dare to talk about the concentration of blacks on welfare, living in public housing, having babies out of wedlock, or committing crimes, we are called "haters of our people" or "good blacks"—because we won't turn a blind eye to the obvious. Democrats love to prescribe more welfare programs as an answer to black economic woes. But it's obvious that black Americans have not benefited from the expansion of the welfare state. Only the Democrat Party has.

The best example of this is the public housing system in America. Though pitched as a gift to "equalize the playing field," welfare was the worst "gift" the Democrats ever bestowed on black America. One of the most durable components of public assistance is America's hundreds of public housing projects, which function as economic graveyards for black Americans. Ironically, they're given names like "Estate," "Village," "Homes," "Farm," and "Gardens," but these developments are wastelands that foster multigenerational black poverty, where crime, nonworking adult males, and single women with numerous children fathered by different men are the norm. And these slums were conceived, executed, and perpetuated by Democrats.

I recently read an article published in the *New York Times* in 1991: "Four Generations in the Projects," by Nicholas Lemann. Lemann tracked the life of Ruby Haynes, a black woman, who along with three of her seven children spent her life in the projects of Chicago. By the time she was fifteen years old, Ruby had had two babies out of wedlock in Mississippi. Her situation did not improve when she moved to Chicago. Ruby met Luther in 1953 in Chicago and had four children with him before marrying him in 1962. The only reason they married was to qualify for one of the 4,300 apartments in the Robert Taylor Homes public housing buildings. At that time the housing authority had a rule stipulating no unmarried women could live in public housing. That rule soon evaporated. "As vacancies developed, the screening procedures became vestigial; almost every new tenant was a single mother on welfare," the *Times* reported.[1]

In 1965 the couple divorced when Luther had an affair with a woman living on the floor beneath them. Through the years Ruby's two youngest sons dropped out of high school and got involved in gangs and drugs. One went to prison. After suffering from depression, Ruby left Chicago in 1979 to return home to Mississippi and live in another housing project there. Her twenty-year-old daughter Juanita, also a high school dropout, took over her apartment, went on welfare, and ultimately had four children by three different men. This disastrous cycle is probably continuing today.

In the *Times* piece, Lemann described the Chicago Democrat machine's vision for its black supporters from the day the Federal Housing Act was passed in 1949 under Democrat president Harry Truman, providing funds to build public housing: "The machine's main goal, during the boom years of public-housing construction in Chicago, was, in a word, segregation. Mayor Daley and his ward leaders (including

Chicago's leading black politician, William L. Dawson) wanted to keep the entire black migration to Chicago housed within the confines of traditionally black neighborhoods."[2]

What Lemann's article makes clear is that public housing projects treat the symptoms of poverty, not the problem itself. Fundamentally, it is not taxpayers' concern to raise other people's children born out of irresponsibility—in fact, all the government help in the world can never be an adequate substitute for responsible parents. I'm not advocating for a heartless government. Our nation should use our resources to improve the lives of the poor. But public housing programs do exactly the opposite. The Democrats have created generations of blacks who feel entitled to government help and are mired in dependency to the point where they demand to stay dependent. That's the attitude the projects foster.

And make no mistake, public housing is mostly a black experience. While blacks represent 13 percent of the nation's population, they make up 45 percent of all public housing residents in the United States, while whites make up 32 percent and Hispanics roughly 20 percent. According to other data from the National Low Income Housing Coalition, more blacks also are using housing vouchers—45 percent of voucher recipients are black, while 35 percent are white and 16 percent are Hispanic. Blacks living in public housing are four times as likely as whites to live in very poor neighborhoods, while blacks participating in the voucher program are three times as likely to live in poor neighborhoods.[3] The statistics don't lie. There is no denying that blacks are using government housing and welfare assistance more than any other race and losing ground economically because of it.

In 2011, according to the Congressional Research Service, 32.5 percent of children receiving welfare assistance (Temporary Assistance to Needy Families) were black, compared to 25.5 percent who were white. Black adults accounted for nearly 34 percent of welfare recipients in 2011 despite being only 13 percent of the population. Whites, who represent about 60 percent of the U.S. population, were only 33.2 percent of welfare recipients.[4] Food stamp assistance is the same story—more blacks than whites rely upon this "social safety net"—which actually helps make the recipients' lives *unsafe* by keeping them mired in poverty and crime. The Pew Research Center found that, as of 2012, 31 percent of blacks reported having been on food stamps at some point in their lives compared with 15 percent of whites.[5]

The residents of the projects aren't just disproportionately black, they are also predominantly women—another constituency the Democrats rely on to stay in power. "Across all housing assistance programs, female-headed households are disproportionately common," concluded the National Low Income Housing Coalition in its November 2012 *Housing Spotlight*. Seventy-five percent of public housing households are headed by single women, and 83 percent of voucher households are headed by single women.[6]

Democrats knew early on that providing publicly subsidized housing would be a useful political tool for making blacks dependent on government and thus capturing their votes. Housing projects first entered the American lexicon as part of Democrat Franklin Roosevelt's 1933–1938 New Deal, the largest expansion of the federal government in history. From 1933 to 1969, Democrat presidents served seven out of the nine presidential terms, and the amount of public housing grew—slowly at first, but undergoing a massive expansion under President Lyndon B. Johnson, who signed into law the Housing and Urban Development Act of 1965 and the Housing Act of 1968. Predictably, as Democrats grew welfare programs upon which blacks became dependent, the percentage of the black vote that went to the Democrats grew as well. Roosevelt won 71 percent of the black vote in 1936.[7] The majority of blacks have voted Democrat in every presidential election since then. In 1964 Lyndon B. Johnson won an unprecedented almost 94 percent of the black vote, and in 1968 Hubert Humphrey took nearly 85 percent.[8]

In the 1930s, New York, Roosevelt's home state, was a prime laboratory for many New Deal programs. Today, New York City has more federally subsidized housing units than any other city in the nation, according to the Furman Center for Real Estate and Urban Policy.[9] Other cities copied the Roosevelt model and today have a high percentage of residents in public housing projects. Chicago, Philadelphia, Baltimore, New Orleans, Boston, and Washington, D.C., have all been governed by Democrat mayors for decades. Washington, a city dominated by black politicians, has elected a Democrat mayor to run the city in every term since 1967. And these liberal cities reward black voters by segregating blacks in ghettos! Roughly 4 million households depend on some kind of federally funded housing assistance program, and most of those 4 million households are located in urban areas[10]— in other words, in the cities where the Democrats have parlayed black voters' dependence on welfare programs into decades of monopoly political power.

There isn't just a one-size-fits-all policy on public housing assistance. Tenants have choices. Section 8 housing is operated by private owners who are paid rent subsidies by the Department of Housing and Urban Development (HUD). Tenants are required to pay only a percentage— capped at 30 percent—of their income toward their monthly rent.[11] Public housing is technically owned by local public housing agencies who receive federal funds from HUD to rent units to low-income Americans, who also pay no more than 30 percent of their income in monthly rent. HUD also runs low-income housing programs for low-income elderly Americans and those with disabilities. Vouchers are also used by HUD to give low-income families the luxury of renting private homes or apartments with most of the rent footed by taxpayers. Under the Housing Choice Voucher Program, HUD makes direct payments to landlords and recipients' monthly rent again is capped at 30 percent of their income.

For example, a mother of two working a minimum-wage, thirty-hour-a-week job and renting an apartment for $700 a month would receive a $440 monthly voucher, according to the Center for Budget and Policy Priorities.[12] "By allowing families to rent a unit of their choice in the private market, vouchers enable them to move to safer neighborhoods with less poverty and higher employment rates. A growing body of evidence indicates that growing up in neighborhoods of concentrated poverty can adversely affect children's health, education, and long-term economic prospects," notes the center.[13] But this liberal think tank doesn't state the obvious: if women weren't having babies without fathers, they would be less likely to live in bad neighborhoods and poverty. When people are given handouts for which they don't have to work, there is less incentive to take responsibility for their actions. And since when are people entitled to live in the neighborhood of their choice and expect other people's money to pay for their housing?

"Federal housing development" is the term that we use to take the sting out of the reality that these projects are ghettos within cities, akin to war zones, full of drugs, crime, and murders. Lemann's article shows blacks will go into the projects, but it's likely they will not come out for generations. Public housing is as much a cesspool of poverty, dysfunction, and crime today as it was in the 1960s. And for this we can thank Democrats, the architects of these segregated ghettos devoid of economic opportunities.

CYCLES OF DEPENDENCY

Democrat politicians love to complain about income inequality between blacks and whites. But since the first black president got elected, the wealth gap between whites and blacks has only gotten worse, turning into a chasm. According to a 2015 analysis by the Urban Institute, in 1983 the median black family had only an eighth of the wealth of the median white family, with total assets of $13,000 compared to $100,000 for the median white family. By 2013 the median white family "had 12 times the wealth" of the median black family.[14] When it comes to retirement savings, the picture for blacks is dire. In 2013 the average white family outpaced blacks with retirement savings of $130,000 compared to $19,000 for the average black family.[15] What have Democrat politicians done about this, especially the first black president? Instead of focusing on policies that help create jobs for blacks and get them off of welfare, Obama has spent seven years focusing on helping gays get married and granting amnesty to illegal aliens.

The more government assistance Democrats shower on blacks, the more black Americans lean on and depend upon this "help" as a crutch, a substitute for personal responsibility. How can #BlackLivesMatter if the Democrats discourage blacks from taking responsibility for our lives and instead encourage us to perpetually ask the government to do something for us? Blacks will continue getting poorer, dumber, and more violent as a race so long as we keep putting our votes into the hands of the Democrat Party. Wishing things will get better won't make it so. It's been fifty years, and Democrats haven't saved blacks yet—not even the first black Democrat to make it to the White House has done anything to help black Americans advance.

Even former D.C. mayor Marion Barry wrote about the need to get residents off the welfare rolls. D.C. is one of the few places in the country allowing residents to receive cash payments indefinitely, a policy that concerned Barry. "Unfortunately," he pointed out in a 2010 op-ed in the *Washington Post*, "this unsound provision in our local law has been coupled with a system that has failed our residents for years. The result has been to enslave residents in joblessness and dependency on the government rather than lifting them up and giving them an opportunity to achieve self-sufficiency through job training and employment."[16]

Another piece in the *Washington Post* confirms the damage that the perpetual enjoyment of welfare is doing to blacks. The article, "Longtime D.C. Welfare Recipients Prepare for Life off the Rolls," profiled four single black welfare mothers with a total of sixteen children and no husbands in sight.[17] While the reporter took great pains to avoid mentioning the women's race because it might offend black people, the photos revealed the truth. One of the main subjects in the piece was single mom

LaTanya Stuckey, who was a high school dropout with four kids by three different men. Formerly an ice cream scooper at Ben & Jerry's, the jobless welfare recipient explained that she wouldn't take just any job: "I won't take a job because TANF wants me to get off TANF," she said. "I just don't want to work at McDonald's. I need something that has a benefits package and that's going to help me in the long run." Let's get this straight. She's getting housing and cash and food from the tax dollars of other people, who had to work to get what this single welfare mother is getting for free, and she's picky about what kind of job she'll work?

Diane Greenfield, a twenty-eight-year-old unmarried welfare mom, had no job and five children, aged three months to six years old, fathered by who knows how many different men. She lived with her boyfriend, a convicted drug dealer recently released from prison, and had been on the welfare rolls in D.C. for seven years, receiving $540 a month in cash payments plus $850 in food stamps. Greenfield was "accustomed" to living off the state—that is, other people's hard-earned money—and found the proposed welfare cuts "scary": "Are they going to guarantee me a job to raise my kids?" Greenfield asked the *Post*. "If they cut me off, how am I supposed to get Pampers, shoes and socks for my babies?" she added.

The Democrats on the D.C. City Council and in the mayor's office should have told women like Greenfield long ago to get a job and stop having kids you can't afford. That's how you pay for diapers and stuff for your kids! If Democrats pushed policies of self-reliance instead of government dependency, blacks would move off the welfare rolls into jobs. That would be Democrats delivering on their years' worth of promises to uplift blacks. But we all know it has no chance of happening.

TRAPPING THEIR VOTERS IN POVERTY

It ought to go without saying: providing people with the comforts of life for free or nearly free encourages them not to work. In long-

Democrat-controlled Maryland and the District of Columbia, welfare recipients are paid more than twice the minimum wage. According to a study conducted by the Cato Institute, Maryland's minimum wage was $7.25 an hour in 2013 and welfare recipients received the equivalent of $18.35 an hour in benefits. Offering even more generous benefits, D.C. paid its welfare recipients the equivalent of $24.43 an hour. This was nearly three times D.C.'s 2013 hourly minimum wage of $8.25. Cato found that thirty-three other states offered similarly rich welfare benefits.[18] Why bother to work?

The federal government puts no limit on how long people can stay on the dole for their housing needs. "You may stay in public housing as long as you comply with the lease," notes HUD on its website.[19] Of course if a recipient's income rises, he or she becomes ineligible for public housing. But with no termination date to the government subsidy gravy train, what incentives are there for welfare recipients to change their behavior?

Every election cycle, Democrats keep blacks on the hook with promises they will make things better—they only need more time and government funding. Then once the black vote puts them in office, those same Democrats give blacks more handouts, never the kind of help that would economically empower us as a race compared to whites. If Democrats were to deliver us from inequality into the arms of opportunity, what would Democrats have left to peddle to blacks for our votes? Nothing. The Democrat Party uses blacks for political expediency, taking our votes for granted, ignoring our real problems—and most of us still keep tagging along for the ride. Maybe it's time for black Americans to take a cold hard look at the party that claims to be lifting us up and get serious about the voting power we hold. As things stand, blacks have become one big joke to the Democrat Party.

A great way to ensure that blacks and single mothers—two of the Democrats' most dependable voting blocs—remain in permanent need of rescue is to keep feeding their dysfunction. Welfare and public housing keep pushing their "beneficiaries" into the black hole of dependence, irresponsibility, poverty, and crime because again black lives don't matter to Democrats as much as black votes. When you give addicts the very thing that feeds their addiction, they become more addicted to what is slowly destroying them, pulling them further away from recovery. Welfare and public housing have become an addiction in America—and the Democrats are dealing the drug.

CHAPTER FOUR

THE PARTY OF ILLEGAL IMMIGRATION

Republican presidential candidate Donald Trump was right when he called the illegals invading America "criminals." According to U.S. immigration law, sneaking across the border into America, working here, and then refusing to leave qualifies an individual as a lawbreaker on multiple counts.

A 2011 Government Accountability Office (GAO) report on "criminal alien statistics" found that about 55,000 criminal aliens were in federal prisons in 2010, SCAAP criminal alien incarcerations in state prison systems and local jails were about 296,000 in 2009, and the majority were from Mexico.[1] (The Department of Justice's State Criminal Alien Assistance Program—SCAAP—reimburses state and local governments for the costs of incarcerating illegals who have committed a felony or have two misdemeanor convictions.)

There are an estimated 11 to 20 million illegal aliens defiantly living and working in America in plain sight and demanding citizenship for their lawlessness because of their sheer numbers. Nothing about this population of criminals is "living in the shadows," as liberals sympathetically describe them. And far too many of them are committing violent crimes. Yet the Democrat Party protects illegals, who break our laws and kill Americans!

In his June 16, 2015, speech announcing his presidential campaign, Trump said: "The U.S. has become a dumping ground for everybody else's problems. [Applause] Thank you. It's true, and these are the best and the finest. When Mexico sends its people, they're not sending their best. They're not sending you. They're not sending you. They're sending people that have lots of problems, and they're bringing those problems with us. They're bringing drugs. They're bringing crime. They're rapists. And some, I assume, are good people."[2]

THE HIGH COST OF ILLEGAL IMMIGRATION

Shortly after Trump's speech, thirty-two-year-old American Kate Steinle was shot to death by an illegal alien from Mexico while she was walking on a pier in San Francisco with her father. Juan Francisco Lopez-Sanchez, whom CNN referred to as an "undocumented immigrant," was a repeat felon who had been deported back to Mexico five times.

Why was this illegal Mexican allowed to keep returning to the United States—and kill Steinle? It's simple. The Democrat Party doesn't believe in immigration enforcement. The Dems have successfully thwarted all efforts to get control of our illegal immigration problem. True, as Donald Trump's campaign has demonstrated by way of contrast, not all Republicans have been as strongly in favor of solving the problem of illegal immigration as they ought to be—too many of them have backed "comprehensive immigration reform," which is really just amnesty for illegals. But however weak some Republicans are on this issue, the Democrats are always 100 percent strong—on the side of the illegals. President Obama's "executive actions" are just the last straw. For *decades* the Democrats have followed the same playbook: make heroes of illegals who break the law to cross our border, ally with La Raza, depend on the Hispanic vote to get elected, and constantly agitate *for* changing our laws to amnesty the illegals already here and *against* enforcing the immigration laws we do have. And then, of course, the Democrats and their willing allies in the liberal media call anyone who disagrees a racist. With one party actively promoting illegal immigration, and the other party afraid to resist it for fear of being called xenophobic, illegals have received the message loud and clear: they will not be deported.

The Democrats' pro–illegal immigrant rhetoric and their lobbying for amnesty is an open invitation for more illegals to cross the border. In 2013 when Congress began intense negotiations to create a path to citizenship for illegals, U.S. Border Patrol agents reported illegal border crossings doubled and tripled in some cases.[3]

And some of these illegals are also violent criminals. From 2010 to 2014, according to U.S. Immigration and Customs Enforcement (ICE), 121 criminal aliens with pending cases before immigration courts committed homicides. They killed and raped Americans while we waited for our officials to enforce our immigration laws.[4]

On May 15, 2013, Ecuadorian alien Henry Estrella-Cordova was arrested in Baltimore for the brutal rape of a nine-year-old girl. The ICE press release announcing Estrella-Cordova's arrest noted that the rapist "was unlawfully present in the United States."[5] If Estrella-Cordova hadn't been in the United States in the first place, he wouldn't have raped this child.

Grant Ronnebeck, a twenty-one-year-old white young man, was another fatality of America's lawless immigration system. In 2015, while Ronnebeck was working the graveyard shift at a convenience store in Mesa, Arizona, twenty-nine-year-old Apolinar Altamirano, a Mexican illegal, shot him in the face. Prior to killing Ronnebeck, Altamirano had been "arrested in 2012 along with two others for kidnapping, sexually assaulting and burglarizing a woman in her apartment."

After pleading guilty to felony burglary in 2013, Altamirano had been sentenced to two years probation and turned over to ICE officials. Because his case was pending before an immigration court in Phoenix and there was no deportation order for him, despite his having a criminal record, ICE officials released him on a $10,000 bond. ICE does not notify local authorities when a detainee is released on bond from ICE custody.

Essentially, Altamirano was set free by American law enforcement to kill.

Prior to his January 22, 2015, arrest for the first-degree murder of Ronnebeck, Altamirano had had two injunctions issued against him, but ICE didn't revoke Altamirano's bond because it wasn't aware of the injunctions until after the Mesa police arrested him for the murder. "There is currently no systematic process for state and local authorities to notify ICE when an injunction or order of protection is served."[6]

"PROSECUTORIAL DISCRETION"

Why wasn't ICE doing its job? Our Democrat president had instructed the agency not to. *The new normal in America is citizens can be arrested and detained for crimes but illegal criminals can't!*

Following the arrest of Estrella-Cordova, the acting field office director for ICE's Enforcement and Removal Operations (ERO) said, "Arresting individuals that are alleged to sexually exploit children and removing them from our streets is an ICE priority in maintaining the safety and quality of life that the citizens of Maryland expect. ICE will continue to identify and arrest child predators unlawfully residing in the United States and protect our communities from threats to public safety."

Obama's ICE says one thing but does another. The reality is this president puts the safety and comfort of criminal illegals above that of American citizens.[7] In 2013 ICE released over thirty-six thousand convicted criminal aliens from its custody, of whom about two hundred had committed murders.[8]

Obama's reinterpretation of America's immigration laws without Congress's approval caused the deaths of innocent Americans like Steinle and Ronnebeck. As the Democrat president explained, "We've expanded my authorities under executive action and prosecutorial discretion."[9] It's not how most of us would choose to use our "discretion." Through these abuses of power, Obama has systematically annihilated our immigration laws.

Our commander in chief has a predilection for referring to illegals as "undocumented" immigrants. For example, when he announced his executive order in November 2014 granting amnesty to some 5 million illegal parents of kids born in the United States: "Undocumented workers broke our immigration laws, and I believe that they must be held accountable." But then he added:

> Let's be honest—tracking down, rounding up, and deporting millions of people isn't realistic. Anyone who suggests otherwise isn't being straight with you.
>
> That's why we're going to keep focusing enforcement resources on actual threats to our security. Felons, not families. Criminals, not children. Gang members, not a mother who's working hard to provide for her kids.[10]

In this same speech, Obama demanded that Congress give these criminals citizenship for breaking our laws. "I know some of the critics of this action call it amnesty. Well, it's not.... To those members of Congress who question my authority to make our immigration system work better, or question the wisdom of me acting where Congress has failed, I have one answer: Pass a bill."[11]

When Congress doesn't give Obama what he wants, Obama unilaterally acts on his own.

In March 2011 ICE director John Morton issued a memo to all ICE employees informing them of Obama's new immigration policy for the "apprehension, detention, and removal of aliens." (Notice how ICE uses the accurate term of "alien" to refer to these criminals.)[12]

"ICE is charged with enforcing the nation's civil immigration laws," the memo noted, but then it went on to say that "it only has resources to remove approximately 400,000 aliens per year, less than 4% of the estimated illegal alien population in the United States." So, essentially, the agency would cherry-pick which of our nation's immigration laws it would enforce.

The agency was given "discretion" by the Democrat administration to follow three immigration enforcement priorities, outlined in order of importance:

Priority 1. Aliens who pose a danger to national security or a risk to public safety

The removal of aliens who pose a danger to national security or a risk to public safety shall be ICE's highest immigration enforcement priority. These aliens include, but are not limited to:

- aliens engaged in or suspected of terrorism or espionage, or who otherwise pose a danger to national security;
- aliens convicted of crimes, with a particular emphasis on violent criminals, felons, and repeat offenders;
- aliens not younger than 16 years of age who participated in organized criminal gangs;
- aliens subject to outstanding criminal warrants; and
- aliens who otherwise pose a serious risk to public safety.

But depending upon the type of felonies these illegals committed, they weren't necessarily high-priority targets within category 1. The other two priority categories:

Priority 2. Recent illegal entrants

In order to maintain control at the border and at ports of entry, and to avoid a return to the prior practice commonly and historically referred to as "catch and release," the removal of aliens who have recently violated immigration controls at the border, at ports of entry, or through the knowing abuse of the visa and visa waiver programs shall be a priority.

Priority 3. Aliens who are fugitives or otherwise obstruct immigration controls

In order to ensure the integrity of the removal and immigration adjudication processes, the removal of aliens who are subject to a final order of removal and abscond, fail to depart, or intentionally obstruct immigration controls, shall be a priority. These aliens include:

- fugitive aliens, in descending priority as follows:
    - fugitive aliens who pose a danger to national security;
    - fugitives aliens convicted of violent crimes or who otherwise pose a threat to the community;
    - fugitive aliens with criminal convictions other than a violent crime;
    - fugitive aliens who have not been convicted of a crime;
- aliens who reenter the country illegally after removal, in descending priority as follows:
    - previously removed aliens who pose a danger to national security;
    - previously removed aliens convicted o f violent crimes or who otherwise pose a threat to the community;
    - previously removed aliens with criminal convictions other than a violent crime;
    - previously removed aliens who have not been convicted of a crime; and

- aliens who obtain admission or status by visa, identification, or immigration benefit fraud.[13]

Wow, no wonder illegals are taking over America and killing Americans. Trying to sort through ICE's four-page maze of a memo is dizzying. When did America's laws become fungible, subject to CliffsNotes interpretation, depending upon who occupies the White House?

"EXECUTIVE ACTION"

Of course this is all of Obama's dirty work. Then, in 2012, the Democrat president did an end run around Congress, issuing an executive order to create the Deferred Action for Childhood Arrivals (DACA), known as the DREAMers Policy for short. Under the order, illegal aliens who were under the age of thirty-one as of June 15, 2012, and had come to the United States illegally before turning sixteen would not be deported for two years, subject to renewal. These "children" must have continuously lived illegally "in the United States since June 15, 2007, up to the present time." What a reward for breaking U.S. immigration laws![14]

With his amnesty-for-kids program and his refusal to deport illegals, Obama broadcast to the world, "If you come, you can stay." And the illegal aliens listened. "If you invite us, we will come," they replied—in Spanish, of course.

And come they did, by the thousands. Mommies and daddies in Latin American countries packed their kids and sent them unaccompanied to break and enter the U.S. border. What did Americans behold during the summer of 2014? A stampede of illegal alien children, about *seventy thousand*, crushing the U.S.-Mexico border and crushing it hard! "By year's end, 70,000 to 90,000 unaccompanied children are expected to cross the border compared to only 24,000 in 2013," according to a *USA Today* article published in 2014.[15]

Under the William Wilberforce Trafficking Victims Protection Reauthorization Act, these children cannot be deported. The law was designed to protect victims of human trafficking and violence fleeing Central America. But with Obama tempting tens of thousands of Latin American children to the United States by promising them amnesty, now the law is being abused by illegals as a loophole for their children.

The Department of Health and Human Services (HHS) is required to care for the "unaccompanied alien children" and find "a suitable family member" in the United States with whom to reunite the children. If a family member cannot be found, HHS must take care of these illegal children through the Unaccompanied Refugee Minor Program at taxpayers' expense.[16]

The long and short of this story is these illegal alien kids get to stay in America—at our expense! This massive wave of illegal children jumping the U.S.-Mexican border forced the Department of Health and Human Services to set up refugee camps to house them. The children brought with them every contagion under the sun: scabies, chicken pox, measles, lice, black bugs, and strep throat. "I would be talking to children and lice would just be climbing down their hair," a worker told Fox News about illegal alien children at Lackland Air Force Base in San Antonio, Texas. A nurse commented, "After we would rinse out their hair, the sink would be loaded with black bugs."[17]

This is your benevolent Democrat Party at work, endangering the health of American citizens to help noncitizens. Redefining illegals as "undocumented residents," as the Democrats love to do, doesn't change the fact that they ARE NOT American citizens. If they can't DOCU-MENT their citizenship with a birth certificate, obviously they're not citizens of America.

Border patrol agents said the children told them they were coming because they believed in Obama's promises that they could stay in America—the magnet for illegal immigration.[18] And a 2015 Government

Accountability Office report concluded that the reason unaccompanied illegal children from El Salvador, Guatemala, and Honduras were rushing our border with Mexico was their perception of our lax immigration policy: "Five agency officials' responses across all three countries identified migrants' perceptions of U.S. immigration policies as a primary cause of UAC [unaccompanied children] migration. For example, the State [Department] official's response for Honduras reported that some Hondurans believed that comprehensive immigration reform in the United States would lead to a path to citizenship for anyone living in the United States at the time of reform."[19]

Adding insult to illegal immigration injury, the United States gives El Salvador, Guatemala, and Honduras millions of dollars in economic aid while thousands of their people are violating our laws. How dumb is this? In 2014 the U.S. Agency for International Development (USAID) and the State Department gave $22 million to El Salvador, $60 million to Guatemala, and $42 million to Honduras. And we're not done. The Millennium Challenge Corporation, another government agency, has committed $277 million to El Salvador and another $15.7 million to Honduras.

The Democrats should be looking out for the safety of Americans by deporting the illegals, not sending their home countries multimillion-dollar aid packages. The president's job is to protect national security, public safety, and border security, but under Obama's direction the agency is running a catch-and-release-and-let-kill program.

We hear constant fervent cries from Democrats that amnesty is the only solution to our illegal immigration problem. That's just not true. If America could figure out a way to send a man to the moon, I'm certain we can figure out how to build a wall to keep illegals out and deport them one by one as they come over. It's not brain surgery, but it does require due diligence by government. Perhaps some of the tens of millions of dollars we're sending in aid to Central American countries could help with the deportation expenses.

THE DEMOCRATS' NEXT PRO-ILLEGALS PRESIDENT?

Democrat presidential frontrunner Hillary Clinton promises to pick up where Obama left off. At a campaign appearance in Las Vegas in May 2015, Clinton said she'll fight against deporting illegals who are "at risk of deportation. And, if Congress refuses to act, as President I will do everything possible under the law to go even further. There are more people—like many parents of DREAMers and others with deep ties and contributions to our communities—who deserve a chance to stay. I'll fight for them too."[20]

Clinton, as her Democrat cohorts regularly do, also bashed Republicans' efforts to protect American citizens, adding, "Today not a single Republican candidate, announced or potential, is clearly and consistently supporting a path to citizenship. Not one. When they talk about 'legal status,' that's code for 'second-class status.'"

Clinton is correct that Republicans support our current immigration laws—not proposed so-called immigration "reforms" that would reward criminals. And let me point out that an illegal alien by definition is not a citizen, much less a "second-class" one.

If the Democrats cared about justice and protecting Americans, Kate Steinle, Grant Ronnebeck, and many others killed by illegals would be alive today. House Democratic Caucus chairman Xavier Becerra has also defended illegal immigration, warning, "Don't take the Donald Trump bait." To the contrary, I think America is long overdue for some straight talk on immigration. It's time for our nation to ditch liberals' politically correct approach to immigration and SEND THE muchachos and muchachas HOME.

TAKING OUR JOBS

Obama's lack of immigration enforcement isn't just costing us American lives; it's killing our jobs too.

The unemployment rate has declined ONLY because Americans either are underemployed or have given up looking for jobs. Those factors make the official unemployment rate look better. But under President Obama's leadership, America has had the lowest labor participation rate—about 62 percent—in nearly forty years. Thank the worst recession since the Great Depression and Obama's amnesty policies.

The labor participation rate measures the number of adults who are either working or looking for work. Americans who fall out of that category aren't even trying to find jobs anymore. So the huge drop in the labor participation rate is an indicator that something is very wrong with our labor market. Could it be the hordes of illegal workers, making the situation worse after one of the worst recessions in U.S. history? In California, 2.6 million illegal aliens make up nearly a tenth of the state's workforce.[21] According to the Pew Hispanic Center, in the twelve months after June 2009 (the end of the Great Recession) foreign-born workers gained 656,000 jobs while native-born workers lost 1.2 million.[22]

The Democrats and the other enablers of illegal immigration like to claim that immigrants take the jobs Americans won't do. But it's not that we won't take these jobs. It's that illegals will work like slaves or indentured servants for ANY WAGE, less than even the federal minimum wage of $7.25 an hour, and work ANYTIME, ANY DAY of the week.

Tell me how these are fair labor practices—a key plank of Democrat Party platform. What's more comical is that Democrat lawmakers from the District of Columbia to California have jacked up the local minimum wages to new heights of $10.50 and $10.00, respectively, and the Democrats are lobbying to more than double the federal minimum wage to $15 an hour. But none of these Democrats are concerned with deporting illegal immigrants, who undercut the minimum wage and take Americans' jobs. Giving safe haven to people who will work for less than the minimum wage DEFEATS the purpose of raising the minimum wage. If illegal aliens weren't here, Americans would be taking these jobs, and employers would be paying Americans a decent wage.

While U.S. citizens overall are harmed economically by illegal workers, black Americans are the biggest losers. Harvard University professor George Borjas has studied this extensively, finding, in a 2010 study that he coauthored, "a strong correlation between immigration and black wages [and] black employment rates.... As immigrants disproportionately increased the supply of workers in a particular skill group, we find a reduction in the wage of black workers in that group [and] a reduction in the employment rate...."[23]

In 2011 the unemployment rate for blacks was 16 percent, the highest since 1984 and almost twice the national average of 9 percent at the time. With its divide-and-conquer identity politics, the Democrat Party can't be all things to all people, and it oftentimes finds itself at odds with the interests of its constituents. There is no better example of the hypocrisy of the Democrats' identity politics than the issue of illegal immigration, which pits blacks against Hispanics. The wonder is how these con artists are able to keep both blacks and illegals convinced that the Democrat Party is on their side.

One of Obama's main agenda items during his 2012 reelection campaign was to serve up amnesty to Hispanics on a silver platter, which would only exacerbate double-digit black unemployment. This is how little the country's black Democrat president thinks of his most loyal constituents, 95 percent of whom voted for him in 2008. In 2012 blacks again showed Obama undying love, with 93 percent of blacks voting for him. But illegal immigration is no friend of blacks in America, and it never will be. Many studies show blacks are harmed more than any other racial group by illegal aliens, mostly Hispanics and Latinos, who broke the law to come here. Blacks also benefit the most when illegal workers are deported!

In a compelling article about why Donald Trump should exploit the illegal immigration issue to win the black vote, Bruce Bartlett observed:

> There is little doubt that immigration depresses the employment and wages of black men. A 2010 study by the economists George Borjas, Jeffrey Grogger and Gordon Hanson found that

a 10 percent immigration-induced increase in the labor supply reduced African Americans' wages by 2.5 percent and the employment rate among blacks by 5.9 percentage points.

Since the 1990s, academics have been studying the political and economic cleavage between blacks and Latinos. A 1997 study by sociologist Roger Waldinger found that employers in Los Angeles favored Latino over black workers, a situation reinforced by tense relations when the two groups worked side by side. A 2006 study by political scientists David O. Sears and Victoria Savalei found that even newly-arrived Latinos were better able to assimilate politically into the broader society than blacks who were still subject to a strict color line.[24]

AN ALTERNATIVE POLICY ON IMMIGRATION AND BLACK UNEMPLOYMENT

While Democrats are enthusiastically trying to take away American jobs from blacks and give them to illegals, Donald Trump wants to do the opposite. At an August 27, 2015, speech in Greenville, South Carolina, Trump made a bid for the black vote by promising to create jobs for blacks, especially black males who suffer from higher unemployment. He said he would bring back jobs that U.S. companies had offshored to China, Japan, and Mexico.[25]

Jamelle Bouie, a reporter for the ultraliberal news outlet Slate, observed that Trump's strategy of winning some of the black vote was the "easiest path for Republicans to take back the White House." As Bouie remarked on CNN, "I don't think I've heard a Republican ever talk specifically about African-American youth unemployment, which is a legitimate problem and a legitimate issue."[26]

Trump is doing more than talking about it. In his immigration plan, Trump describes how America's bad policies have killed opportunity for blacks. "Decades of disastrous trade deals and immigration policies have destroyed our middle class. Today, nearly 40% of black teenagers are unemployed. Nearly 30% of Hispanic teenagers are unemployed. For black Americans without high school diplomas, the bottom has fallen out: more than 70% were employed in 1960, compared to less than 40% in 2000."[27]

Trump's straight talk and solutions to problems had him leading in every national poll among Republican presidential contenders during the summer of 2015, and he's making huge waves with black voters. Two black women have become a viral sensation by producing videos on DiamondandSilkInc.com showing their unfettered support for Trump. They encouraged Trump to bust open the truth about illegal immigration like "a piñata": "If we commit a crime in this country, we gon' go to jail for it. So why is it, they can commit a crime by crossing that border illegal [sic] and once they do that we give 'em shelter?" the sisters asked in one video.[28]

REPUBLICANS VS. DEMOCRATS ON ENFORCEMENT

In 2006 Crider Inc. in Georgia was raided by ICE, which found 75 percent of its nine hundred mostly Hispanic workers were illegals. After the raid, the company hired mostly black workers. Ironically, a decade before, blacks had represented 70 percent of the company's workers, but blacks began leaving "with the arrival of so many immigrants willing to toil for rock-bottom wages on brutal round-the-clock shifts."[29]

These raids were conducted under Republican President George W. Bush. The Democrat Obama regime virtually stopped ICE worksite raids and prosecuting illegal workers. "Instead, they conduct I-9 audits and release the illegal workers so they can walk down the street and take another job from an American worker," remarked then–House Judiciary Committee chairman Lamar Smith at a March 1, 2011, House Subcommittee on Immigration Policy and Enforcement hearing on "Making Immigration Work for American Minorities."[30]

Once again we see Republicans concerned about protecting Americans against illegal aliens and the Democrats taking the side of illegals. At the same hearing, ranking Democrat Representative John Conyers said, "Now this is a very sensitive subject because if we are not careful—and I have a very optimistic and expanded view of what we can accomplish here today—but the notion that is underneath the surface of pitting African-American workers against Hispanic workers and immigrants is so abhorrent and repulsive to me that I want to get it on the table right now."

From the mouth of a Democrat, no less, Conyers virtually confesses to his party's dirty politics of racial division. Americans who support the Democrat Party, particularly blacks, should be very offended by Democrats' support of illegal immigration, which is at direct odds with their prosperity.

Conyers asked the panel of witnesses at the hearing if they believed America should enforce our immigration laws—but he asked the question as if the very possibility were ridiculous: "Well, let me just close with a question about the subject. How many here of the four of you believe that we ought to really just remove all the nonlegal immigrants in the country? Just take them right out of the fields, wherever they work. Or if they are not working, period."

After fifty years of blacks' allowing Democrats to pimp them at the ballot box, we deserve more from the Civil Rights Party that claims to have our backs. Black lives may matter, but clearly whether blacks have jobs doesn't.

Once again adding insult to injury, Democrats regularly make "the comparison that somehow immigrants or undocumented immigrants are in an analogous position to African Americans in the civil rights struggle," as Frank L. Morris of Progressives for Immigration Reform testified at that House hearing. How do the two groups really compare? Blacks were brought forcibly to America in bondage and worked without being paid, then were denied access to jobs during segregation. Illegals, on the other hand, force their way into the country and steal jobs from blacks and other citizens.

Vanderbilt University professor Carol Swain, another expert who testified at the hearing on the impact of illegal immigration on minorities, expressed her dismay at "the fact that the Black leadership, whether we are talking about the NAACP or the Congressional Black Caucus, has done a very poor job of representing the interests of Black Americans."

Conyers snapped back: "Dr. Swain never misses an opportunity to denigrate the CBC, which is frequently regarded to be the conscience of the Congress." ("Conscience of the Congress"—talk about a con job! See chapter 12 for more on the Congressional Black Caucus.)

"I have been reelected 23 times in a row and am now the second most-senior Member of the Congress," Conyers ranted. But that doesn't mean he's done his black constituents any good.

Swain continued her testimony, putting her finger on the conflict between the pro–illegal immigration agenda the Democrats are pushing and the true interests of the constituents they claim to represent.

> I would like to be able to elaborate, and I would also like to be able to say to you, Mr. Conyers, that the [virtually 100 percent Democrat] Congressional Black Caucus, over the decades, they have done a great job. But it seems like somewhere along the way, they just lost their way.
>
> And I think that we can trace the shift in the Congressional Black Caucus's position on immigration enforcement and that they seem to be more responsive now to interest groups rather than to the people that vote for them. And Black people vote for you and for the other Black members because they are very loyal. They love you. We love you. I love you.
>
> But I wish the Congressional Black Caucus would do a better job of really representing the downtrodden, their constituents who are of different races and not one particular race.

Well, as a black person, I don't love Conyers or respect him. But Swain is right that the Democrats in the CBC have utterly failed black people on immigration—and many other issues. Over the past fifty years, beginning at the very time blacks began voting almost exclusively Democrat, we have suffered higher unemployment rates than other racial groups.

AMNESTY BY EXECUTIVE ORDER

On November 20, 2014, again acting unilaterally, President Obama announced he would use an executive order to stop the deportation of the parents of U.S. citizens and green card holders. These are people who knowingly broke the law to enter the United States—many of whom are the parents of "anchor babies."[31]

You broke the law, no problem. Obama rewarded you with a path toward amnesty and citizenship. The president's plan will allow about 5 million illegal aliens to remain in the country. It bears repeating AGAIN and AGAIN that these are people who knowingly broke the law to enter the United States, but Obama AGAIN rewards them with what looks and sounds like citizenship.

No way was this good news for blacks, who in the fall of 2014 had an unemployment rate of 11.2 percent, nearly twice the national average of about 6 percent.[32]

Obama's granting amnesty to 5 million illegal immigrants makes the job market even more hostile to blacks competing for the same blue-collar jobs that illegals are taking. The Bureau of Labor Statistics found the unemployment rate for "the foreign born," which includes both legal and illegal immigrants, declined from 8.1 percent in 2012 to 5.6 percent in 2014, while the unemployment rate for native-born blacks remained in the double digits.[33] The BLS also found that the majority of foreign-born workers are employed in blue-collar service jobs—the same jobs that in decades past had been filled by blacks. Foreign-born workers are also driving down wages. In 2014 the median weekly income of foreign-born, full-time workers was $664, a figure that is about 81 percent of the weekly income of native-born, full-time workers.[34] Illegal immigration has always been bad for black Americans. The CBC knows it, Democrats know it, and so does Obama!

Of particular insult to blacks is the propaganda "African American" tab on the Democratic National Committee (DNC) website, which reads, "But the economic crisis has had an especially brutal impact on minority communities—communities that were already struggling long before the financial crisis hit."

What is the Democrat Party's solution to help blacks economically? Support a fast track to citizenship for illegal aliens and a virtual ban on deportation to help them continue to steal jobs from blacks. This makes perfect sense in the minds of liberals.

"For decades, Democrats have stood with the African American community in the struggle for equality and the enduring struggle to perfect our nation itself," brags the DNC website.

Democrats have stood with blacks all right—on a crumbling sand-castle of hypocrisy. Instead of taking the side of American citizens, and particularly some of their most loyal constituents, such as blacks, Democrats side with noncitizens.

"The Congressional Black Caucus and the Congressional Hispanic Caucus have been at the forefront in championing progressive policies that take into account the challenges that American minorities confront. One need only review the Republicans' voting records to understand their political priorities, and it does not include a deep concern for the working class or American minorities," remarked Democrat Representative Maxine Waters of California at the "Making Immigration Work for American Minorities" hearing.

Republicans are the ones who vote to secure our borders, deport illegal aliens, and enforce existing immigration laws. Democrats have consistently opposed all three things.

Democrats believe illegal aliens deserve easy access to what is our birthright because they've had the audacity to live and work in America ILLEGALLY for years.

TEARING AMERICA APART

"We cannot afford to allow people who have political agendas to divide us," added Waters. Voters should think about that. The Democrat Party's immigration agenda is designed to do just that—tear America apart. Illegal immigrants are future Democrat voters. The blacks whose jobs they're taking are the Democrat Party's most loyal voting bloc as long as they're in desperate need of government rescue from their economic plight. Cries of "racism" against anyone who points out how illegal immigration is hurting Americans keep the Republicans on the defensive and help the Democrats win elections. And if, in the process, American citizens get killed or raped by illegal immigrants, what do the Democrats care?

A 2011 *Columbus Post Dispatch* investigation of illegals in Ohio "revealed that it is common for deported immigrants to return to the United States despite the threat of felony charges." The report included an array of thugs, from domestic violence abusers to drug dealers with "serious criminal histories" who become repeat offenders once they return to the United States. In 2011 prosecutors charged more than one hundred illegals in federal court in Columbus with breaking the law by returning illegally after being deported.[35] Tragically, Mexico isn't "sending their best," as Trump said in his campaign announcement.[36]

Let's be honest, Trump just said what most Americans think but are afraid to say for fear of public backlash from liberal hyenas calling them racists. Knee-jerk accusations of "racism" work just as well to shut down honest discussion on the subject of illegal immigration as they do the subject of the crimes being committed by young "unarmed black men." And in both cases, the beneficiaries at the ballot box are the Democrats. If the American people are not even allowed to *discuss* the damage the Democrats' irresponsible policies are causing, how can we correct course? That's why Donald Trump is really scaring the Dems and their allies in the mainstream media.

The mainstream media went ballistic over Trump's remarks. They were shocked and appalled by his bluntness—and terrified by the fact that political correctness doesn't work to shut him up.

Washington Post columnist Jonathan Capehart referred to Trump's remarks about Mexicans as "nasty" and "harsh."[37] Univision host Jorge Ramos decried his comments as "absurd" and "prejudiced."[38] The *Christian Science Monitor* found them "insulting."[39]

But apparently not all insults are created equal. The liberal media didn't have a problem when British celebrity Kelly Osbourne appeared on *The View* on August 4, 2015, and said this: "If you kick every Latino out of this country, then who is going to be cleaning your toilet, Donald Trump?"[40]

You can't get more racist than that. I wonder what Osbourne thinks blacks are good at—picking cotton? Instead of lambasting her as they did Trump, liberal *View* cohosts Whoopi Goldberg and Raven-Symoné defended her as not being a racist. Whoopi said Osbourne just "stepped in dog doo."

The most obvious racism doesn't really offend the Democrats—except when they can use their outrage to attack Republicans and win elections. And apparently illegal immigrants' crimes don't upset them either. It's the Republicans who are VILLAINS for wanting to secure our borders and deport illegal aliens. In the world according to Democrats, U.S. lawmakers elected by Americans should serve the interests of illegals.

When Trump released his immigration plan in August of 2015, the liberal media were aghast that a presidential candidate had the nerve to use the word "deportation." Aside from calling for the removal of these criminals, Trump's plan also would end birthright citizenship, which illegals abuse. As if it's not outrageous enough that illegal aliens invade our borders, they also give birth to "anchor babies" who automatically become citizens under the Fourteenth Amendment. Republican members of Congress like Representative Steve King of Iowa have long championed this issue, introducing bills to end birthright citizenship.[41]

Trump has also warned that if he's elected president, he will build a wall along the two-thousand-mile Mexican border—and make Mexico pay for it! That only seems appropriate, since more illegals enter our country from theirs than from any other nation. Ironically, the headline of the *Washington Post*'s August 18, 2015, editorial read, "Donald Trump's Immigration Plan Would Wreak Havoc on U.S. Society." Perhaps the paper's editorial team missed the havoc illegals have already wreaked on American citizens—stealing our jobs and killing us.

Another *Washington Post* article described Trump pushing "fringe" ideas and driving "a debate over harsh immigration measures." Mexicans are scared and offended by the prospect of a Trump presidency. And they should be. For a long time, Americans have been offended by their disregard for our laws and demands that we owe them something for violating them. The only thing America owes illegal immigrants is a swift kick in the butt back over the border.

Gustavo Vega Canovas, a professor at the College of Mexico, compared Trump's comments to what the Nazis did to the Jews.[42] But Trump's not calling for genocide of Mexicans, he's calling for the deportation of illegals back to their own country. There's a big difference.

When did enforcing U.S. laws become harsh? Since Democrats became cheerleaders for illegal aliens over Americans.

CHAPTER FIVE

THE PARTY OF SANCTUARY CITIES

The Democrat Party is like a drug dealer: it derives its power from selling bad things like abortion and crime to good people and getting them hooked—addicted to the bad life. "Sanctuary cities" are another evil addiction the Democrat Party markets and sells to its constituents like a hooker seducing a teenage boy.

Please don't be misled or confused by the name. Sanctuary cities aren't places for religious worship or calming retreats. They are cities in our nation, largely governed by Democrats, that not only welcome illegals with open arms but give them the same rights as American citizens. Law enforcement in these cities shields illegal criminals from prosecution and deportation, allowing them to threaten the safety of lawful residents.

Were it not for Democrat-governed sanctuary cities' giving refuge to illegal aliens, Kate Steinle, Jamiel Shaw II, Grant Ronnebeck, and many other Americans would be alive today.

Democrat lawmakers in these cities are violating the 1996 Illegal Immigration Reform and Immigrant Responsibility Act, which requires local

passed at request of President Clinton

governments to assist the Department of Homeland Security's Immigration and Customs Enforcement to apprehend and deport illegal aliens.[1]

But in sanctuary cities, Democrat politicians ignore this and many other immigration laws with downright indignant impunity, as if the laws do NOT exist.

Kate Steinle was murdered in San Francisco, a Democrat-dominated "sanctuary city" that refuses to cooperate with the enforcement of our immigration laws. The relevant part of the San Francisco code reads:

> No department, agency, commission, officer or employee of the City and County of San Francisco shall use any City funds or resources to assist in the enforcement of federal immigration law or to gather or disseminate information regarding the immigration status of individuals in the City and County of San Francisco unless such assistance is required by federal or State statute, regulation or court decision.[2]

Like many American cities governed by Democrats, San Francisco welcomes illegals with open arms, allowing them to steal jobs from Americans and harm residents. Francisco Lopez-Sanchez, the five-times deported illegal alien who killed Kate Steinle, had numerous convictions for drug offenses. He had been released from federal prison to the custody of U.S. Immigration and Customs Enforcement. The agency turned him over to the San Francisco County Sheriff deputies, who in turn released this criminal into the streets of San Francisco to kill Steinle.[3] It's the equivalent of rewarding rapists with a get-out-of-jail-free card and then putting them up in a sorority house.

THE JAMIEL SHAW CASE

In 2008 another illegal alien killed a seventeen-year-old unarmed black teen, Jamiel Shaw II, in Los Angeles—another sanctuary city run by a Democrat mayor. Pedro Espinoza, a nineteen-year-old illegal Mexican, had been released from jail the day before he gunned down Shaw. Espinoza had a prior record of three gun charges and had served four months of an eight-month jail sentence for assaulting a police officer with a deadly weapon. Espinoza received the death penalty for the murder, but that was too late to save Shaw—his illegal alien murderer should never have been in the country in the first place.[4]

Jamiel Shaw's father gave agonizing testimony about his son's death on February 25, 2015, at the House Government Oversight and Reform hearing on the Department of Homeland Security's policies toward "non-citizens unlawfully present in the United States." (ICE is part of DHS.)

"Why was this violent illegal alien allowed to walk the streets of America instead of being deported?" Shaw asked members of Congress.

> Why was ICE not called to pick up this violent invader? We were promised that the federal government would keep us safe from violent illegal aliens....
>
> I see in here black politicians, black athletes, black stars say "hands up, don't shoot." My son was shot in the head by an illegal alien gangbanger while he lay on his back with his hands up. He still shot him through his hand and into his head and killed him....
>
> ... The duty of the U.S. government is to always put American families first.[5]

Mr. Shaw, your son died because Democrats value the rights of illegal alien gangbangers over the lives of U.S. citizens. That's the raw, ugly truth. After America has defended itself against so many enemy combatants for over two hundred years, Democrats are now welcoming the enemy to our homeland.

WHEN BLACK LIVES DON'T MATTER TO THE DEMOCRATS

Mr. Shaw's son's death didn't inspire marches or hashtags on Twitter. Democrats like President Obama and presidential candidate Hillary Clinton didn't speak out about this young unarmed black man's death. Why? Because black lives only matter to liberals when a white man kills a black man—and the Democrat Party can leverage the racially divisive, sensational headlines into votes.

Obama found time to speak on multiple occasions about the deaths of Freddie Gray, Trayvon Martin, and Michael Brown, holding press conferences and issuing statements.[6]

July 19, 2013—White House Press Briefing about the Martin Trial Verdict

First of all, I want to make sure that, once again, I send my thoughts and prayers, as well as Michelle's, to the family of Trayvon Martin, and to remark on the incredible grace and dignity with which they've dealt with the entire situation. I can only imagine what they're going through, and it's remarkable how they've handled it....

You know, when Trayvon Martin was first shot I said that this could have been my son.[7]

August 14, 2014—Statement on Brown's Death While on Vacation in Martha's Vineyard

We lost a young man, Michael Brown, in heartbreaking and tragic circumstances. He was 18 years old. His family will never hold Michael in their arms again. And when something like this happens, the local authorities—including the police— have a responsibility to be open and transparent about how they are investigating that death, and how they are protecting the people in their communities.[8]

The president also sent administration officials to Brown's funeral.[9]

April 28, 2015—Remarks by Obama in the Rose Garden, Included Comments on Gray

First, obviously our thoughts continue to be with the family of Freddie Gray. Understandably, they want answers....

I think there are police departments that have to do some soul searching. I think there are some communities that have to do some soul searching. But I think we, as a country, have to do some soul searching. This is not new. It's been going on for decades.[10]

Brown and Martin were thugs in the making who caused their own deaths. The jury is still out on what caused that of ex-con Gray. But Jamiel Shaw was an innocent, unarmed teen killed by an illegal immigrant, and Obama said zero about his death.

Obama also snubbed the vicious murder of Kate Steinle, an unarmed white woman, in the same way. Our commander in chief extended no condolences, "thoughts," or "prayers" to Steinle's family. Obama sent no one to Steinle's funeral. He made no calls for police departments and sanctuary cities to do some "soul searching" about harboring illegals. Even though our illegal immigration problem "isn't new" and has been "happening for decades"!

In heart-wrenching testimony before a Senate Judiciary Committee hearing about Obama's immigration policy on July 21, 2015, Jim Steinle said the last words he heard his daughter utter were, "Help me, Dad." "The U.S. has suffered a self-inflicted wound in the murder of our daughter by the hand of a person that should have never been on the streets of this country," Steinle told the committee.[11]

DEMOCRATS: ILLEGALS' STRONGEST CHAMPIONS

Mr. Steinle can thank the Democrats for his daughter's murder. They have fought tooth and nail to keep illegals on the streets. On its website, the House Democratic Caucus boasts its support for "President Obama's executive actions to fix our country's broken immigration system."[12] Democrats are the party that defends illegals who kill Americans.

On July 23, 2015, the Republican-controlled House voted 241 to 179 in favor of the Enforce the Law for Sanctuary Cities Act. The bill, which was drafted in direct response to Kate Steinle's murder, would deny funding to state and local police who refuse to enforce our immigration laws. Of course Obama vowed to veto it because, as a Democrat, he'd rather protect the criminals.[13]

Criticizing the bill as anti-immigrant, Chairman Xavier Becerra of the House Democratic Caucus said on the House floor: "This is not the way we do justice in America. And it is wrong...."

What's wrong is Becerra and other Democrats encouraging illegal immigration.

THE PAYOFF

Why would Democrats support amnesty havens that harm Americans—and some of their constituents in the process?

Votes, votes, votes! It turns out that #HispanicVotesMatter a lot more than black lives, or any American lives. Hispanics are the fastest-growing demographic in America thanks to the nonenforcement of the nation's immigration laws. Dividing and conquering the electorate based on race, ethnicity, gender, and sexuality is the Democrat Party way.

By supporting illegal immigration, Democrats win the Hispanic vote because Hispanics know they can count on Democrats like Obama to allow their friends and family to keep jumping the borders like rabbits procreating. The endgame for the Democrats, as Obama has demonstrated through his executive orders, is to reward these criminals with citizenship so they will vote Democrat.

Every election cycle, Democrat politicians suck up to pro-amnesty groups like the National Council of La Raza, the Mexican American Legal Defense and Education Fund, and the League of United Latin American Citizens and promise to ignore our immigration laws. In exchange, these groups tell their brown constituents to vote Democrat, and so it goes. Rinse, recycle, and repeat the amnesty message!

Thanks to Democrats, sanctuary cities are fast becoming as dangerous as our inner-city black ghettos. Instead of blacks' occupying and terrorizing the streets, it's illegal aliens. And Democrats are perfectly okay with this. No one feels safe in America's ghettos, and soon no one will feel safe in cities like Los Angeles. As you will see, sanctuary cities are literally becoming like the Wild West, where Annie better get her gun or die not having one.

According to the Center for Immigration Studies (CIS), there are more than two hundred sanctuary cities, counties, and states across the United States that protect criminal aliens from deportation. Using data collected from ICE, CIS concluded that these jurisdictions "have policies, laws, executive orders, or regulations...[that] obstruct federal law authorizing U.S. Immigration and Customs Enforcement (ICE) to administratively deport illegal aliens without seeking criminal warrants or convictions from federal, state, or local courts."[14]

According to the House Judiciary Committee, "Specifically, sanctuary jurisdictions refuse to comply with U.S. Immigration and Customs Enforcement (ICE) detainers or notification requests, which are the tools that federal immigration enforcement agents use to pick up criminal aliens in local jails."[15]

But then again these local and state authorities are just doing what Obama has instructed them to do—not follow our nation's immigration laws. On November 20, 2014, Obama announced the Priority Enforcement Program. Among other things, PEP gives local and state authorities the CHOICE to inform ICE and other federal agencies when local police release illegals who have committed crimes.

"Detainers" are ICE requests to police or other law enforcement agencies to hold illegals for up to forty-eight hours "after their scheduled release from custody" so that ICE can pick them up. Because local law enforcement refused to comply with ICE, the administration's new PEP policy relies less on detainers and more on "requests for notification," which only ask local jurisdictions to *notify* ICE forty-eight hours before releasing an illegal from custody rather than actually hold onto him.

A 2015 *Washington Post* article outlined another "key change" in policy:

> … ICE will file the requests in cases where the immigrant has been convicted of a crime; before, the requests included those only charged.
>
> The new program is part of a broader shift in DHS's priorities in which the department has been narrowing enforcement efforts to three groups of illegal migrants: convicted criminals, terrorism threats or those who recently crossed the southwest border.[16]

CITIES SHIELDING ILLEGALS FROM DEPORTATION

The Democrat Party should create a bumper sticker that reads: "Sanctuary Cities Are Us!" Democrat mayors of sanctuary cities flat-out REFUSE to cooperate with ICE because they think it's mean or not fair.

Breaking another country's laws is a bitch, I guess. But if Americans have to follow the laws, invaders of our homeland should too.

Philadelphia's Democrat mayor Michael A. Nutter refuses to cooperate with the Department of Homeland Security's immigration enforcement guidelines. In April 2014, Nutter signed an executive order that the city would not comply with ICE's detainer requests, because of the federal government's "overly aggressive use of these detainers." Hey moron, it's called enforcement of immigration laws.[17]

Nutter is a black mayor serving Philadelphia, a city with a large black population. A study conducted by Drexel University's Center for Labor Markets and Policy found that only one in ten young black men in Philadelphia was employed in 2012–13. This ranked as one of the lowest black employment rates among big cities.[18]

So why would Nutter act like such a nut, making it easier for illegals to get jobs in Philly and harder for blacks? The hypocrisy of Democrats— saying one thing but doing another, harming their constituents. Mayor Nutter talks a good game. You can watch him on YouTube announcing the reestablishment of the Mayor's Commission on African American Males, to address the "far too many African American males" in Philadelphia who are "uneducated, unemployed, and unhealthy."[19] But meanwhile he's harboring illegals who take jobs from blacks.

New York City, which has the largest police department in the nation and is run by Democrat mayor and cop-hater Bill de Blasio, also refuses to comply with ICE detainers.

The District of Columbia is another sanctuary city governed by a Democrat—Mayor Muriel Bowser, who is black, no less, and harming her own. The city "scaled back its cooperation with ICE several years ago."[20]

Black residents make up the largest group of residents in D.C. and are four times as likely as white residents to be unemployed. In 2013 the unemployment rate for blacks in the city was 16 percent, more than double the unemployment rate for Hispanic residents and more than quadruple the unemployment rate for white residents.[21]

By not enforcing the country's immigration laws in D.C., Democrats are making it even harder for black citizens to get jobs.

Thanks to the pro-amnesty climate Obama has created in the past six years, when a governor tries to work with ICE, all hell breaks loose from the Democrats. On August 13, 2015, Republican Governor Larry Hogan of Maryland announced he would comply with ICE and notify federal officials forty-eight hours before releasing an illegal targeted for deportation.

Hogan was assailed by advocates of illegal immigration, who don't want states and cities to follow our laws. Dozens of amnesty lovers—including probably illegals themselves—protested in front of the governor's mansion in Annapolis.[22] A group of twenty-five pro-amnesty groups sent Hogan a letter asking him to "opt out" of complying with our immigration laws: "Until [Immigration and Customs Enforcement] can prove itself worthy of trust, we ask that you decline to send notification to it about release." Can you believe this, the illegals' enablers asking the state to simply "decline" to assist in enforcing our immigration laws? "In light of the enormous federal failure to repair a broken immigration system, we ask that you remain focused on building the strongest local communities possible." Once again the illegals and their friends in the Democrat Party are dictating the debate. America's immigration laws need to be enforced. And when the laws are enforced and governors and mayors assist ICE in deporting illegals, American cities are made safer. If Hogan had been governor in 2013, maybe Ecuadorian alien Henry Estrella-Cordova would have been deported by ICE and would not have raped a nine-year-old girl in Baltimore.

"Advocates worry that the action could lead to the deportations of people who haven't committed serious crimes," reported the *Washington Post*. They *should* be worried about their illegal friends getting booted from America. But illegals have been allowed to flout our laws and live and work in America like squatters in a person's home for so long that now they think they're entitled to amnesty. Their outrageous behavior is condoned, perpetuated, and encouraged by the Democrat Party.

In contrast to Hogan's trying to make Maryland inhospitable to illegals, San Francisco has long been "a haven for illegal immigration"— which is exactly why Kate Steinle is dead today. San Francisco adopted its "City and County of Refuge" law in 1989 to ban city employees from cooperating with or using government funds and resources to assist federal immigration enforcement officials to deport illegal immigrants unless compelled by court order or state law.[23] Police officers and other city employees in San Francisco are prohibited from asking a person's immigration status.[24]

original reason for sanctuary

The law was inspired by churches in cities like San Francisco seeking to give refuge to people who were fleeing violence in Central America but whom the federal government wouldn't grant asylum. Now, of course, the laws are being used by Democrats and the illegals they shelter to abuse our immigration system.[25]

In February 2007, Democrat San Francisco mayor Gavin Newsom rolled out the red carpet for illegals, issuing an executive order mandating that the city's government agencies develop protocols and training to aid and abet illegal aliens.[26] Newsom followed his executive order with an $83,000 taxpayer-funded public awareness campaign promoting San Francisco's Sanctuary City Outreach Program.[27]

From 2005 to July 2008, San Francisco spent $2.3 million to provide housing for 162 illegal alien youths. The city also spent $38,955 in two years to fly illegal kids who had committed crimes back to Honduras, American Samoa, and Mexico.[28]

Here's a novel idea. How about lawless Democrat mayors like Newsom start following U.S. immigration laws and deport these little thugs?

Long before Kate Steinle was killed, other innocent Americans were dying because San Francisco's sanctuary status attracted the "worst of the worst" to the city, causing a rise in violent crime committed by illegals. In 2008 a local CBS affiliate poll found that 79 percent of people living in San Francisco believed the city should "turn over convicted illegal immigrants for deportation."[29]

THE BOLOGNA CASE

That's not what happened. In June of 2008, Tony Bologna, forty-eight years old, and his sixteen- and twenty-year-old sons, Matthew and Michael, were murdered by Edwin Ramos, an illegal alien from El Salvador. The Bolognas were just a few blocks from their home in the Excelsior district of the city, driving back from a family picnic, when they accidentally blocked Ramos's car from making a left turn. When the father backed up to allow Ramos's car to pass, Ramos fired bullets at them, killing the three men.[30] Tony Bologna's third son, Andrew, survived.

Not only was Ramos a member of Mara Salvatrucha (MS-13), he had had numerous run-ins with the police before he killed the Bolognas. Ramos had been arrested on felony weapons charges but wasn't prosecuted because of a lack of evidence and was NEVER deported. The triple murder was one of the most notorious crimes ever committed in San Francisco. In 2012 Ramos was convicted and sentenced to three consecutive life sentences without the possibility of parole.[31]

Proving that Democrats are more concerned about the well-being of murderous noncitizens than the safety of law-abiding citizens, San Francisco Democrat district attorney Kamala Harris decided not to pursue the death penalty in the case despite objections from the victims' wife and mother, Danielle Bologna. Now Harris is campaigning to win the Democrat Senate nomination to fill Senator Barbara Boxer's seat in 2016. Illegals and their Democrat sympathizers can rest assured that if elected, Harris will be a cheerleader for amnesty and sanctuary cities.

According to investigators, the Bolognas' tragic deaths were a result of mistaken identity; apparently Ramos thought they were enemies of

MS-13. But the real mistake was San Francisco refusing to enforce the country's immigration laws. Thanks to Mayor Newsom and the rest of his Democrat clan, the Bolognas are dead.

PUTTING OUT THE WELCOME MAT FOR CRIMINALS

Illegals have bombarded our borders by the millions; apparently they don't think the rules should apply to them. It takes a long time to become a U.S. citizen, and none of the 11 to 20 million illegals in America meet the requirements listed on the U.S. Citizenship and Immigration Services website.[32]

According to U.S. Citizenship and Immigration Services, to be eligible for naturalization you must:

- Be age 18 or older; and
- Be a permanent resident [green card holder] for a certain amount of time (usually 5 years or 3 years, depending on how you obtained status); and
- Be a person of good moral character; and
- Have a basic knowledge of U.S. government (this, too, can be excepted due to permanent physical or mental impairment); and
- Have a period of continuous residence and physical presence in the United States; and
- Be able to read, write, and speak basic English. There are exceptions to this rule....

Before immigrants can even get to the step of applying for citizenship, they must have a green card, a document NO illegal has. We also know that for THE VAST MAJORITY of these illegals English is a second language; most never have "basic" understanding of it. (Ever tried communicating with the illegal busboys in U.S. restaurants? They give new meaning to the word "clueless"—unless you speak Spanish to them. But I digress.)

Obviously illegals certainly don't fit the eligibility requirement of being "persons of good moral character"—they've established that they're criminals by breaking our laws to come here. One would think any elected official would seek to work with ICE to deport these criminals so they can't harm Americans. Yet in sanctuary cities, Democrat lawmakers give illegals the respect due to U.S. citizens though it's not their birthright and they haven't earned it.

Noticing a trend here? Most sane people close their doors to criminals, alarm their homes, put locks on their doors, and the like. When it comes to illegal immigration, Democrats leave the doors to America wide open and welcome the criminals. Our borders have no padlocks, alarms, barricades, or—dare anyone suggest it—wall.

According to the Center for Immigration Studies, "Although federal regulations plainly require cooperation, the federal government has never sued nor sanctioned a sanctuary jurisdiction, nor denied federal funds."

COLLUSION: NATIONAL DEMS SMILE ON SANCTUARY CITIES

Thank Obama, America's first black Democrat president, and Jeh Johnson, the *black* Department of Homeland Security secretary who is his chief unenforcer. The two of them should just start contracting buses to bring illegals over the border. There would be more honesty in that because Obama's policies have legitimized illegal immigration.

Testifying before the House Judiciary Committee on July 14, 2015, Johnson opined that it would be "controversial" to force sanctuary cities to follow our immigration laws.

"I do not believe that mandating through federal legislation conduct of sheriffs and police chiefs is the way to go," he said. "I think it will be hugely controversial; I think it will have problems with the Constitution.

I want to see us work cooperatively with state and local law enforcement and I believe they are poised to do that."[33]

Johnson pretended to Congress that the federal government is impotent to enforce our immigration laws. It would have been more honest if he had simply told Congress that Obama wants to allow sanctuary cities to ignore our laws. Because Obama knows that his collusion with sanctuary city policies flies in the face of federal law. On September 26, 2007, at a presidential debate held at Dartmouth College, NBC's Tim Russert asked Obama what he'd do about sanctuary cities. Our future president answered, "The federal law is not being enforced not because of failures of local communities, because the federal government has not done the job that it needs to do."[34] So in 2007 Obama blamed President George W. Bush for not enforcing our laws. But now it's okay for Obama to do the same, only to a far greater extreme.

And if Hillary Clinton wins in 2016 she'll keep that illegal love train going just like Obama. When Russert asked Clinton in that 2007 debate, "But you would allow the sanctuary cities to disobey the federal law?" she answered, "Well, I don't think there is any choice." At least the Democrats are consistent—they all pretend there's nothing they can do to enforce our immigration laws.

America's Democrat Party has its priorities completely screwed up, and yet people keep voting for them. I'm pretty sure the Fourteenth Amendment to the Constitution defines U.S. citizens as "All persons born or naturalized in the United States and subject to the jurisdiction thereof." If you can't check either of those boxes, our laws say you ain't a citizen and therefore must be deported. That's the law the director of homeland security should follow. But instead Johnson is looking out for the rights of noncitizen criminals.

Johnson has made it his top priority NOT to enforce America's immigration laws. As we have seen, the president's "prosecutorial discretion" allows ICE not to deport criminal aliens who are not considered high enough "priorities." In 2014 Johnson issued guidelines allowing law enforcement to ignore "fugitive aliens" who had previously been flagged as priorities for deportation, if their removal order was issued before January 1, 2014. This edict amounts to Obama rewriting our immigration laws into nonexistence and giving criminals a get-out-of-jail-free card.[35]

ICE admitted to releasing 30,558 aliens with criminal convictions in 2014. The agency may as well put loaded guns to Americans' heads. While Obama isn't the only president to blame for our illegals problem, it has spun out of control on his watch, as House Judiciary Committee chairman Bob Goodlatte remarked at the same DHS hearing at which Johnson testified: "Unfortunately, new priorities issued by Secretary Johnson last November have turned the flight from enforcement into a headlong rush."

The lack of immigration enforcement in prior administrations has led to 180,000 convicted criminal aliens currently awaiting deportation and another 170,000 convicted criminal aliens who have been ordered to leave but refused to. Since 2012, thanks to Obama's nonenforcement policy, the number of criminal aliens roaming our streets has risen 28 percent.[36]

BLOOD ON THEIR HANDS

Obama and the Democrats have American blood on their hands, lots of it, for putting criminal noncitizens before Americans. Josh Wilkerson's, for example. On November 16, 2010, in Houston, Texas, Josh was killed by a classmate, Hermilio Moralez, who had been brought illegally to the United States from Belize by his parents. Because Moralez was ten years old at the time he broke our immigration laws, he would qualify as a DREAMer under Obama's amnesty-for-illegal-kids program. Mrs. Wilkerson describes the murder of her son in horrific detail.

"We found out later that what he did was he asked Josh for a ride home from school and Josh said, 'sure,'" Mrs. Wilkerson said.

I think he'd given him a ride home two or three times before. He took him actually to his parents' house. For some reason, we found out later why, what he did to Josh was he hit him in the nose, and this is what the kid tells from the stand, he hit him in the nose so hard that it would blind him so that he couldn't fight back. Then he kicked him so hard in the stomach. Josh was about this big around and he weighed about 100 pounds in the body bag. He kicked him so hard in the stomach that his liver sliced in two and his spine sliced in two. He ruptured his spleen. He took a closet rod and beat Josh over the head so hard with it that it broke in four pieces. He strangled him, then let him go. Strangled him, let him go. Per the medical examiner, it was just torturous. After he murdered him, as he said, when Josh quit having bloody bubbles come out of his nose, he knew he was gone, he tied him up like an animal with about 13 ropes from the back of his neck to the back of his hands, to the back of his feet. He covered his head with his school shirt. Then he put him in the back of my son's truck and he drove around and he took two dollars out of Josh's wallet and he stopped and bought gas. Then he took him to a field and he took his wallet and school ID out and just placed it by the body. Then he doused him with gas and set him on fire. It was just incredible. You just don't even believe something like this will happen to your family, let alone to just your kid. What we saw in the beginning of the trial, in the opening, was the police going out to this itty bitty trail and there you saw, when they finally got to Josh, you finally saw him in the fetal position, barefooted, charred, bound up. The policeman said he looked like a doll. He didn't even look real. He looked so tiny. Then after that in the trial the next picture was of his face after they removed his shirt. It was horribly disfigured by the closet rod.[37]

The autopsy report noted that Josh's charred body was found with one stick of gum and a tardy slip in his pocket. During the trial, Mrs. Wilkerson said, Moralez showed no remorse, but rather was excited about what he had done.[38]

When the detective told Joshua's mother they had found Moralez, she asked where Moralez's parents were. The detective explained that he wasn't allowed to ask Moralez those questions because Houston was a sanctuary city and didn't ask illegals their immigration status. Mrs. Wilkerson pointed out to the detective how screwed up America's priorities have become when police don't hold illegals accountable to our laws.

Moralez was sentenced to life in prison, but Mrs. Wilkerson testified at a congressional hearing that when Moralez is up for parole in thirty years he'll only be forty-nine, and she doubts he'll ever be deported.

This is utterly reprehensible policy. As Josh Wilkerson's mother told members of Congress, they're elected to serve and protect Americans, not illegal alien criminals. Under the auspices of compassion, Democrat politicians are spending taxpayer dollars to protect a tsunami of foreign invaders terrorizing our country.[39] But compassion is only the excuse. The truth is, the "sanctuary city" farce helps Democrats keep a lock on the Hispanic vote.

SANCTUARY CITY SLUSH FUND

Just when you thought our nation's immigration policy couldn't be any more lawless and corrupt, there's the Justice Department's State Criminal Alien Assistance Program, which provides federal funds— taxpayer dollars—to states and localities for the jailing of illegal aliens. For the local jurisdictions to qualify for the funds, illegals must be convicted of a felony or two misdemeanors and be incarcerated or detained by local law enforcement for at least four days. SCAAP is giving money to sanctuary cities—in yet another example of Democrat *follow the money*

politicians' fueling our illegal immigration problem and the violent crime that comes with it.[40]

It's no surprise that the program has flourished under Obama. In 2010 SCAAP gave $400 million in grants to about 850 cities, counties, and states. Twenty-seven sanctuary cities received over $62 million to continue to serve as refuges for criminals. They included D.C., home to our nation's government; Fresno County, Los Angeles County, San Francisco, Sonoma County, and Santa Clara County in California; Cook County, Illinois; Montgomery County, Maryland; New York City; Arlington County and Alexandria, Virginia; and more.[41]

"This is a nonsensical situation. These jurisdictions, some of which are home to the largest concentrations of illegal aliens in their state, have policies in place designed to impede federal immigration law enforcement—and yet year after year they ask the federal government to reimburse them for costs associated with a problem that their own policies make worse," observed Jessica Vaughan and Russ Doubleday in a 2010 piece written for the Center for Immigration Studies.

The 2011 GAO report on criminal aliens collected data from five states—Arizona, California, Florida, New York, and Texas. All these states contain sanctuary cities, with California, New York, and Texas being among the worst offenders. The GAO selected these states because of their high concentrations of illegals who had committed crimes. Collectively, these five states accounted for 70 percent of the SCAAP criminal alien population in 2008, which means they received the most funding from the program.[42]

The highest percentage of convictions overall was for drug-related offenses, but in New York the main offense for illegals was homicide. The GAO found that criminal aliens had an average of seven arrests and that about 90 percent of the ones sentenced in federal court in 2009 were convicted of immigration and drug-related offenses.

The cost to imprison illegal aliens in federal prisons and reimburse states and cities through the SCAAP program is about $1.5 billion to

$1.6 billion a year. To point out the obvious, why don't we just deport them? It would reduce the costs of our already overburdened U.S. prison system—and, by the way, enforce our immigration laws. What a concept.

"Sanctuary city policies needlessly endanger American lives by refusing to honor the federal government's authority to enforce immigration laws. Unfortunately, the Obama Administration's own foolish policies enable rogue local governments to defy federal immigration laws. All too often, these reckless policies create preventable tragedies," House Judiciary Committee chairman Bob Goodlatte, a Virginia Republican, has said.

DEMOCRATS VERSUS OUR CIVIL RIGHTS

The United States of America shouldn't be in the position of having to ask illegals to "pretty please" leave our country because Democrats care more about these criminals than they do about the safety of U.S. citizens. Democrat politicians' defying the laws of our land by harboring illegal aliens is tantamount to the racist Democrat politicians' protecting white murderers of blacks in the South during the civil rights movement.

Josh Wilkerson's murder at the hands of an illegal is eerily reminiscent of the 1955 murder of Emmett Till, one of the most important civil rights cases in history. While visiting his uncle in Mississippi that summer, Till stuttered at a white woman in a store, who accused Till of whistling at her. In the segregated South, blacks dared not look a white person in the eye, much less speak to him or her first.

As retribution for his act, Till was hunted down by two white men, J. W. Milam and Roy Bryant, who brutalized him before shooting him in the head and gouging out one of his eyes. Then they tied a seventy-pound cotton gin to his neck with barbed wire to ensure that Till would sink to the bottom of the Tallahatchie River, where they dumped him. When his body was found, it was bloated beyond recognition. His mother was able to identify his body only because of the ring he wore, which had belonged to his father.

In a historic travesty of justice, an all-white jury found Emmett Till's killers not guilty. The crimes committed by illegal immigrants are the modern-day equivalent. Today illegals are given the same freedom to kill as the white racists in the segregated South were in the sixties—by the same Democrat Party. We can thank the Democrats and their sanctuary city policies for the illegals' ability to terrorize American citizens in our homeland. The Democrat Party has let loose an epidemic of violent crime in this country. Consider the following astonishing statistics, collected by the GAO and reported by former congressman Tom Tancredo on Breitbart. In the six years leading up to 2014, *38 percent* of the murderers convicted in the states of New York, Arizona, Texas, California, and Florida were illegal immigrants—even though illegals make up just *5.6 percent* of the population of those five states. That's 7,085 murders that wouldn't have happened if the Democrats weren't making it impossible to deport the criminals who have broken our immigration laws.[43]

Whose side are Democrats on, anyway? When will they start defending law-abiding American citizens instead of illegal hoodlums?

Speaking at a Center for Security Policy conference in 2015 about the Democrats' goal of "erasing America through illegal immigration," James Simpson explained the Democrat Party: "The Left doesn't care about you. They don't care about me. They don't care about immigrants. They don't care about the environment. They don't care about gays. They don't care about anything except their agenda, and their agenda can be described in two words: *power* and *wealth*. That's all they care about. They wrap themselves in the mantle of compassion and good intentions but that's a tactical ploy."[44]

Truer words were never spoken. The Democrats are pulling a con job on the American people. Their "compassion" for illegals is a mirage. The reality behind it is their duplicitous scheme to win votes, which translate into political power.

CHAPTER SIX

THE PARTY OF ABORTION PROFITEERS

The Democrat Party is having a grisly and highly profitable love affair with abortion. "Abortions are very common. In fact, 3 out of 10 women in the U.S. have an abortion by the time they are 45 years old," Planned Parenthood, one of the Democrats' staunchest allies, brags on its website.[1]

Yikes! Really? What about former Democrat president Bill Clinton's promise at the 1996 Democratic National Convention that "abortion should not only be safe and legal, it should be rare"? Another Democrat lie![2]

Baby killing is very lucrative for the number one "pro-choice" organization in the country. In its 2013–14 annual report, Planned Parenthood reported racking up $1.3 billion in revenue, 41 percent of which was of taxpayer money in "government health services grants and reimbursements." In the same period, it performed over three hundred thousand abortions. Why are taxpayers forced to subsidize this baby-butcher factory with our hard-earned dollars?[3]

There's no "family planning" in Planned Parenthood's advocating that women assassinate their babies. In fact, *unplanned* parenthood is what drives so much of the organization's gruesome business. People who PLAN to have babies do just that—anticipate, look forward with joy, and plan for their child's arrival, not their demise.

Referred to as "pro-choice," let's face it, supporters of abortion are really pro-death. Abortion gives women the right to kill their unborn babies. Planned Parenthood should really be named Planned Butcherhood. Abortion is legal, but it's anything but an optimal choice for women. A truly pro-woman agenda would encourage women to take precautions to avoid unplanned pregnancies rather than terminate life. Still, Planned Parenthood–allied Democrats keep racking up women's votes. Pro-choice Obama won 55 percent of women's votes in 2012 against Republican presidential candidate Mitt Romney.

Planned Parenthood is the nation's largest provider of abortions, with seven hundred centers across the country. The group, which is subsidized by the federal government, became embroiled in controversy when undercover videos revealed Planned Parenthood doctors treating human fetuses like garbage.

HORRIFIC UNDERCOVER STING VIDEOS

In the summer of 2015, the Center for Medical Progress (CMP) released a series of videos it had secretly recorded of Planned Parenthood doctors laughing about selling fetal body parts to medical research firms. Federal law prohibits the sale of fetal tissue but allows nonprofit organizations like Planned Parenthood to donate the tissue for research if women give their consent.[4]

Planned Parenthood denied any wrongdoing. It insisted that the payments discussed in the videos were just reimbursement to its centers for the time it took their employees to pick through baby parts to "donate" them to medical research firms. Presumably, "donate" is the new word for "sell." All very legal, you see—according to Planned Parenthood, that is.

Watching the videos challenged my moral conscience and turned my stomach. As I cried seeing Planned Parenthood technicians treating babies like garbage, straining fetuses over a Pyrex dish for their organs, all I could do was think about the babies I'll never have. Something I mourn daily is the fact that I haven't married and my biological clock is toward the end of its reproductive years. I would relish the chance to be able to carry one of these babies, and people were dismembering their tiny bodies, harvesting their hands and feet with tweezers as if in a game of Operation. It was gruesome.

Planned Parenthood is a baby slaughterhouse.

In "Human Capital—Episode 1: Planned Parenthood's Black Market in Baby Parts," Holly O'Donnell, an ex–procurement technician, narrates the horrifying six months she worked for StemExpress, LLC, a customer company of Planned Parenthood based in Placerville, California. (Following the release of the CMP videos, StemExpress decided to "terminate activities" with Planned Parenthood.)[5] On its website StemExpress states it is a multimillion-dollar company that supplies fetal and adult human tissues to biomedical researchers around the world.

This is how O'Donnell described the company she worked for: "StemExpress is a company that hires procurement techs to draw blood and dissect dead fetuses and sell the parts to researchers. They partner with Planned Parenthood and they get part of the money 'cause we pay them to use their facilities and they get paid from it. They do get some kind of benefit. We were asked to procure certain tissues like brain, liver, sinus, pancreas, heart, lungs, and pretty much anything on the fetus. It's basically human trafficking of fetal tissues."[6] As O'Donnell explains on video, "The harder and more valuable the tissue, the more money you get. So if you can somehow procure a brain or a heart, you're going to get more money."

O'Donnell describes StemExpress as "making a lot of money off of poor girls who half the time don't want to get abortions. It's a pretty sick company." And the Dems defend Planned Parenthood because it provides "access" to abortions.

For a nonprofit, it's making a lot of money off its services. The 1976 Hyde Amendment prohibits ANY taxpayer money from paying for abortions. But the money that Planned Parenthood receives is comingled. It's impossible to separate federal dollars from other dollars.

Recalling her first day working at the Planned Parenthood Concord Clinic in California, O'Donnell says she watched someone come into a room with a bottle of bloody contents and pour it into a strainer over a sink. Then the person put the remains in a clear pie dish with a light under it.

> My trainer comes over. She puts on gloves and grabs some tweezers and she's taking the parts away from the vaginal tissue…. Literally, she has tweezers and she's like, "Okay well this is the head, this is the arm, this is a leg." She hands 'em over. "Oh, here you go, can you show me some of the parts I just showed you?"
>
> And I grabbed the tweezers because I didn't want to lose this job, I didn't know…. So I did what she said and the moment I took the tweezers and put 'em in the dish. And I remember grabbing a leg and I said "This is the leg," and the moment I picked it up I could feel like death and pain. Like shoot up through my body and I blacked out basically.

Dr. Mary Gatter, president of the Medical Directors' Council of the Planned Parenthood Federation of America, was also featured in the videos—laughing as she offered to sell baby parts for "$75 a specimen" to CMP's investigative reporter. This is what Democrats think of human life.

How proud the supporters of the Democrat Party must be.

When the undercover investigator offered to pay $100 for the parts, Gatter demurred, saying she needed to check with the California affiliates first. She added that if they needed to "bump it" to a higher price, the company could do that later. In the next breath, Gatter said, laughing, "I want a Lamborghini"—suggesting she wanted to use any extra profit Planned Parenthood made off selling baby parts to buy an expensive Italian sports car.

PROFITING FROM ABORTION

Americans can thank Democrat president Bill Clinton for creating the dead-baby-parts-farming business. In 1993 Clinton signed the National Institutes of Health Revitalization Act of 1993, which legalized government-funded research using aborted fetal tissue for the first time in U.S. history.[7]

I don't know how any woman could work for Planned Parenthood. But Planned Parenthood president Cecile Richards, who should be called the chief baby butcher, has the stomach for it. In a video statement released July 16, 2015, Richards denied any wrongdoing: "I want to be really clear: the allegation that Planned Parenthood profits in any way from tissue donation is not true!"[8]

That's not what the undercover videos showed. Moreover, StemExpress's advertising material explains how providers can make "financial profits" by supplying baby parts to them. As the flyer advises, it's an "Easy to Implement Program." But I thought it was against federal law for people to sell fetal tissue![9]

It's all right there in the StemExpress flyer: "StemExpress promotes global biomedical research while also providing a financial benefit to your clinic. By partnering with StemExpress, not only are you offering a way for your clients to participate in the unique opportunity to facilitate life-saving research, but you will also be contributing to the fiscal growth of your own clinic. The stem cell rich blood and raw materials that are usually discarded during procedures can, instead, be expedited through StemExpress to research laboratories with complete professionalism and source anonymity."

Planned Parenthood president Cecile Richards claimed that over her organization's hundred-year history it has worked diligently with leading medical experts to develop its "high standards." Since when did selling aborted baby parts to the highest bidder become an example of standing on high moral ground? How is it compatible with the Hippocratic oath's pledge to "first do no harm"?

Planned Parenthood clinics don't just abort babies; they treat baby parts like items on a fast food menu. In the Center for Medical Progress's sixth undercover video about Planned Parenthood, former StemExpress technician O'Donnell describes how she placed orders for "a fifteen-week fetus," eyes, lungs, whatever she wanted.[10]

O'Donnell reveals in graphic detail the gruesome story of the profitable abortion industry in America, built on lies, deception, and exploitation of the poor. Nurses at Planned Parenthood clinics would give StemExpress technicians sheets of paper listing every woman who was coming in that day, along with the medical procedure she was receiving, from ultrasounds to abortions. Then, O'Donnell explains, the technicians would place their orders with the nurses, telling them what parts they wanted that day.

"The environment is morbid," O'Donnell says, describing the "high-volume" Planned Parenthood abortion clinic in Fresno, California. "Fresno was in, uhm, actually in an alley. The areas like Fresno where it's dirt-cheap and the area's not good, there were so many, so many…40 something patients [a day]." So much for Planned Parenthood's posing as the polar opposite of the notorious back-alley abortions of the bad old days before *Roe v. Wade*. In fact, the Fresno Planned Parenthood clinic sounds like a baby-killing factory. O'Donnell explains that Dr. Ron Berman, who worked at the clinic, "had a reputation for going viciously fast." He would pace the halls impatiently if he didn't have abortions to perform. On the video, O'Donnell says she felt like telling women not to go to that clinic. "It's almost like he wanted to do it," she says, disgusted.

Despite the legal requirement to get mothers to sign consent forms, O'Donnell reveals that her coworkers often just took "what they wanted"—as in whatever fetal tissue and baby parts they had orders for—without the mother's consent. "They were cold. They just wanted their money," she testifies. "Imagine you were an abortion patient and someone was going in stealing your baby's parts," O'Donnell adds on the tape.

Half the women were undecided as to whether they wanted to have an abortion, according to O'Donnell. Girls were throwing up in trash-cans, asking O'Donnell if they should get the abortion. O'Donnell says she wasn't going "to tell a girl to kill her baby so I can get money"—something she says StemExpress pushed her to do.

BABY HEADS IN THE MAIL

The biggest indictment against the American abortion industry in this video is O'Donnell's description of baby parts being treated with NO dignity, with complete callousness, the way you'd handle an item purchased online. At the end of her work day at any clinic, O'Donnell says, she would put the baby parts she had acquired in tubes, label them with stickers, update her paperwork on "how many" she had gotten, and ship everything in a FedEx box.

When the FedEx worker would ask her what was in the box, O'Donnell explains, she didn't want to say, "Dead baby parts." On its website, FedEx states it has "a comprehensive library of shipping labels" to help customers identify special package-handling needs. I wonder if it has a label that states: *CAUTION! Dead baby parts, handle with care!*?

The shipping giant also has a 183-page service guide that includes guidelines for shipping dangerous goods and hazardous material. I did a search and couldn't find any guidelines for shipping sacred human remains. But I did notice that the list of items that FedEx prohibits from shipment includes "human corpses, human body parts, human embryos," along with dead animals, explosives, live insects, lottery tickets, and cash. Of course the disclaimer at the end of the list of prohibited items states FedEx isn't liable for ANYTHING if the shipper doesn't disclose to FedEx what's in the box.

The eighth undercover video shows Cate Dyer, the CEO of StemExpress, talking about shipping whole dead babies and baby heads.[11] Or, as the *Weekly Standard* headlined its story, "Planned Parenthood Baby Parts Buyer Laughs about Shipping Severed Heads."[12] "Oh yeah, if you had intact cases, which we've done a lot, we sometimes ship those back to our lab in its entirety." It turns out that receiving a baby head in the mail can be a shock for some of the folks working at the research labs that StemExpress sells baby brains to: "Tell the lab it's coming! They'll open the box, go, 'Oh God!' [laughter] So yeah, whereas so many of the academic labs cannot fly like that, they're just not capable…. It's almost like they don't want to know where it comes from. I can see that. Where they're like, 'We need limbs, but no hands and feet need to be attached….' They want you to take it all off, like, 'Make it so that we don't know what it is'…. And their lab techs freak out, and have meltdowns, and so it's just like, yeah."

ABORTION: UNSAFE, ANYTHING BUT RARE—AND LEGAL ONLY BECAUSE OF THE DEMOCRATS

Apparently StemExpress liked working with Planned Parenthood because it's "a volume institution." As Dyer says, "We're working with, you know, almost like triple digit number clinics [a figure that apparently included independent abortion clinics as well as Planned Parenthood clinics, which made up something like 50 percent of StemExpress's business]. So it's a lot on volume, and we still need more than what we do."

Dyer tells the undercover reporter that StemExpress could use "another fifty livers a week." We know that the Democrats' promise to keep abortion "rare" is a farce, don't we?

And the same undercover video shows that it's not exactly "safe," either. StemExpress's CEO complains about how the samples she gets are sometimes contaminated with bacteria and yeast from abortion clinics: "Contamination-wise is another big issue. I mean, so you know, we've seen all sorts of things but yeast contamination, that can be an issue.... I've seen really rampant problems with bacteria in certain clinics. Some where you're kind of like in question of really, should they really, you know.... I've seen staph come out of clinics."

Those "safe," "legal," and "rare" promises were just part of the Dems' con job. The only thing they care about is the "legal" part. And, honestly, should it be legal to kill babies? Not to mention, to chop their bodies up afterward and sell the parts? This is the abortion regime the Democrats have ardently defended for the past forty years, running "pro-choice" candidates, assaulting the Republicans for the imaginary "war on women," torpedoing Supreme Court nominations, all in defense of the "right" to turn unborn children into medical waste.

And apparently the harvesting of the baby parts isn't always done *after* death. In the seventh undercover video, former StemExpress technician Holly O'Donnell explains she harvested a brain by cutting with scissors through the face of a fetus whose heart was beating.[13]

This horror story is what the Democrat Party has given America.

And the Democrat Party is still defending it. Not only are they pulling out every stop to keep abortion legal. They also insist that the nation's premier abortion provider must be *funded with our tax dollars*. Of course it was the Democrats who made sure that government funding kept flowing to the abortion profiteers even in the wake of the videos' release. After those videos exposed Planned Parenthood as purveyors of dead baby parts in the summer of 2015, Republicans tried once again to do something to at least chip away at the outrageous abortion-on-demand regime in America. Senate Republicans Joni Ernst, Rand Paul, and James Lankford introduced a bill to strip Planned Parenthood of its government funding. Of course Democrat President Obama threatened to veto the bill. But he didn't need to, because Democrats in the Senate roundly defeated it. Apparently they love subsidizing the baby parts–farming business.[14] That includes two supposedly pro-life Democrat senators, Bob Casey and Heidi Heitkamp. (Bob Casey Sr., the Pennsylvania senator's father, actually was pro-life, but the Democrat Party has become even more committed to abortion over the decades, and the son now apparently feels he must side with Planned Parenthood over the babies they kill.)[15]

A PRO-ABORTION *COMEDY*

Should we really be surprised, though, at the Dems' circling the wagons for their closest allies in the abortion business, even after the horrors revealed in the videos? It's been clear for a long time, to anyone who took the trouble to pay attention, that the Democrats and their "pro-choice" allies are utterly callous. The Planned Parenthood we see on the undercover videos is the same Planned Parenthood that helped Hollywood produce a *comedy* about a young woman having an abortion. Yep, you heard me correctly. In its 2013–14 annual report, Planned Parenthood bragged that one of its proudest accomplishments was working for years with the writer, director, and producer of the film *Obvious Child*. Planned Parenthood opened up its Hudson Peconic Health Center to be used by Hollywood to shoot this "breakthrough" film, and some PP employees appear in it as extras. Debuting to critical acclaim in 2014, *Obvious Child* was described in Planned Parenthood's report as "an edgy, hip, funny, remarkably honest story revolving around one woman's abortion." Of course the abortion cheerleaders in the media praised the film. *Vanity Fair* found it "wildly funny and exceptionally raw and honest."[16]

I have to admit I haven't forced myself to sit through the movie, but without watching it, I will bet you there is no scene in the film showing Planned Parenthood technicians dismembering a fetus in a pie dish and joking, "Another boy!" Planned Parenthood reviewed the script in advance. How did they miss including this critical scene that would have given the film that real-world "honest" feel?

Here's *Obvious Child*'s plot summary, from iTunes:

> For aspiring comedian Donna Stern, everyday life as a female twenty-something provides ample material for her hysterical and relatable brand of humor. On stage, Donna is unapologetically herself, joking about topics as intimate as her sex life and as crude as her day-old underwear. But when Donna winds up unexpectedly pregnant after a one-night stand, she is forced to face the uncomfortable realities of independent womanhood for the first time. Donna's drunken hookup—and epic lapse in prophylactic judgment—turns out to be the beginning of a hilarious and totally unplanned journey of self-discovery and empowerment. Anchored by a star-making performance from Jenny Slate, OBVIOUS CHILD is a true Sundance gem: a heartfelt discovery packed tight with raw, energetic comedy and moments of poignant honesty and vulnerability. Writer/Director Gillian Robespierre handles the topic of Donna's unwanted pregnancy with a refreshing matter-of-factness rarely seen onscreen. And with Donna, Slate and Robespierre have crafted a character for the ages—a female that audiences will recognize, cheer for, and love.[17]

Planned Parenthood's president Cecile Richards praised the film for depicting a young woman "making the serious decision to end a pregnancy and still having a full and fun life."[18] Since when is having an abortion fun? Apparently that's how the abortion industry hopes to stay in business—by marketing abortion as fun. And by brazenly denying and even doing their best to cover up the video evidence of their grisly deeds—with the help of their staunch defenders in the Democrat Party and its allied media.

THE DEMS' FULL-THROATED DEFENSE OF THE INDEFENSIBLE

When the video proof of Planned Parenthood's abortion profiteering came out, how did Democrat politicians respond? By circling the wagons. The Democrats fought tooth and nail to defend the indefensible. They mindlessly repeated the mantra about the supposedly "heavily edited videos"—despite the fact that the Center for Medical Progress released *unedited* versions of all the videos at the very same time that they released the edited ones.

Josh Earnest, Obama's press secretary, repeatedly told the press that he didn't know whether the president had seen any of the videos. He hadn't watched them himself, but he confidently told the White House press corps that they were "fraudulent." When he was asked where he got that information, he admitted he was just regurgitating Planned Parenthood's spin. Our Democrat president's spokesman makes a pretty good mouthpiece for the abortion profiteers:

> Planned Parenthood has been quite specific about the policy and procedures that they have in place and I know that they have described those procedures as reaching the highest ethical standards.... Based on the essentially fraudulent way these videos have been released, there is not a lot of evidence that Planned Parenthood hasn't lived up to those standards....
>
> There is ample reason to think that this is merely the tried and true tactic we've seen from extremists on the right to edit

this video and selectively release an edited version of the video that grossly distorts the positions of the person who is in the video....[19]

Senator Elizabeth Warren, a potential Democrat presidential candidate, also sprang to Planned Parenthood's defense:

Republicans have had a plan for years to strip away women's rights to make choices over their own bodies.... The Republican scheme to defund Planned Parenthood is not some sort of surprised response to some highly edited video. Nope, the Republican vote to defund Planned Parenthood is just one more piece of a deliberate, methodical, orchestrated, right-wing attack on women's rights. And I'm sick and tired of it. Women everywhere are sick and tired of it. The American people are sick and tired of it.... I stand with Planned Parenthood and I hope my colleagues will do the same.[20]

But Hillary Clinton outdid them all in defending the indefensible. That was no surprise. The front-running Democrat presidential candidate has been carrying water for abortionists for decades. There is no bigger advocate of the "pro-choice" movement than Hillary Clinton: "Abortion access as a fundamental human right has long been a core principle for Mrs. Clinton. On the very first day of her husband Bill Clinton's presidency in 1993, which nearly coincided with the twentieth anniversary of *Roe v. Wade*, she pushed him to sign five executive orders authorizing federal funding for and involvement with abortion—both of which had been banned under Presidents Bush and Reagan."[21]

At a 1994 UN conference on population and development in Cairo, the Clintons stacked the U.S. delegation with pro-abortion representatives to pressure world leaders to include access to abortion in their definition of "reproductive health care." But the conference rejected it.[22]

And as *National Review* reported, "Planned Parenthood's international arm received $26 million in foreign-aid money during Hillary Clinton's last two years at the State Department, a new report points out, thanks to the Obama administration's policies."[23]

Clinton's hypocrisy knows no bounds. Her Twitter biography reads, "Wife, mom, grandma, women+kids advocate, FLOTUS, Senator, Sec-State, hair icon, pantsuit aficionado, 2016 presidential candidate. Tweets from Hillary signed –H." She forgot to include "abortion advocate." Something tells me that as a new grandmother, Hillary wouldn't have wanted Chelsea to abort her daughter Charlotte and have Planned Parenthood sell Charlotte's baby parts. Hillary's pro-abortion rhetoric is contradicted by the fact that she knows a fetus is in fact a baby—you can tell from the fact that when she announced news of Chelsea's pregnancy, Hillary didn't refer to the baby as a fetus but as a child. She tweeted, "My most exciting title yet: Grandmother-To-Be! @billclinton and I are thrilled Chelsea and Marc are expecting their first child!"[24]

"MORE CHILDREN FROM THE FIT, LESS FROM THE UNFIT"

In 2009 Clinton received Planned Parenthood's "highest honor," the Margaret Sanger Award. "Secretary Clinton received this award for her unwavering support of women's health and rights throughout her public service career," noted the press release.

It's astonishing that a woman who is campaigning so feverishly for the black vote was proud to receive an award named after the founder of Planned Parenthood, an avowed racist and eugenicist—Margaret Sanger, who in 1921 founded the American Birth Control League, which in 1942 was renamed Planned Parenthood Federation of America.[25]

Sanger made no bones about her eugenic goals: "More children from the fit, less from the unfit—that is the chief aim of birth control," said her *Birth Control Review*. She spoke to a Ku Klux Klan rally in 1926 in

Silver Lakes, New Jersey. She created the "Negro Project" to decrease the black population by convincing black community leaders and pastors to promote birth control use to blacks.[26] That's why black pastors are asking the Smithsonian to get rid of its statue of the Planned Parenthood founder.[27]

Sadly, Planned Parenthood has achieved Sanger's goal. Black women are having abortions at a disproportionate rate compared with any other race. Though we make up only 13 percent of the U.S. population, blacks account for about 36 to 37 percent of the nation's abortions. About 13 million abortions have been performed on black women since 1973, when the Supreme Court legalized abortion in *Roe v. Wade*. According to the Alan Guttmacher Institute, a pro-abortion group, a total of 50 million abortions have been performed in the United States since that time. Tell me again how the Democrats were going to make abortion "rare" and how black lives matter to them?[28]

Accepting the Sanger award, Clinton said she was in awe of this racist abortion promoter:

> Now, I have to tell you that it was a great privilege when I was told that I would receive this award. I admire Margaret Sanger enormously, her courage, her tenacity, her vision.... And when I think about what she did all those years ago in Brooklyn, taking on archetypes, taking on attitudes and accusations flowing from all directions, I am really in awe of her.
>
> And there are a lot of lessons that we can learn from her life and from the cause she launched and fought for and sacrificed so bravely.[29]

Hillary's going to have to come up with a good reason why blacks should vote for a candidate that supports an infanticidal organization whose priority is killing black babies. *For blacks to support any Democrat flies in the face of our survival.* The Democrat Party and its handmaiden Planned Parenthood are exterminating black babies like Hitler had the Nazis exterminate the Jews. It's an ugly comparison, but it's true.

Black lives really DON'T matter to Democrats. In 2015 Planned Parenthood once again outright lied to black Americans, covering up its racist history in a hypocritical celebration of Black History Month. It honored ninety-nine "Dream Keepers," or black leaders, one for every year since Planned Parenthood was founded. "Planned Parenthood has a complicated history, but since our founding, we have worked with the community to increase opportunity and access to health care for everyone," read the statement about the initiative. Complicated to say the least! In her book *Woman, Morality and Birth Control*, published in 1922, Sanger wrote about using black ministers to encourage blacks to have abortions: "We should hire three or four colored ministers, preferably with social-service backgrounds, and with engaging personalities. The most successful educational approach to the Negro is through a religious appeal. We don't want the word to go out that we want to exterminate the Negro population, and the minister is the man who can straighten out that idea if it ever occurs to any of their more rebellious members."[30] Planned Parenthood celebrating Black History Month is like the Nazis celebrating Yom Kippur.

In the announcement of its Black History Month initiative, Planned Parenthood boasted it was working with black women to serve their best interests:

> Together we are fighting to protect against dangerous legislation that is harmful to women and families, and deny access to critical services.
>
> We are partnering with young black women and men—the next generation of leaders in the movement for reproductive freedom. We are spreading the word that finally, health insurance is more affordable for millions of people who are

uninsured. We are working hard to end racial health disparities and for the community to be the healthiest it can be.[31]

In reality nothing about Planned Parenthood is helpful to blacks.

The only thing Planned Parenthood is partnering with blacks to do is to promote their demise as a race. And blacks are unwittingly carrying out Sanger's plans when they continue to vote for a party in bed with her organization.

According to a 2012 New York City Department of Health and Mental Hygiene report, more black babies were aborted than were born in the city that year—31,328 abortions versus 24,758 births. Black babies accounted for 42.5 percent of all abortions performed that year in the city.[32] Planned Parenthood's main offices are in New York City and Washington, D.C. According to its website, it is "the leading advocate for reproductive health care in the United States today."[33] How is encouraging black women to go through a surgical procedure that harms their reproductive health and kills their babies providing them healthcare?

Why would any black American, regardless of political affiliation, support a racist organization like Planned Parenthood? I'm sure most black women who go to a Planned Parenthood center to abort their babies don't know the organization's history or goals. It's grotesque and inappropriate for Planned Parenthood to honor the achievements of blacks because its purpose is to kill black babies before they can achieve anything.

Seventy-nine percent of Planned Parenthood's surgical abortion facilities are strategically placed near black or Hispanic communities.[34] Why is that? Because Planned Parenthood is still carrying out Sanger's mission of exterminating blacks.

A SHOCKING BUT ACCURATE COMPARISON

In their article "Video 5: Planned Parenthood's *Uncle Tom's Cabin*," Jason Jones and John Zmirak of the Stream compare abortion to slavery because both institutions profited off "a profound moral evil." When I first heard of their comparison, I was skeptical. But reading their article, I was surprised to find myself agreeing with them.

Planned Parenthood is profiting off of poor black women today just as American slave owners profited off of black slaves. Pro-slavery advocates—who ironically were also Democrats—justified the heinous institution. They defended it as an idyllic arrangement: the master loved the slave and had to take care of blacks who were intellectually inferior to whites. Thomas Jefferson, a founding father of our nation and the Democrat Party, wrote at length about black inferiority to justify his slave ownership. Today, Democrats defend the abortion profiteers at Planned Parenthood with the same hypocrisy and paternalism, pretending that abortion is good for women and blacks.

As a black woman who grew up in the South—in Richmond, Virginia, the capital of the Confederacy—I'm keenly aware from history that slavery was no picnic. Black women were routinely raped and impregnated by their white slave masters. Men and women were beaten with leather whips or killed by dogs as punishment. As Jones and Zmirak note, "Even well-meaning slave-owners, when their gambling debts needed paying, routinely had black children ripped out of their mothers' arms and sold 'down the river' to perish in the brutal cane-fields of Louisiana, or be prostituted to sate the lusts of 'honorable' Southern gentlemen."

Today, Planned Parenthood, its army of abortion doctors, and its loyal fans in the Democrat Party are "harvest[ing] the children of the poor and cannibaliz[ing] them for parts, like stolen cars in a chop-shop." As Jones and Zmirak point out, "They plant their clinics in ghettos and abort 94 percent of the babies they encounter, then pretend that they serve the poor and honor African-Americans." Planned Parenthood is the modern-day slave master, and abortion is one of the biggest civil rights issues of our time.

And once again the Democrats are on the wrong side. The writers remind us that Planned Parenthood and their Democrat allies like Hillary and Obama keep justifying this amoral practice, just as defenders of slav-ery did: "*Keep talking about the mammograms—it doesn't matter that PP doesn't offer them. Keep using words like 'health,' 'choice' and even 'adoption.' Who cares if PP's ratio of abortion to adoption is 117 to 1? Just stay with the spin, and wait the opposition out. The money will keep on coming* [emphasis in the original]."

The Democrats fighting today to save Planned Parenthood are like the Democrats who fought during the Civil War to maintain slavery: both profit off of human misery. Like the slavery proponents of yesterday, Planned Parenthood is raking in millions if not billions "by selling their victims. Like slaves."

In a July 20, 2015, Facebook chat for her campaign, Hillary Clinton responded to a question about racial justice in America: "Black lives matter. Everyone in this country should stand firmly behind that. We need to acknowledge some hard truths about race and justice in this country, and one of those hard truths is that that racial inequality is not merely a symptom of economic inequality."[35]

HILLARY CLINTON GOES ON THE OFFENSIVE

Clinton is right, racial inequality is real—with Planned Parenthood's assault on the black woman's womb. When will black Americans, who vote overwhelmingly Democrat, be outraged by Democrats' murdering black lives? By championing abortion, Democrats are able to harm, profit off, and secure votes from two of their constituencies—blacks and women—for the price of one.

Clinton's ties with Planned Parenthood run deep and strong. So when the video sting operation became public, Clinton leapt to the abortion profiteers' defense. The videos were so shocking that she found it prudent initially to concede that "I have seen pictures from them and obviously find them disturbing." But at the same time, she wasn't backing down from her long love affair with abortion, or her alliance with the baby parts–profiteering organization: "I will defend a woman's right to choose, and I will defend Planned Parenthood," she roared at campaign events in July 2015, the month the first four undercover videos were released.

The Democrat frontrunner's support of Planned Parenthood was "a forgone conclusion" reported *Politico*: "Hillary Clinton is friends with Planned Parenthood's president and took a rare pause from her duties as secretary of state to keynote a Planned Parenthood gala, while her family foundation [the corrupt Clinton Foundation] has worked with the group to promote birth control."

But in August 2015 Clinton really pulled out all the stops. Just days after the release of the video proving that StemExpress, a "volume" purchaser of aborted baby parts from Planned Parenthood, had shipped severed heads to research laboratories, Hillary compared *critics* of Planned Parenthood to... *ISIS*: "Now, extreme views about women, we expect that from some of the terrorist groups, we expect that from people who don't want to live in the modern world, but it's a little hard to take coming from Republicans who want to be the president of the United States. Yet they espouse out-of-date and out-of-touch policies. They are dead wrong for twenty-first-century America. We are going forward, we are not going back."[36]

OPPOSITION RESEARCH

The Democrats are joined at the hip to the abortion profiteers at Planned Parenthood. Former Democratic National Committee spokeswoman Lily Adams, who is the daughter of Planned Parenthood president Cecile Richards, works as Iowa press secretary for Clinton's campaign. Many of the biggest donors to the Planned Parenthood Action Fund, the organization's political action committee, are also longtime Clinton donors and contributed the maximum amount $2,700 her primary campaign in 2015.[37]

So when Planned Parenthood needed to pay for a skewed "forensic report" alleging that the sting video footage was unfairly "manipulated" to make Planned Parenthood look bad, naturally they turned to "Fusion GPS.... an opposition research firm with ties to the Democratic party" that "has a history of harassing socially conservative Republican donors, possibly on behalf of the Obama campaign." That information is from the *Weekly Standard*. We would never have learned the facts from the Democrat-dominated mainstream media. In fact, both *Politico* and the *New York Times* reported that the videos had been judged by experts to be "manipulated" without revealing those supposed experts' ties to the Democrat Party. What's more, even the shills for the Democrats at Fusion GPS admitted that "there was no widespread evidence of video manipulation" and no evidence of made-up dialogue.[38]

The evidence on the undercover videos is incontrovertible. The Democrats' loyal allies in Planned Parenthood are exploiting women (disproportionately black women), killing their babies, and selling their body parts. And the Dems have hardly paused in their nuclear defense of these atrocities—that's how invested they are in this evil.

CHAPTER SEVEN

THE PARTY OF BABY BUTCHERS

Babies' feet stored in jars and aborted fetuses crammed into milk cartons and orange juice containers. These were a few of Dr. Kermit Gosnell's favorite things that he kept as souvenirs of the murders he committed. Practicing in Philadelphia, Gosnell was an abortionist who ran a "criminal enterprise motivated by greed," according to the grand jury report on his crimes.[1] This should make the Democrat Party extremely proud! After all, it was the "pro-choice" regime in Pennsylvania that made sure Gosnell's clinic wasn't inspected for *seventeen years*.[2]

In May 2013, Gosnell received a life sentence without parole for murdering three babies outside the womb by cutting their necks with scissors as they "writhed in pain." He also was found guilty of involuntary manslaughter in the death of a woman.[3]

But deaths of women at the hands of abortionists has never stopped the Democrats from accusing abortion *opponents* of waging a "war on women." If pro-lifers are fighting a war on women, how come all the killings are done by the "pro-choice" side?

"If you willfully disregard a deadly risk to the mother's life, and kill her, you will be charged with murder. If you deliver a viable baby, born alive, and kill it, you will be charged with murder," noted the grand jury report.[4]

BLACK GENOCIDE

For almost forty years, Gosnell, who ironically was a black man himself, carried out Sanger's life mission of exterminating black babies with relentless enthusiasm. What better way to annihilate a race than by starting at the womb, the place of conception—which is exactly why Margaret Sanger founded Planned Parenthood.

Making his practice of pure evil even more sinister, Gosnell set aside Sundays, the Christian Sabbath, to perform illegal late-term abortions and kill babies born alive. Degenerates like Gosnell exist thanks to Democrats and their handmaiden Planned Parenthood. Let's face it, only one person has a choice in the abortion equation, and it's not the baby. *Meditate long and hard on that for a moment.*

Democrats and their liberal-leaning allies chant and rant that BLACK LIVES MATTER to win votes, and this pandering works. But behind the scenes, Democrats do everything they can to end black lives. As we have seen, many more black women abort their babies than women of other races—so much so that blacks, who make up only 13 percent of the population, make up *more than three times as high a percentage of the abortions.* Make no mistake, this is genocide. Nothing illustrates the Democrats' real disdain for their black constituents more than the party's "pro-choice" stance and its shielding of bad actors like Gosnell from inspections.

Gosnell performed over sixteen thousand abortions over his career, many of them illegal late-term abortions on mostly poor black women at his Women's Medical Society clinic in Philadelphia. Gosnell "treated his patients with condescension—slapping them, providing abysmal care, and often refusing even to see or talk to them—unless they were Caucasian, or had money," according to the grand jury report. But Planned Parenthood will tell you the abortion industry doesn't prey on poor women, or on blacks.

Gosnell

INFANTICIDE AND THIRD-DEGREE MURDER

Pennsylvania law allows late-term abortions to be performed on babies up to twenty-four weeks gestation—when they can easily survive outside the womb. Nonetheless, the district attorney called what Gosnell did infanticide. The federal Born-Alive Infants Protection Act defines a human as "somebody who's been completely expelled from the mother and has either a heartbeat, pulsating cord, or is moving." Those are the babies Gosnell stabbed through the neck with his scissors.

Gosnell was not an obstetrician or gynecologist, but he made a killing off killing babies, racking up about $1.8 million a year, virtually all of it in cash to maximize profits. While Gosnell's grim-reaper practice didn't amass the $1 billion annual revenue of Planned Parenthood, both figures show how profitable the abortion industry is—from the bottom to the top.

Gosnell was charged with third-degree murder in the death of forty-one-year-old Karnamaya Mongar, a refugee who had come to the United States from a resettlement camp in Nepal. Gosnell gave Mongar too much of the sedative Demerol, and she stopped breathing. Gosnell tried CPR, but his defibrillator was broken and there were no medications on site to restart her heart. So the woman died.[5]

COUNTENANCING FILTH AND HORROR

Latosha Lewis, one of Gosnell's many unlicensed workers, told the grand jury that lots of times women would deliver babies sitting on the toilet and wait there for hours before Gosnell arrived. A cleaner at the clinic, James Johnson, testified that sometimes patients "miscarried or whatever it was" into the toilet and clogged it. Johnson described how he had to remove the toilet "so that someone else—he said it was too disgusting for him—could get the fetuses out of the pipes."

The 281-page grand jury report reads like an unimaginable horror story. It should be mandatory reading for any woman contemplating an abortion. Of course the Democrats would never let that happen. They would rather let women be endangered in filthy clinics like Gosnell's than allow any challenge to abortion on demand.

"This case is about a doctor who killed babies and endangered women. What we mean is that he regularly and illegally delivered live, viable, babies in the third trimester of pregnancy—and then murdered these newborns by severing their spinal cords with scissors," says the grand jury report. Women's Medical Society was a "sham medical practice" in the business of making profit, not promoting health. "By day it was a prescription mill; by night an abortion mill."

Gosnell ran a filthy, highly profitable abortion business. The price to end a human life in the womb was cheap early on but increased as the baby grew bigger. Gosnell's abortion fees:

6 weeks to 12 weeks: $330
13 weeks to 14 weeks: $440
15 weeks to 16 weeks: $540
17 weeks to 18 weeks: $750
19 weeks to 20 weeks: $950
21 weeks to 22 weeks: $1,180
23 weeks to 24 weeks: $1,625

He charged a bounty of as much as $3,000 to perform illegal late-term abortions after twenty-four weeks. "The bigger the baby, the more he charged," as the grand jury report explains.

A stench enveloped the clinic, which was cleaned only once a week. Stirrups were caked with dried blood, as was waiting room furniture, and the walls were stained with urine. There was no nurse on staff, and assistants as young as fifteen helped Gosnell perform abortions. Because he didn't come to work until the evening, Gosnell left behind pre-signed, blank prescription pads for staff to fill with "prescriptions for Oxycontin and other controlled substances, for themselves and their friends."

As the grand jury report explains, "With abortion, as with prescriptions, Gosnell's approach was simple: keep volume high, expenses low—and break the law. That was his competitive edge." Ignoring all Pennsylvania abortion laws—twenty-four-hour waiting period, age limit, gestational limit—he performed abortions on demand.

HOW ABORTION PAVED THE WAY FOR INFANTICIDE

Women in their third trimester would come to the clinic during the day when Gosnell wasn't there to pay and pick up a prescription for labor-inducing medication. Gosnell wouldn't show up for work sometimes till as late as 10:00 p.m., by which time many of the women had already returned and given birth.

"By 24 weeks, most babies born prematurely will survive if they receive appropriate medical care. But that was not what the Women's Medical Society was about. Gosnell had a simple solution for the unwanted babies he delivered: he killed them."

He stabbed the baby's neck with scissors and called it "snipping."

According to the grand jury report, "Baby Boy A" was breathing and moving when his seventeen-year-old mother gave birth to him in July 2008 after being in labor for over thirteen hours. She delivered a seven-and-a-half-month (29.4-week) baby who breathed for ten to twenty seconds after he was born—until Gosnell murdered him. In testimony before the grand jury, Kareema Cross, who worked at Gosnell's clinic, explained that the baby was eighteen to nineteen inches long, nearly the size of her own newborn daughter, who was six pounds, six ounces at birth.

Upon delivering the boy, Gosnell joked that "this baby is big enough to walk around with me or walk me to the bus stop." Then Gosnell cut the baby's neck with scissors, and, Cross said, she watched in horror as the baby moved. Gosnell shrugged it off, telling her, "It's the baby's reflexes." He tossed the baby in a plastic shoebox. Cross said its feet and arms were hanging out of the sides because it was so developed.

A neonatologist testified to the grand jury, "If a baby moves, it is alive. Equally troubling, it feels a 'tremendous amount of pain' when its spinal cord is severed. So, the fact that Baby Boy A continued to move after his spinal cord was cut with scissors means that he did not die instantly. Maybe the cord was not completely severed. In any case, his few moments of life were spent in excruciating pain."

When asked why she and other workers at the clinic took photos of the baby boy, Cross explained, "Because it was big and it was wrong and we knew it. We knew something was wrong."

She said, "I'm not sure who took the picture first, but when we seen this baby, it was—it was a shock to us because I never seen a baby that big that he had done. So it was—I knew something was wrong because everything, like you can see everything, the hair, eyes, everything. And I never seen for any other procedure that he did, I never seen any like that."

Gosnell treated these babies with the same indecency as the Stem-Express workers who ship aborted fetal parts in FedEx boxes. Human life is treated like garbage by the abortion industry, absolute garbage. And the Democrats are more outraged at calls for illegal immigrants to be deported from America than at doctors killing babies.

Sadly, this wasn't the only viable baby Gosnell or his staff murdered. There were dozens upon dozens of viable babies killed. Cross testified that between 2005 and 2008 she saw Steven Massof, an unlicensed medical school graduate, sever the spinal cords of at least ten babies who were breathing and about five who were moving.

After Massof left the clinic in 2008, Lynda Williams took over the job of cutting babies' necks in Gosnell's absence. "Baby C" was moving and breathing for about twenty minutes. Cross testified that "Gosnell had delivered the baby and put it on a counter while he suctioned the placenta from the mother. Williams called Cross over to look at the baby because it was breathing and moving its arms when Williams pulled on them. After playing with the baby, Williams slit its neck."

Just when you think the story couldn't get more gruesome, you read that investigators found "Baby Boy B," a twenty-eight-week-old nearly full-term baby found frozen in a gallon-size spring-water bottle with placenta and gauze. The medical examiner determined the baby would have lived had he not been murdered by Gosnell, who made a surgical incision in the back of his neck, severing the first and second vertebrae.

DEMOCRATS DEFENDING PARTIAL-BIRTH ABORTION, JUST A STEP SHORT OF INFANTICIDE

Every medical expert who testified before the grand jury agreed that doctors wouldn't treat a corpse the way Gosnell treated these babies. Investigators had first thought that Gosnell was performing partial-birth abortions, which were banned in 2007. But they later confirmed that he waited until after the babies were born to crush their skulls and suck out their brains, though there was no medical reason to do so.

It's worth taking a slight detour from Gosnell's story to mention that partial-birth abortions were banned under Republican President George W. Bush because people found them an affront to human decency. Before the ban, in order to abort babies beyond seventeen weeks gestation, doctors would suck the brain matter out of the baby's skull while it was still in the womb, then remove the fetus. This horrific procedure would have been outlawed nine years earlier if DEMOCRAT President Bill Clinton hadn't vetoed the 1996 Partial-Birth Abortion Ban Act, which would have prohibited this inhumane procedure unless the mother's life was in danger.[6] Clinton's excuse was that he wanted a broader exemption, including language about "averting serious health consequences to the mother," which Republicans pointed out would create a loophole for women to have these gruesome abortions.[7]

Even the liberal-leaning, pro-Clinton network CNN said at the time how heinous the procedure was: "In the grisly procedure, a fetus is partially extracted from the womb, a catheter inserted in the skull and the brain removed before the fetus is taken out."[8]

The Republican-led Congress passed the bill again in 1997, and again Clinton vetoed it—even after the American Medical Association came out in support of the bill and a "prominent supporter of the techniques [used in partial-birth abortion] admitted that he had lied" about how many of these abortions were done annually.[9]

By protecting a woman's right to kill her baby at any point in her pregnancy, Democrats have been enablers of abortionists for decades. Gosnell just took abortion to its logical conclusion and started murdering babies who were a few minutes past the point where he could kill them legally.

All the medical experts who testified before the grand jury confirmed that by twenty-four weeks babies can survive outside the womb and sometimes breathe on their own, though many require assistance. Thus it is routine medical practice for doctors to resuscitate a baby delivered at twenty-four weeks or later. A doctor's failure to provide medical assistance to a baby is infanticide under Pennsylvania law. By not hiring medically licensed employees or having functioning life-saving equipment, "Gosnell's intent...was not to try to revive live, viable babies. It was to kill them."

A BUTCHER

During the trial, a woman who started working for Gosnell when she was fifteen years old testified that she witnessed Gosnell abort babies "screeching" and that the chest of one "was moving." Massof testified that "it would rain fetuses."[10]

Investigators referred to Gosnell as a "butcher." He botched abortions, puncturing his patients' uteruses, cervixes, and colons, leaving the women on dirty exam floors bleeding and in some cases near death. Harming women and killing babies—all in pursuit of money. Women got venereal diseases because Gosnell used unsterilized instruments, transferring germs from one patient to another.

When Drug Enforcement Agency (DEA) agents raided the clinic on February 18, 2010, they encountered a ghoulish scene: bloodstained lounge chairs and fetal remains stored in bags, milk jugs, orange juice cartons, catfood containers, and a refrigerator. A row of jars containing the sawed-off feet of fetuses decorated the clinic, as if Gosnell were keeping trophies of what he had done, remarked Joanne Pescatore, one of the state prosecutors.[11]

What agents discovered that night was deplorable—to put it mildly. Medical waste was piled high in the basement. There were bloodstained, rusty surgical instruments and forty-five fetuses strewn about the building. The Philadelphia medical examiner confirmed that at least two fetuses and maybe a third had been born alive.

Employees from the Pennsylvania Department of State (which regulates doctors and the practice of medicine) and the Pennsylvania Department of Health (which regulates health care facilities) joined the DEA in the raid. It had been over fifteen years since anyone from these agencies had bothered to visit Gosnell's clinic despite numerous complaints, including notification of Mongar's death months earlier.

"There was blood on the floor. A stench of urine filled the air. A flea-infested cat was wandering through the facility, and there were cat feces on the stairs. Semi-conscious women scheduled for abortions were moaning in the waiting room or the recovery room, where they sat on dirty recliners covered with blood-stained blankets."

Gosnell's mistreatment of women was nothing new to the women of Philadelphia—or the women from Virginia, Delaware, Maryland, and North Carolina who came to him for "care." His baby killing and women maiming had gone on for decades.

In 1972 Gosnell already showed himself to be the relentless murderer he would be known as in the future. It was then that he was responsible for the "Mother's Day Massacre," as it was called, which was worse than a slasher film. On Mother's Day 1972, Gosnell performed abortions on fifteen poor women in the second trimester of their pregnancies. Thinking they would receive a safe abortion, the women had taken a bus from Chicago to his clinic. What they got from Gosnell was botched abortions using an illegal device called a "super coil," developed by Harvey Karman, a California man who had performed illegal abortions in the 1950s.

The super coil was a ball made of plastic razors coated in a gel to keep them closed. After it was inserted into the woman's uterus, her body temperature would melt the gel. Karman told Gosnell that the coils would spring open and cut up the fetus, and it would be expelled from the woman's uterus.

This device had never been tested on animals, though Karman had tested it on pregnant women before, in Bangladesh, with little success and a high rate of complications. Needless to say, the super coil was most certainly not approved by the FDA. It was "just something that Gosnell…and this guy decided they were going to use on these women," according to the grand jury investigation into Gosnell's later murders. Karman joined Gosnell that day in using the super coils on these unwitting women.

The results were horrific. Women retained fetal remains inside their uteruses, suffering infections and hemorrhages, among other complications. Yet the Pennsylvania Board of Medicine took no action against Gosnell. As a February 25, 2010, article published in the *Philadelphia Inquirer* after Gosnell's license was suspended—over three decades after the Mother's Day Massacre—reported:

> The federal Centers for Disease Control and Prevention and
> the Philadelphia Department of Public Health subsequently did
> an investigation that detailed serious complications suffered by

nine of the 15 women, including one who needed a hysterectomy.

The CDC researchers recommended strict controls on any
future testing of the device....

Karman spent two years in court battles in Philadelphia.
He was convicted of practicing medicine without a license,
but a Common Pleas Court judge overturned the conviction
in 1974, saying then–District Attorney Arlen Specter had
failed to show which women Karman had treated.

Gosnell—who testified that Karman had done an "innoc-
uous" part of the procedures but not fetal extractions—was
not charged with anything.

Does this look like women's health services to you? What Gosnell
did to these women is eerily reminiscent of the Nazis' experiments on
the Jews during the Holocaust—pure and utter evil. Gosnell and his
practices were morally corrupt and repugnant. This is the face of abortion, albeit illegal abortion, but it still gives one a clear idea of what is
going on—MURDER.

HOW HE GOT AWAY WITH IT FOR SO LONG

Pennsylvania's Board of Medicine continued to ignore Gosnell's
atrocities as he performed illegal abortions and hired unlicensed staff
for more than thirty years after the 1972 massacre. From 2002 to 2009,
lawyers for the board reviewed five cases involving malpractice against
Gosnell, but all were closed without any action being taken against
him.

Dating back to the 1980s, Pennsylvania's Department of Health had
received complaints from patients and employees and issued citations
against Gosnell, but he was allowed to continue operating a filthy abortion clinic where he was performing illegal abortions. The grand jury

report concluded that "assuring safety at abortion clinics has been a low priority for Pennsylvania's Department of Health for decades."

None of the agencies responsible for oversight of abortion clinics—the Pennsylvania Department of Health, the Pennsylvania Department of State's Board of Medicine, and the Philadelphia Department of Public Health—did anything to stop Gosnell's carnage, even though they had years' worth of evidence about his horrific practices. The grand jury report called it a "complete regulatory collapse."

The Hospital of the University of Pennsylvania and its subsidiary, Penn Presbyterian Medical Center, located in the same neighborhood as Gosnell's office, also dropped the ball. "State law requires hospitals to report complications from abortion," noted the grand jury report. But HUP only filed a report for one patient who died at its hospital a decade ago, even though other victims "kept coming in."

The grand jury also noted in its report that the National Abortion Federation failed in its oversight:

> NAF is an association of abortion providers that upholds the strictest health and legal standards for its members. Gosnell, bizarrely, applied for admission shortly after Karnamaya Mongar's death. Despite his various efforts to fool her, the evaluator from NAF readily noted that records were not properly kept, that risks were not explained, that patients were not monitored, that equipment was not available, that anesthesia was misused. It was the worst abortion clinic she had ever inspected. Of course, she rejected Gosnell's application. She just never told anyone in authority about all the horrible, dangerous things she had seen.

If it hadn't been for the DEA's raiding the clinic to find evidence that Gosnell was illegally selling prescriptions, the baby butcher would never have been caught. Four days after the raid, on February 22, 2010, the

Pennsylvania Board of Medicine finally had the guts and moral fortitude to suspend Gosnell's medical license, citing "an immediate and clear danger to the public health and safety."

Less than a month later, in March of 2010, the Department of Health finally did its job and began the process of closing Gosnell's butcher shop for good. Pennsylvania's action against Gosnell was more than thirty years too late. No wonder many people have no confidence in government to do its job.

How could this happen? Because the politics and power of the Democrat abortion lobby always supersede what's right and decent. Officials had long since stopped conducting inspections of abortion clinics in Pennsylvania for fear that they would be accused of trying to strip women of their "right" to abortion. Thanks to the Democrats and their allies in the abortion lobby, it was easier for government officials to ignore the problem while babies and women died.

On the day the verdict was handed down in Gosnell's case, Planned Parenthood issued an ironic, deceitful statement: "This case has made clear that we must have and enforce laws that protect access to safe and legal abortion, and we must reject misguided laws that would limit women's options and force them to seek treatment from criminals like Kermit Gosnell."[12]

But Kermit Gosnell flourished—butchering women and children for a third of a century—under the legal abortion regime that has been passionately defended by Democrats the entire time. Pennsylvania's abortion laws were not enforced, because those in charge were afraid of being publicly assailed by the abortion lobby for "limiting women's options" to kill their babies. If Pennsylvania and Philadelphia government officials had done their job, maybe those babies would be alive today. But any time a Republican attempts to tighten regulation on abortion or even enforce existing laws, the Democrat backlash is like a nuclear bomb going off: not only are Republicans going to limit abortion, but they're going to outlaw birth control and close down women's health clinics.

Democrats would rather keep abortion sacred and untouchable than improve the care that women—especially black women—receive.

Even in the immediate aftermath of Gosnell's conviction, in May 2013, when Republican Senator Mike Lee introduced a resolution to hold hearings to review the public policies that had allowed Gosnell to go on maiming and killing for years, Senate Democrats were outraged! They opposed any such review. Again, we see Democrats coming to the defense of abortion, even in its most illegal, immoral form.

Senator Lee's resolution, which had twenty-six cosponsors, would have directed Congress and the states to "gather information about and correct abusive, unsanitary, and illegal abortion practices and the inter-state referral of women and girls to facilities engaged in dangerous or illegal second- and third-trimester procedures."[13] That seems like a no-brainer. We know that Kermit Gosnell got away with butchering babies and women for decades. Shouldn't we find out whether similar atrocities are still happening? We might prevent some illegal abortions from being done on fetuses developed enough to survive outside the womb—or at least save some women from doctors who give them STDs and perform surgery with filthy instruments. Who could object to that? The Democrats, of course. And yet somehow the Democrat Party gets away with posing as women's champions against the mean old Republicans who want to take us back to barefoot and pregnant.

The Philadelphia District Attorney's office said the Gosnell case was about "a doctor who killed babies and endangered women" and added "disregard of the law and disdain for the lives and health of mothers and infants." Isn't that what abortion really is, whether Gosnell is the perpe-trator or not? Abortion is not birth control or family planning. Absti-nence, birth control pills, condoms, and the like are examples of birth control. Abortion is about family destruction. You tell me who's waging the war on women.

It's worth noting that many Americans are beginning to find the Democrat Party's support of on-demand abortion and even infanticide to be morally repugnant. There is no federal ban on late-term abortions, but recent surveys conducted by The Polling Company and Quinnipiac found that 60 percent or more of people would support a law banning abortion after twenty weeks unless the mother's life was in danger.[14]

Gosnell, who has been described as "America's biggest serial killer,"[15] did a jailhouse interview with writer Ann McElhinney in 2015. "Gosnell is a complete narcissistic," she told the *National Journal*. McElhinney is writing a book (to be published by Regnery, my publisher) and working on a movie about Gosnell, both of which are expected in 2016.[16]

Prior to her in-person interview, McElhinney talked with Gosnell numerous times over the phone. But it's her description of the face-to-face encounter with Gosnell that's really scary. It makes the hairs on your body stand on end. McElhinney said Gosnell, speaking with her for two hours, smiled, broke into song, and was generally delusional throughout the entire interview. He's convinced of his innocence and believes he will one day be released from prison. Gosnell repeatedly touched McElhinney's leg and "didn't give me any room to avoid these unwelcome touches," she explained.

When McElhinney asked Gosnell about Baby Boy A, the baby Gosnell joked was SO big he could walk him to the bus stop, he said he "didn't remember that." As McElhinney reports, "He lied about everything and if he wasn't lying he was concocting elaborate stories to explain away the horror of what really happened at 3801 Lancaster Ave."[17]

I ache for the babies Gosnell says he "doesn't remember" and the excruciating pain they must have felt before they died. It's an outrage, but despite the fact that the grand jury report concluded Gosnell "killed live, viable, moving, breathing, crying babies," and he was convicted and given a life sentence for his crimes against humanity, his trial received scant coverage from the Democrat-allied mainstream media.

Cecil, the lion who was killed by an American dentist in Zimbabwe while on safari in 2015, received nonstop media coverage and public outrage from the same liberals who ignored the Gosnell trial. The lion was protected by Zimbabwe. Don't get me wrong, I love animals. But there is something very disturbing about the Left's outpouring of sorrow for an endangered animal and dead silence about a doctor taking human life in its most innocent form—a baby. It's contemptible to see the Democrat Party continually beating back attempts to protect women from the harm of abortion, which is no longer "rare"—but, thanks to their enthusiastic defense of the indefensible, all too frequent and sinister.

Gosnell is not an anomaly or outlier among abortionists, as Democrats would have Americans believe. Dr. Michael Roth, an obstetrician/gynecologist from the wealthy town West Bloomfield, Michigan, also seems to have a lust for performing botched, illegal abortions and keeping baby parts as souvenirs. In October 2015, while driving his car, the good doctor hit and critically injured a special needs child. Police obtained a search warrant to retrieve the car's "black box" data as evidence. What they found was shocking to the conscience. In the trunk of the car, Roth had a grisly stash of fourteen containers filled with what appeared to be "fetuses, medical equipment and large amounts of Fentanyl," a drug used to control pain during abortions.[18]

Michigan's attorney general began an investigation to determine if Roth was illegally performing abortions in his home or the homes of his patients. (Roth was evicted from his abortion clinic—Novi Laser and Aesthetic Center—in October of 2014.)[19]

Since the state passed comprehensive legislation in 2012 to tighten oversight of the abortion industry and shut down unscrupulous actors, Michigan has closed sixteen abortion clinics, mostly because of filthy, unsanitary practices.[20]

But baby murderers like Roth still manage to escape detection. Democrats seem to enjoy giving "doctors" like Roth and Gosnell room to kill and immunity from punishment, all in the name of preserving a woman's right to choose—even if it means losing her life.

Like Gosnell, Roth had performed abortions for over thirty years and racked up a long rap sheet of complaints, malpractice lawsuits, and state disciplinary actions against him. In 2003 the Michigan Board of Medicine fined Roth $15,000 and put him on a six-month probationary period for health violations. Roth was fined again, $2,000, in 2012 for violating health codes, including using the wrong size dilator on a patient and leaving the clinic without explaining why he had to delay the abortion.[21]

Roth also had several lawsuits filed against him, one of which he settled by paying $200,000 to the victim of a botched abortion at Henry Ford Hospital.[22]

In 1988 Dr. Weiss of the same hospital wrote a memo stating, "There was perforation of the uterus, hemorrhage and hysterectomy" in a patient on whom Roth performed an abortion.

And according to a 2012 report from Right to Life of Michigan, "Abortion Abuses and State Regulatory Agency Failure," Roth had been "disciplined in 2002 for drug-related violations, including prescribing drugs without a license. He was disciplined in 2004 for violating patient consent laws and was accused of falsifying medical records by a former employee."[23]

Notorious "serial killers" of babies don't look so rare after all. I wonder how many more doctors like Roth and Gosnell there are openly practicing their butchery for years while the authorities turn a blind eye to their crimes. Again, I ask you, which party is waging a war against women? Democrats encourage women to destroy a life growing in their womb and allow abortionists to injure and maim their so-called patients. Republicans encourage women to CHOOSE to protect their lives and those of their unborn babies. Which party is pro-choice?

CHAPTER EIGHT

THE PARTY OF FAMILY BREAKDOWN

As if abortion doesn't kill enough black babies, Democrats also support an equally powerful weapon that will ultimately annihilate the black race—out-of-wedlock births and the complete destruction of the black family. What better way to ensure that an entire race has slim economic opportunity—and thus remains as loyal to the Democrat Party as a baby to a pacifier—than by rewarding the women with government assistance for raising babies without fathers? Blacks are literally addicted to this dope of destruction that Democrats are selling them by the mouthful, election after election, generation after generation. Over 70 percent of black babies in America are born out of wedlock. The Democrats have normalized this behavior among blacks, pushing it on them like a drug dealer selling crack.

It's well known how in 1965 Daniel Patrick Moynihan, assistant secretary of labor to Democrat President Johnson, warned that the black family was on the verge of a "complete breakdown" because of growing illegitimacy rates: in 1963 the out-of-wedlock birthrate for whites was

3 percent, and for blacks it was 23.6 percent. Moynihan was part of a generation of Democrats who cared about lifting blacks up into the ranks of equal opportunity with whites, back in the days before the Democrat Party became completely morally corrupt.

A "TANGLE OF PATHOLOGY" ENABLED BY THE DEMOCRATS FOR FIFTY YEARS

In his 1965 *The Negro Family: The Case for National Action*, Moynihan observed that because more blacks were being born into unmarried homes, more blacks were becoming dependent on welfare to survive. Then, as now, blacks represented only a small percentage of the U.S. population but a disproportionate percentage of people relying on public assistance. At the center of this "tangle of pathology," as Moynihan called it, was "the weakness of the family structure" among blacks. "Once or twice removed, it will be found to be the principal source of most of the aberrant, inadequate, or antisocial behavior that did not establish, but now serves to perpetuate the cycle of poverty and deprivation."[1]

Ever since, the problem has only gotten worse. Thanks to our self-appointed political guardians in the Democrat Party, blacks have literally become addicted to birthing bastards. As ugly as that sounds, it is true. No wonder black America is in a total state of disrepair. The majority of black babies are being born to single mothers—a prescription for a life of poverty and crime. And despite the warnings that have sounded off loudly for over half a century, Democrats have done nothing to stop blacks, their most steadfast constituents, from having babies they can't take care of. This problem has perpetuated itself for generations, producing generational poverty among blacks.

If black lives truly matter, as Democrats shout at the top of their lungs, why don't they promulgate policies that encourage blacks to get married before they have kids? Blacks' voting overwhelmingly for

Democrats over the past half century is the quintessential definition of political suicide. But what's bad for blacks translates into a high rate of return on investment for Democrats. Marketing the "no baby daddy" syndrome to blacks has translated into votes, lots of votes, approaching 100 percent from blacks over the past half century. And the black family has been dismembered in the process, like the fetuses Planned Parenthood chops up to sell for profit. Democrats don't quit while they're ahead. No, the donkey party doubles down on evil.

In his 1992 acceptance speech for the Democrat presidential nomination, Bill Clinton declared, "Governments don't raise children; parents do. And you should."[2]

Clinton meant to say, "If you're white, I expect you to raise your kids"—because Democrats have made it their priority for society to normalize the idea that the federal government should be responsible for parenting blacks and their children. Neither Clinton nor any Democrat president since Johnson has done anything effective to ask black Americans as a race to take responsibility for raising our kids.

No greater or more glaring example of liberals' profiting politically off of black people's misery can be seen than the Democrats' refusal to address the illegitimate birthrate spiraling out of control among blacks. More black babies are born out of wedlock today (72 percent) than into married homes. That's dramatically worse than when Moynihan initially raised the issue (when it was 23 percent)—thanks to fifty years of encouragement by the Democrat Party. In other words, in America today, it is rare for black babies to be born to married parents. Black fathers are simply not part of the black family equation. Think about that.

"YOU CAN HAVE A HUSBAND?"

A few years ago, my mother tutored a four-year-old black girl in pre-K at a Richmond, Virginia, public school. It was part of an after-school program organized by her church's outreach ministry. One afternoon in February, my mother was explaining to the little girl the meaning of Valentine's Day's. Helping the child make a card for her mother, my mother told her that she was going to give Valentine's Day cards to special people like her husband and her children.

The little girl looked up at my mother in disbelief, asking, "You can have a husband?"

Slightly shocked and a little taken aback, my mother simply responded, "Yes."

It's a sad state of affairs when the word *husband* is a foreign word to a little black girl.

A few weeks later, around Easter, the little girl asked my mother again, "Mrs. Wright, you have a husband?"

"Yes," my mother responded.

"Husbands, friends, they're all the same," replied the little girl.

No, they certainly are not all the same. But the little girl probably had gone home and asked her single mother what a husband was, and her mother had told her that. It's difficult to have a conversation with a four-year-old about the importance of marriage. But the problem is that this little girl will grow up with her mother's message that husbands are just the same as boyfriends. Based on the statistics, she will likely follow her mother's bad example and have a baby out of wedlock.

WE KNOW WHAT WORKS

Women having babies without fathers isn't just a sign of the moral collapse of our culture, it's hazardous to the child. When a child is born into a single-parent home, the chances of that child's growing up in poverty are much greater. According to a Brookings Institution study published in 2009, if a person graduates from high school, works a full-time job, and waits until twenty-one to get married and have children, his or her chance of succeeding in life and becoming a member of the middle class rises to 76 percent. If a person doesn't finish high school, doesn't marry, and has a baby before the age of twenty-one, his or her chance of becoming poor soars to 74 percent.[3]

One of the anti-poverty solutions the Brookings study recommended was for the federal government to advocate policies that strengthen families, such as programs "to reduce unplanned pregnancies for teens and twenty-somethings." The Brookings researchers seem to have understood that the breakdown of the black family has been the main driver *Key* of the chronic wealth gap between whites and blacks over the past five decades. The lack of intact families among blacks leads to a lack of education and jobs, which translates into higher rates of crime and government dependency among blacks. Eureka! You don't have to be a neurosurgeon to see that a child born to an unmarried teenage mother isn't going to have a rosy future in life. The conclusions of the Brookings research are obvious, but Democrats continue to ignore the plain truth.

Back in 1965, Moynihan was pelted with virulent criticism for telling the truth about black America. Things have only gotten worse since then. Today Democrats express open hostility toward anyone remotely suggesting that blacks' choices may be responsible for the misery our race is trapped in, or that we should take individual responsibility to clean it up. If you're white or a Republican and you talk about the subject, you're "a racist." If you're a black Republican like me, you're an "Uncle Tom" and you "hate your people."

FEEDING THE PATHOLOGY

While "racist" Republicans promote marriage and teen abstinence, Democrats feed the pathology of single motherhood. If a Republican dares to suggest telling teens not to have sex until they are married or at least adults, the Democrats respond with mockery. They say, "Teenagers are gonna have sex, you can't stop them." But if a four-year-old prekindergartner can be taught there's no difference between a husband and "friend," you can teach a teenager premarital sex is bad.

Democrats are even pushing government-funded day care programs in public schools for teen moms. This only encourages young women to continue to have babies out of wedlock because they know that the government will help them take care of the babies. There's zero personal responsibility in this attitude. Programs from Maryland to New York are subsidized by the state and federal governments—with taxpayer money. The District of Columbia operates free day care centers in four high schools: Bell Multicultural, Ballou, Dunbar, and Luke C. Moore. In 2012 the D.C. government paid $40.70 to $54.41 per day per child to care for kids in these high school day care centers. The centers also received funding from the federal government's Head Start program. Teen day care centers in Prince George's County, Maryland, Northwestern and Bladensburg public high schools "received $200,000 from the county to provide programs, summer employment and transportation for high school students with children."[4] High school is a place for learning, not for taking care of babies! Other teens shouldn't have to be distracted by their classmates' babies. Worse, day care centers in high schools send the message that teens can have sex without repercussions.

People, including teens, can have all the babies they want. It's a free country. But other people's hard-earned money shouldn't be paying for the consequences of their irresponsible actions. Of course the Democrats don't see it that way. The victimization policies promoted by Democrats make it far too easy for black Americans to keep doing what harms our race the most—having babies out of wedlock and becoming dependent upon the government to raise them. It's like giving an alcoholic a drink, it will never cure his problem, only make it worse. That's exactly what's happening to blacks. Democrats are enabling black Americans' baby mama drama.

One need to look no further than a provision in Obamacare, a law envisioned and passed by Democrats, to see the Democrats' continued passion for feeding black America's harmful addiction to out-of-wedlock births. (It's worth noting that not a single Republican member of

Congress voted for the 2010 bill aimed at providing health insurance to all Americans through mandated coverage and taxpayer-funded subsidies.) Funded by Obamacare, the Nurse-Family Partnership strives to reduce the nation's infant mortality rate. But instead of addressing the real problem by discouraging single black teen mothers from having babies they can't parent, the program—pushed by Obama during his first presidential campaign—treats only the end results of irresponsibility. In over eight hundred cities across the country, the federal government pays nurses to make home visits to poor mothers to teach them how to care for their babies—how not to do things like "shake them when they cry or feed them Coca-Cola." In participating cities like Memphis, most of the mothers are "young, black, poor and single," according to a *New York Times* article on the initiative. "Few had fathers in their lives as children, and their children are often repeating the same broken pattern."[5] Interestingly, after making the mistake of having one baby they can't take care of properly, many of these women continue having more babies without husbands because liberal policies enable their bad behavior. Shirita Corley, a twenty-eight-year-old unmarried black woman in Memphis who received home visits, had a two-year-old son and a four-month-old son. She complained about meeting deadbeat men but wasn't doing anything to stop getting pregnant—perhaps because she, like so many other black women in her shoes, knows that Democrats will make sure she can get her government benefits.

The only way the government is going to change this bad habit is to implement pregnancy prevention policies. Prevention is cheaper than spending billions of dollars growing the black American government-dependency rolls. But Democrats will never allow policies that would decrease out-of-wedlock births to black mothers to see the light of day because there's no political power in that for them. Instead Democrats will assiduously support policies that keep the black underclass in a permanent state of victimhood.

LOW EXPECTATIONS

In 2014 President Obama announced a White House program dubbed "My Brother's Keeper" designed to teach young black men how to be responsible (because their parents aren't). The goal was, according to Obama, "to help young men of color stay out of prison, stay out of jail."[6] What high aspirations Obama has for young black men! The program should have been called "The Government's Nanny Program for Black Men," because that's really what it is. In addition to all the welfare programs enabling the dysfunctional behavior pervasive in black society in America, Obama now wants the federal government to parent young black males because so many are coming from fatherless homes. Wow, talk about the politics of low, low, low expectations. Why didn't Obama have the audacity to announce "My Caucasian Keeper" for white young men? Because, as someone told me when I posed the question on Twitter, "white people don't need it." This is true. Society doesn't accept it as normal for white men to indiscriminately father a bunch of babies out of wedlock and expect the government to raise them.

To even suggest such a thing would be laughable and offensive to white people because society—including even the Democrats—expects white men to take responsibility for their actions. But when Obama announced My Brother's Keeper, blacks embraced it like the victims Democrats have taught us to be. Sounds like black junkies to me, buying into the rhetoric Democrats are feeding them and believing that this government stuff is good for them. How sad is that? But the Democrats know what they're doing. They're feeding blacks bad policies disguised as good because it all translates into votes for the Democrat Party.

My Brother's Keeper aims to spend $200 million over five years, much of it from businesses and nonprofits, to test which strategies work in helping black boys "stay on track and reach their full potential."[7] But the Obama administration has also allocated $500 million to fund a sixteen-course curriculum of fatherhood classes around the country to teach black male teenagers how to parent.[8] Although it may seem prudent for the government to spend taxpayer dollars to prevent more black men from becoming criminals and populating our costly prisons, these liberal policies continually treat the symptoms rather than the underlying problem of black irresponsibility.

America doesn't need yet another Great Society–style government program and more money to find out what works. We already KNOW what works. Black men become successful when they are born into stable married homes with TWO PARENTS—A MOTHER AND A FATHER. We need to tell black men and women to stop having babies out of wedlock in the first place. The message should be to finish high school, delay sexual activity, go to college or get a job, get married before having a baby, and exercise self-discipline. "If you work hard, if you take responsibility, then you can make it in this country," said the president in his speech about My Brother's Keeper. But this is NOT what Democrat policies promote or strive to achieve. There's a double standard in America when it comes to taking responsibility. Whites must be held accountable while blacks can make everyone else (the government, white people, the Democrats) responsible for their lives. In the end, this keeps blacks coming back for more government help from their drug dealer, the Democrat Party. Blacks pay for their drug with their votes—for Democrats!

Obama observed that "50 years after King talked about his dream for America's children, the stubborn fact is that the life chances of a black or brown child born in this country lags behind by almost every measure...."[9] Obama continued, "If you're African American, there's about a one in two chance you grow up without a father in your house." Yet he never states the obvious reason why black kids are growing up without fathers—because the ugly truth about their unacceptable behavior would offend blacks. Frankly, blacks need to be offended and shamed because that's the only way this "tangle of pathology" dragging us down as a race, generation after generation, will end.

During the course of Obama's nearly thirty-minute speech about how helping black men was an issue of national importance, Obama referenced the fact that a father has "to play an active role in his son's life." How can a black father do that when he's missing in action from the point of birth? Obama rattled off statistics we already know, about how black boys and young men are "dropping out, unemployed, involved in negative behavior, going to jail." Blah, blah, blah, most black boys can't even read at grade level. According to the White House, 86 percent of black boys read below proficiency levels by the fourth grade—compared to 58 percent of white boys.

Then the president demanded that everyone but wayward black males themselves take responsibility for America's long-standing problem of the wayward black male. "We all have a job to do and we can do it together—black and white, urban and rural, Democrat and Republican," Obama said. Apparently that job, for which the entire American society—from parents and teachers to business, tech, and faith leaders—is responsible, is to parent black boys in America. How utterly demeaning to blacks and insulting to every other American. Yet blacks eat it up and keep voting for the hand that feeds them this poison—the Democrat Party!

The country's first black president was insistent that we must take collective responsibility for black boys because their black parents are incapable of that task. My Brother's Keeper is a disgrace! And blacks should be disgusted that fifty years after breaking free from the humiliating shackles of segregation to gain equality, blacks are still treated as second-class citizens by Democrats. But again, blacks are too addicted to the smack Democrats are slinging us to see how we're being oppressed for our votes.

THE ETERNAL CHARITY CASE

I'm frequently asked by black Democrats on social media, "What have you done for my people?" My response always is, "The only person I'm obligated to do anything for in life is me." Democrats never think of asking whites to "take care of their people" because white people are expected to take care of themselves and exert individual responsibility over their lives. You will never hear a white person ask another white person, "What have you done for your people?" Charity for people in need is something all races believe in. The problem is that Democrats view the black race as one big charity case. When it comes to us, deviance is treated as normal. So the black race is *always* going to be a charity case. That's been the problem weighing down blacks for generations. There's always either the collective "we" for blacks to fall back on, or worse, the government.

The Democrats have been heaping money on black America for decades, and nothing has changed—because they don't want anything to change. When Republicans propose ideas such as funding abstinence education programs to stem the main cause of black poverty and crime—the out-of-control out-of-wedlock birthrate—Democrats balk. Rather than asking businesses to throw away $200 million creating more excuses for black pathology, the Obama White House and Democrats should direct businesses to fund abstinence programs like the Best Friends Foundation, with a character-building curriculum program that has taught young girls from fourth through twelfth grades to delay sexual activity, graduate from high school, and go to college.

Best Friends had a companion program for boys, also taught during the school day, called the Best Men Program. Boys were taught by staff and mentors about the definition of manhood and taking responsibility for their actions. In other words, the program was trying to SOLVE the problem of illegitimacy, not PERPETUATE it. Boys and girls in grades four through twelve were taught the negative consequences of violent behavior and abusing drugs and alcohol and why fathering a baby out of wedlock wasn't a good thing. The programs operated in public schools in nearly twenty states nationwide—until their funding was cut by the Obama administration.

In a 2005 *Washington Post* column "A Poverty of Thought," George Will wrote about how Hurricane Katrina had exposed the generational poverty infecting black Americans since 1964. Most of Katrina's victims in New Orleans were black women with children but no husbands, Will wrote: "Given that most African Americans are middle class and almost half live outside central cities, and that 76 percent of all births to Louisiana African Americans were to unmarried women, it is a safe surmise that more than 80 percent of African American births in inner-city New Orleans—as in some other inner cities—were to women without husbands. That translates into a large and constantly renewed cohort of lightly parented adolescent males, and that translates into chaos in neighborhoods and schools, come rain or come shine."[10]

Will handily refuted then–Illinois senator Barack Obama's September 2005 remarks on the *Week* criticizing President George W. Bush's handling of Katrina for inadequate "empathy" and blaming the government's "historic indifference" and "passive indifference," which Obama called "as bad as active malice," as missing the point. As Will pointed out, Obama's claims of neglected victimhood were ridiculous. From 1964 to 2005, the government had doled out "more than $6.6 *trillion* in anti-poverty spending." If trillions of dollars hasn't solved black poverty in forty-one years, more money won't. This is the hypocrisy of the Democrat Party. The Democrats constantly argue that more money will fix the problem of cultural collapse in black America, but behind the scenes they know the money fixes nothing—but it does win elections for politicians like Obama. The best vaccination against poverty hasn't changed in centuries. "Graduate from high school, don't have a baby until you are married, don't marry while you are a teenager. Among people who obey those rules, poverty is minimal," wrote Will.

DEFINING DEVIANCY DOWN

Nearly ten years later, Obama announced the $200 million My Brother's Keeper Initiative, and he is still claiming that the problem with black America is that the rest of America isn't spending or doing enough to fix it. Taking a sanctimonious tone in his remarks about the program, Obama called the state of black men in America old news: "And the worst part is we've become numb to these statistics. We're not surprised by them. We take them as the norm. We just assume this is an inevitable part of American life, instead of the outrage that it is."[11] Remember what Moynihan warned about politicians defining deviancy down? It leads to an increase in very bad behaviors in society.

Yes, the Democrat Party, Obama's party, has been guilty not only of accepting the appalling statistics as normal for blacks but also of feeding the cancer of family breakdown to keep the black man hooked on the Democrat Party. Today's modern-day Democrats seem no better than their white supremacist forefathers, the Dixiecrats of the segregation-era South. Black intellectual Shelby Steele explains how it works in *White Guilt*: White liberals see themselves as superior to blacks, masters responsible for "black uplift," because blacks can't do any better. In the white liberal's mind, blacks aren't equal to whites. They can't control their libidos, much less be expected to excel in education. Essentially, today's Democrats may as well be saying out loud what their attitudes and policies convey: "Blacks are niggers," inferior to whites in every way. "Whites are agents; blacks are agented," as Steele describes it.[12] While I don't make analogies to slavery lightly, it does look and feel like blacks have empowered Democrats to be masters over our destiny. The aspirations Democrats have for blacks are bleak—just stay out of jail and prison. Not a destiny any white Democrat would want for himself, but something that is enough for young black men.

Democrats can't offer blacks anything more than demeaning insults and offers to be caretakers of their problems in exchange for their votes. Yet blacks keep returning to the Democrat Party for more. As the old saying goes, if you keep doing the same thing, you'll keep getting the same results. It's just not smart. You know the old line from the Negro College Fund ads? "A mind is a terrible thing to waste." But the reality is that black minds, like black lives, don't really matter to the Democrats.

They want blacks to remain political zombies. Obama sounds a lot like President Johnson did fifty years ago, bursting with promises of "hope and change" for everyone—except nothing changes for blacks. Of all the Democrat Party's constituents, blacks chronically remain the worst off, stuck in the status quo of government dependency generation after generation—while the Democrat Party continues to solidify its political power at our expense.

CHAPTER NINE

THE PARTY OF RACIAL DIVISION

Imagine politicians telling white people that because of the color of their skin they must vote only for one political party—even if that party doesn't address their concerns. And imagine those same politicians and the news media publicly ridiculing and mocking whites if they fail to show allegiance to this one party. People would be outraged and call that political party racist. But that's exactly how the Democrat Party talks to blacks day in and day out, and every election cycle year in and year out. Democrat politicians demand blacks be members of their party or suffer public embarrassment and verbal lynching. Pitting blacks against whites has been the bread and butter of this party's existence for hundreds of years—and the key to Democrats winning elections. The Democrat Party has grown from being outright racists from the time of Thomas Jefferson through the time of the civil rights movement, to being covert racists today.

You can tell today's Democrats are still racists because of the way they use and abuse black voters who help keep them in power. The

Democrat Party employs a divide-and-conquer strategy, deliberately feeding blacks' distrust and resentment of white people—especially of white conservatives and Republicans—in order to keep black votes on lockdown with the Democrats.

We have already seen how, during the high-profile shootings of unarmed young black men from 2012 to 2015, the Democrats made white police officers the enemy to curry electoral support from blacks. In the course of perpetuating the LIE that young black men are most in danger from racist white cops, instead of from each other, the Democrats and their sleazy friends in the race-baiting business intimidated law enforcement out of doing their jobs for fear of being pilloried as racists— "the Ferguson effect." In the process, they succeeded in creating a crime wave in which hundreds of black citizens are being murdered.

When the hashtag #BlackLivesMatter started trending on Twitter in 2014, Democrat presidential candidates like Hillary Clinton and Martin O'Malley turned their pandering up to eleven to pretend to black voters that #BlackLivesMatter more than white ones. "All lives matter" was not enough. O'Malley tried that at a campaign appearance at a Netroots Nation conference in Arizona, and was loudly booed for it. Realizing he hadn't pandered enough, O'Malley later apologized for not saying black lives mattered more than white lives.[1] Can anyone imagine a Republican getting away with this outright racism?

KEEPING THE BLACK VOTE ON LOCKDOWN FOR THE DEMOCRAT PARTY

Affirmative action programs that lower standards for minorities— ironically, in the name of equality—are a crucial tactic in the Democrats' divide-and-conquer strategy. When colleges, private companies, and government agencies are required to accept blacks and other minorities with lower qualifications than those of white candidates, it inflames racial animosity. Whites resent the unfairness, Democrats label that resentment "racism," and the whole cycle of racial tension keeps black voters captive to the Democrat Party as the big strong friend that will protect them from the evil white racist Republicans.

As Supreme Court justice Clarence Thomas has argued powerfully, affirmative action and other racial preferences do blacks no favors. These programs, created by the Democrats and touted by them as help for which the black race should be grateful, only diminish the genuine accomplishments of black Americans—because affirmative action makes it impossible to tell which achievements are genuinely earned, and which are the gift of affirmative action. Thus in his autobiography, *My Grandfather's Son*, Thomas tells the story of how he decorated his Yale Law School diploma with a "15 cents" sticker and relegated it to his basement because affirmative action had made his prestigious degree practically worthless for getting a job: "I learned the hard way that a law degree from Yale meant one thing for white graduates and another for blacks, no matter how much any one denied it. I'd graduated from one of America's top law schools, but racial preference had robbed my achievement of its true value."[2] To Thomas, affirmative action rewards weakness. He believes the point of higher education is to educate blacks, not fill racial quotas: "Merely to enroll a black in a predominantly white college means nothing. What matters most is what happens next. An education is meaningless unless it equips students to have a better life."[3]

The racist insults heaped on "Uncle Tom Clarence Thomas" are Exhibit A demonstrating the shameful way the Democrats inevitably treat any black person who dares to disagree with their politics. That's the ugly nickname that Democrat Representative Bennie Thompson of Mississippi gave the only black person on the Supreme Court in a radio interview with the Nation of Islam.[4] You only have to listen to the way the Democrats talk about blacks who question the value of their liberal policies—and thus threaten the Dems' monopoly on the black vote—in order to hear their racism loud and clear.

In 2002 Neil Rogers, a gay liberal Florida talk radio host, thought it would be fun to air a racist rant against Condoleezza Rice, who is a black Republican and at the time was serving as President George W. Bush's national security advisor. Rogers sang the below lyrics with an Amos 'n' Andy accent to the tune of Nat King Cole's "Mona Lisa":

> Condoleezza, Condoleezza, what you be doin'? That neo-
>   fascist black-haired token schwarze dog.
> Is you there 'cause you a high-toned public Negro?
> Is you their black-haired answer-mammy who be smart?
> Does they like how you shine their shoes, Condoleezza?
> Or the way you wash and park the whitey's cars.
> Georgie junior says he trusts you, Condoleezza.
> Who said our [unintelligible] off the greedy oil woes.
> But then he make you clean all the White House
>   bathrooms.
> The public sink, the toilet and let's scrub the floors.[5]

Rogers also unapologetically told FoxNews.com that Rice was Bush's "house negro."[6] If Rush Limbaugh or any prominent conservative talk radio host sang such a song about President Obama, the liberal press would have had wall-to-wall coverage of the incident and the host would have been fired.

But the Democrats don't just fling racist epithets around. They will say anything to ridicule and isolate blacks who rebel against the Democrat orthodoxy. They will do their best to read black conservatives out of the black race, in order to keep black voters from taking their ideas seriously. The same Representative Thompson who called the only black on the Supreme Court "Uncle Tom Clarence Thomas" commented on Thomas's votes on affirmative action cases before the court:[7] "When I look at decisions he's been a part of on that court, it's almost to the point saying this man doesn't like black people, he doesn't like being black. Because every decision where color has something to do with it, he votes against it."[8] Because Thomas doesn't conform to the Democrats' line that blacks can't succeed without affirmative action, Thompson concludes that Thomas hates himself and all black people—a ridiculous idea. Black Americans should be insulted by such racist comments from Democrats like Thompson, who demand that our politics be skin deep, not the fruit of serious reflection. In their view, all blacks should think alike.

The Democrat Party dictates to us how we should think and vote solely based upon the color of our skin. When it comes to the black race, political choice is not allowed! Anyone who dares to defy the unanimity the Democrats require of our race must be insulted and marginalized, lest other African Americans listen and question our monolithic support for the Democrat Party. After all, the Democrats have been able to rely on the black vote since 1964; over 80 percent of blacks have voted Democrat in every presidential election since.[9] Today, many blacks don't even know why they vote Democrat, but won't consider voting any other way. When asked why they make this political choice, they can't come up with any better answers than that it's because their parents did, or because Republicans are unworthy of their vote because they are "racists."

When it comes to riding herd on black people to keep them in line, the Democrats have no more useful allies than the liberal media. Journalists literally snicker when interviewing black Republicans, acting like we're aliens or some kind of freaks. CNN's Kyra Phillips's 2012 live interview of Mia Love is a good example. At the time, Love was victorious after winning the Republican primary for a congressional seat in Utah. In 2014 she won the general election, becoming the first black Republican woman ever elected to Congress. Mia Love is a substantial political figure, but CNN's Phillips seemed to think she was some kind of joke, chuckling as she interviewed her:

PHILLIPS: Mia, Good to see you.
LOVE: Thank you, thank you for having me.

PHILLIPS: I tell you, I tell you what, you fascinate me. Conservative, Mormon, African American woman, living in Utah. You're a daughter of Haitian immigrants. Anything else you want to tell me that makes you even more unbelievably unique. (Laughs)

LOVE: Well I don't know if it's unbelievably unique but I run also and I enjoy running because it just keeps my head straight and keeps my priorities and makes sure my body's healthy. So, I love running.[10]

Phillips would never insult a white candidate in the same position. But in her mind and the minds of most liberals, it is perfectly okay to be dismissive of black Republicans because we're not supposed to exist. Mocking black conservatives publicly is a way to keep us in our place politically where we can be controlled by Democrats. But more important, it is a way to discourage any liberal rebellion among blacks who are considering voting Republican.

I know what it's like to be the target of ridicule as a black Republican. In 2012 I participated in a panel discussion entitled "Why Voting Matters for African Americans," hosted by the Congressional Black Caucus's Annual Legislative Conference. Ron Christie, a former aide to Vice President Dick Cheney, and I were the only two black Republicans on the panel, joining the five black Democrat panelists: Representatives Marcia Fudge, John Lewis, and Mel Watt, political strategist Donna Brazile, and "activist" Al Sharpton. We spoke to a crowd of over six hundred people, largely black and Democrat. Obviously, the deck was stacked against the Republican point of view for a reason—to keep blacks politically unawakened, so they would stay members of the Democrat herd. Before moderator Marc Lamont Hill, a black Democrat pundit and Columbia University professor—you may remember him as the commentator who insisted the Baltimore riots were really "uprisings"—introduced the panelists, he made Republicans the butt of his jokes on the issue of voter ID laws:

> ... this is an important conversation we are going to have today about voter discrimination, about voter ID laws and how it constitutes really the new form, twenty-first century form of racial discrimination. There's a lot of conversation going on right now about what these voter IDs mean. The Republicans say it means one thing, Democrats say it means another.
>
> I think they want me to be nonpartisan and objective, and I will when the panel comes out, but before they come out, while they're getting their make up on I'm going to tell you all something. **This is not anything to be objective about. This is a clear case of racial discrimination.** What is going on now is important [applause] because this election will be decided by these types of issues. **Republicans don't win by genius. They don't win because they make a compelling argument.**[11] [emphasis in the original]

By stating that there was nothing to be objective about when talking about voter ID laws, Hill was trying to poison the minds of the virtually all-black Democrat audience against anything Ron and I had to say. When Lamont introduced the Republican panelists, he continued poking fun at us: "Now I said this was going to be a diverse panel. Why are you laughing? We have some conservatives. We went through the whole CBC and found the black Republicans—both of them. First up, Ms. Crystal Wright [applause] and we have Mr. Ron Christie [cheers and applause]."

I guess Ron and I should be glad that Hill didn't introduce us as "house negroes" or "sellouts." But like Representative Thompson and CNN's Kyra Phillips, he was sending the message: *These guys are not normal black people, and you don't want to be one of them.* There's certainly power in numbers—and sometimes ignorance in numbers, too. The more black people continue to vote solidly Democrat without questioning why, the more power the party has over blacks to do absolutely nothing for us. Democrats know they can count on the black vote decade in and decade out without delivering results, so they laugh all the way to the ballot box.

TARGETED ON TWITTER

More recently, following Obama's sixth State of the Union address, black Democrats attempted to shame me into silence again. In a January 2015 article, "#BlackTwitter Responds to the State of the Union," published on NBCBLK, the microsite for blacks at NBCNews.com, Danielle Belton wrote about black Twitter users' reactions to Obama's State of the Union speech. In the story, she included a tweet of mine reacting to Obama's proposal to provide free community college to all Americans at the whopping price tag of $60 billion over ten years:

> **@GOPBlackChick**
> Sending Congress plan to lower cost of college to 0. (Correction paid for by tax hikes on rich). #SOTU

I was the only black conservative quoted in Belton's article, and blacks loyal to the Democrat Party line unleashed a torrent of insults at me on Twitter:

> **Bert Maclin, FBI @_CasanovaJr**
> NBC news putting a tweet from @GOPBlackChick in an article about "Black Twitter" just shows how little they know about #BlackTwitter

> **Twice Sifted @twice_sifted**

Dear @NBCNews, Perhaps you missed THIS on #Black-Twitter, but we traded @GOPBlackChick in the racial draft 2 yrs ago. Also Stacy Dash. FYI.

I am She-Ra @AskShaaB
Every black person is not black twitter, but clearly they don't know that since they included Crystal Wright in that piece.

Dorianna Gray @blurbette
So, @NBC actually put Crystal Wright's tweets in an article about #BlackTwitter live tweeting the #SOTU. Like, really???[12]

In other words, to be black meant I had to be Democrat, so I don't belong on #BlackTwitter. As a black Republican, I must be banished from my race. I for one don't know why NBC felt a need to create a microsite devoted to "elevating America's conversation about black identity, politics & culture" in the first place. Such a focus on tailoring the news to one racial group further perpetuates the racial divide in this country—to the Democrats' electoral advantage.

All these tactics, both subtle and overt, are tools of intimidation used by Democrats to bully black Republicans into silence and scare other blacks from daring to have any political free thought, much less free will. The resounding message is that to be black is to be born Democrat—a proposition extremely convenient for the electoral fortunes of America's progressive party.

KEEPING BLACK POLITICIANS IN LINE

In a January 2014 speech to NAACP members in Columbia, South Carolina, North Carolina NAACP president Reverend William Barber mocked Senator Tim Scott of South Carolina, the only black Republican in the U.S. Senate: "A ventriloquist can always find a good dummy...the extreme right wing down here finds a black guy to be senator and claims he's the first black senator since Reconstruction and then he goes to Washington, D.C., and articulates the agenda of the Tea Party."[13]

Ironically, Barber's speech also celebrated the legacy of Martin Luther King Jr., who fought for the government to give blacks equality, as in the 1965 Voting Rights Act, which guaranteed blacks not only the right to vote but also the freedom to choose which political party they would support. Ridiculing Scott like that was a gross insult to King's legacy.

In 2014 Democrat Representative James Clyburn, a black congressman from South Carolina and at the time the assistant Democratic leader, also assailed Scott for having the audacity to be a black Republican: "If you call progress electing a person with the pigmentation that he has, who votes against the interest and aspirations of 95 percent of the black people in South Carolina, then I guess that's progress," Clyburn told the *Washington Post*.[14] According to Clyburn's logic, Scott should automatically be a Democrat solely because of his race. Apparently Clyburn believes Scott has committed a betrayal of his people by supporting conservative policies. Would Clyburn talk this way if Scott were white? Of course not. It's only blacks who are required to kowtow to the Democrat Party or be labeled traitors to their race.

As a Republican, Scott believes that blacks, like all Americans, benefit more from policies that encourage individual prosperity through hard work than from policies that encourage reliance on government programs. As a Democrat, Clyburn thinks the interests of black people in South Carolina are for government to take care of them. But how well has that policy worked out? After half a century of welfare programs pushed by the Democrats since the Johnson administration, blacks are more than twice as likely as whites to have gone on food stamps and been unemployed.[15] Based on that result, it is not Republican Scott but rather the Democrats who are the politicians voting against "the interest and aspirations of 95 percent of the black people in South Carolina."[16]

KEEPING BLACKS IN A STATE OF EMERGENCY

To the shock and awe of liberals, 2016 Republican presidential candidate Donald Trump had the audacity to blast Democrat President Barack Obama's record as "a shame."[17] In an August 2, 2015, appearance on ABC's *This Week*, Trump said he didn't think the country would elect another black president for generations "because I think that he has set a very poor standard. I think that he has set a very low bar, and I think it's a shame for the African-American people."[18]

Black lives really don't matter under Obama. But don't take my word for it as a black woman. Look at the facts—as laid out by none other than Democrat Representative G. K. Butterfield in his January 7, 2015, speech as incoming chairman of the Congressional Black Caucus: "As we stand here now on the dawn of a new Congress, the 114th Congress, we must tell the full story—for many Black Americans, they are not even close to realizing the American dream. Depending on where they live, an economic depression hangs over their head, and it is burdening their potential and the potential of their children. Black America is in a state of emergency today as it was at the turn of the century!"[19] Butterfield added that in 2015 "the statistics tell the story." In his words:

- Twenty-five percent of black households live below the poverty line as compared to eight percent for white households.
- One out of three black children lives in poverty.
- African Americans are twice as likely as whites to be unemployed.
- African Americans earn $13,000 less per year than their white counterparts.

- The unemployment rate of African Americans has consistently been twice as high as for whites over the last 50 years.
- For every $100 in wealth of a white household, the black household only has $6 in wealth.[20]

The statistics Representative Butterfield listed are utterly embarrassing—for him and his fellow Democrats! The liberal policies they've been pushing for the last fifty years, with at least 80 percent support from black voters in every single presidential election, have left blacks in a "state of emergency." And the first black president, another Democrat, has done nothing to help blacks either. Emanuel Cleaver, a former chair of the CBC, has admitted as much: "Look, as the chair of the Black Caucus I've got to tell you, we are always hesitant to criticize the president. With 14% black unemployment, if we had a white president we'd be marching around the White House. However, I [also] don't think the Irish would do that to the first Irish president or Jews would do that to the first Jewish president; but we're human and we have a sense of pride about the president. The president knows we are going to act in deference to him in a way we wouldn't to someone white," Cleaver unapologetically told The Root.[21] White people are free to complain when white presidents screw them over, but blacks are supposed to be like happy children devoted to Democrats. Cleaver joked that if Hillary Clinton had won the presidency in 2008 and seen black unemployment as high as it was under Obama, he'd be singing a different tune: "As much as I love Sen. Clinton I would have been all over her on 14 percent unemployment for African Americans. I would have said, 'My sister, I love you, but this has got to go.'"[22] Well, let's see if Cleaver does that if Hillary gets elected president. Somehow it's never the right time for the black voters who keep the Democrat Party in power to mention that Democrats are doing nothing for blacks.

Our first black president has had time to advocate for gays—getting them gay marriage, repealing the U.S. military's prohibition on openly gay and lesbian soldiers serving in the military. He's done a lot for immigrants, too. Through executive order, Obama prevented millions of illegal aliens ages thirty-one and under from being deported from America. But blacks, who voted at a rate of 95 percent for Democrat Obama in 2008 and 93 percent for him in 2012, have gotten a lump of coal—at best—from their black messiah. The Democrat president's record with blacks as the nation's first black president should give blacks pause or even paralysis before voting another Democrat brother into the White House. But it's not all President Obama's fault. Unfortunately, Obama's failure to make black lives better is very typical of Democrat presidents over the past half century—when blacks were guaranteeing them electoral victories.

It all began with Democrat President Lyndon B. Johnson's Great Society agenda in 1964. The "Great Society" should actually be called the "Government-Dependency Society," at least where blacks are concerned, because ever since 1964 Democrat policies in areas like education, employment, welfare, and poverty have kept blacks in a fifty-year "state of emergency," to quote Representative Butterfield, and most definitely unequal to whites. Democrats have successfully continued funding for these destructive programs ever since LBJ. With the amount of government money poured into improving the lives of blacks over the years, you would think it was time for the Democrats to put up or shut up—to demonstrate that these programs have helped blacks by now, or to quit pushing the same failed programs that have kept us in this "state of emergency" for decades.

In his inaugural speech to the Congressional Black Caucus, Democrat Representative Butterfield urged his colleagues that it was time to "learn from our past, but boldly confront an uncertain future." What's profoundly embarrassing is that the Democrats haven't learned anything from the past fifty years—except how to lock up the black vote.

The Democrats keep advancing policies that don't reduce racial disparities but rather increase them. Key planks of the agenda of the

Democrats in the CBC are protecting "the social safety net that our communities depend on," advancing "anti-poverty" programs, and defending affirmative action. None of these things has helped pull blacks out of the "state of emergency" Butterfield was complaining about—quite the opposite! Blacks are still on welfare at higher per capita rates than whites.[23] Even in absolute numbers, despite the fact that we're a mere 13 percent of the U.S. population, more blacks are incarcerated than whites.[24] Blacks are poorer than whites. According to a 2013 study by Brandeis University, the wealth gap between blacks and whites has tripled over the past twenty-five years due to inequality in education, income, homeownership, and inheritances. As of 2009, white families had a median net worth of over $265,000 while black families had a median net worth of only $28,500.[25]

At this point, blacks should have serious doubts that Democrats will ever fight for racial equality. It's simply not part of the Democrat Party's DNA. Stoking racial division, not creating prosperity for all, is what helps Democrats at the ballot box. "A rising tide lifts all boats" isn't the Democrat motto; it's more like "Divide and conquer."

THE DEMOCRATS: CYNICS ON RACE SINCE 1964

But how did the Democrats get such a tight lock on the black vote to begin with? Before 1964, the presidential black vote averaged about 30 percent Republican.[26] President Dwight D. Eisenhower actually won 39 percent of the black vote in his 1956 election largely because of his civil rights agenda. He used his executive power to end segregation in the District of Columbia and the federal government and was the first president to appoint a black person, E. Frederic Morrow, to a senior position in the White House.

But after President Johnson signed the Civil Rights Act into law, Democrats became adroit at manipulating blacks with rhetoric suggesting that whites in general and Republicans in particular were evil racists intent on keeping the black man down. That's ironic, because Johnson himself had appealed to the racism of white voters. His motives in passing the Civil Rights Act of 1964 were anything but pure. Often revered as the champion of civil rights, Johnson was more of a racist who profiteered politically first by supporting segregation and then by posing as the generous benefactor giving blacks the civil rights that they had literally died to achieve. Blacks were becoming a growing and influential voting bloc, and Johnson saw the handwriting on the wall. So he changed course and got behind the civil rights movement in a reversal that "was motivated as much by what was right for him politically as what was right for the country," as Bruce Bartlett writes in *Wrong on Race*.[27]

Before Johnson was against segregation, he was for it. Johnson was first elected as a Democrat/Dixiecrat, and according to Bartlett when he was sent "to the Senate from the old confederate state of Texas in 1948" he "had an impeccable record of supporting the Southern position on race."[28] By 1955 he was elected Senate majority leader by racist Southern Dixiecrats in the Democrat-controlled Senate on his promise of blocking any civil rights legislation. In 1957 President Eisenhower lobbied Congress to finally pass a civil rights bill. Johnson, like the caucus of racists he led, didn't want to give blacks equal rights, but he saw a political opportunity to get the Senate to pass a civil rights bill, which would buoy his ambition to run for president in 1960. In an exchange with Georgia Democrat senator Richard Russell, Johnson betrayed his animosity toward blacks: "These Negros, they're getting uppity these days and that's a problem for us since they've got something now they never had before, the political pull to back up their uppityness. Now, we've got to do something about this, we've got to give them a little something, just enough to quiet them down not enough to make a difference. For if we don't move at all, then their allies will line up against us and there'll be no way of stopping them, we'll lose the filibuster and there'll be no way of putting a brake on all sorts of wild legislation. It'll be Reconstruction all over again."[29]

good to know truth!

Of course, returning to the days of Reconstruction, when blacks had gained many civil rights, was a terrifying prospect to Johnson—to any racist Democrat at the time. From 1865 to 1875, the Republicans had controlled Congress, passing two dozen civil rights bills, including the Thirteenth Amendment, ending slavery; the Fourteenth Amendment, counting blacks as citizens; and the Fifteenth Amendment, granting black men the right to vote.[30] State legislatures at the time were also dominated by Republicans, and the first seven blacks elected to Congress were Republicans elected during Reconstruction: Senator Hiram Rhodes Revels of Mississippi, Representative Benjamin Turner of Alabama, Representative Robert De Large of South Carolina, Representative Josiah Walls of Florida, Representative Jefferson Long of Georgia, and Representatives Joseph Hayne Rainey and Robert Brown Elliott of South Carolina.[31] Altogether twenty-three black Republicans were elected to Congress during Reconstruction. As Dave Barton, in *Setting the Record Straight: American History in Black and White*, noted of the five years after the Republican-dominated U.S. Congress passed the Thirteenth Amendment, "Blacks went from being slaves to becoming members of Congress."[32]

Of course Johnson didn't want to return to the days of Reconstruction—no Southern racist did. In a 1960 interview with *Jet* magazine reporter Simeon Booker, Republican National Committee chairman William Miller described Johnson's duplicity: "His vice-presidential platform favored sit in demonstrations. His state platform called for enforcement of laws designed to protect private property…from physical occupation. His national platform favored school desegregation. His state platform pledged to protect the decisions of the people of local school districts in operation and control of their schools."[33]

Johnson was a confirmed racist who backed the Civil Rights Act of 1964 for political convenience, and the Democrat Party has been using and abusing black voters in the same exact way ever since. The Democrats' reputation as heroes who fight for black America is the biggest con job in the history of the country.

Take a look at these comparisons between black America in the 1960s and today:

Incarceration Rates

According to Pew Research Center, "Black men were more than six times as likely as white men to be incarcerated in federal and state prisons, and local jails.... That is an increase from 1960, when black men were five times as likely as whites to be incarcerated."[34]

High School Graduation

In 1967, 71.4 percent of blacks graduated high school, versus 84.6 percent of whites.[35]

In the 2011–2012 school year, 68 percent of blacks graduated from high school on time, versus 85 percent of whites.[36]

College

Only 5 percent of U.S. blacks were enrolled in college in 1964, versus 10 percent of whites.[37]

Today, nearly 70 percent of white high school graduates go to college, versus 65 percent of blacks.[38]

But among students who started at four-year schools in 2006, 62.5 percent of whites graduated within six years versus 40.2 percent of blacks.[39]

Out-of-Wedlock Births

In 1965, 24 percent of black infants and 3.1 percent of white infants were born to single mothers.[40]

In 2013, whites had an out-of-wedlock birthrate of 29 percent, versus blacks' rate of 72 percent.[41]

Black author Shelby Steele, a fellow at Stanford's Hoover Institute, has asked a profound question: "If the Great Society was so good, why did black America produce its first true underclass after it was over?"[42] Black America in 2015 looks like it's beyond a state of emergency. It looks more like it's on life support.

One definition of insanity is doing the same thing over and over again but expecting different results. In the case of black Americans' blind loyalty to the Democrat Party, we're coming up empty handed over and over again. No other political party but the Democrats tells blacks they love us the most yet gives us less than they give to any other group of their constituents. *Ebony* magazine had this to say about the black vote in 2016: "In the era (or perhaps, the dawn) of #BlackLivesMatter, it is unlikely that a Democratic candidate will be able to carry the critical Black vote without making criminal justice reform central to his or her campaign."[43] Unfortunately, that's nonsense. The Democrat candidate for president in 2016 will carry the black vote just as the party has for decades, by saying a lot and doing nothing for blacks. If the Democrats are reelected, we can look forward to four more years of economic stagnation for blacks, cynical race baiting that pits us against our white neighbors, and Democrat-enabled violence that is killing our young men. When will we stop allowing ourselves to be made fools of at the ballot box and diversify our politics? How idiotic can black people be?

CHAPTER TEN

THE PARTY OF IDENTITY POLITICS

The Democratic National Committee's outline of the constituents it serves reads like a U.S. Census questionnaire. On the bottom of the homepage of its website, the DNC lists nineteen groups in all, including everyone from "Democrats Abroad" and "Asian Americans and Pacific Islanders" to "Rural Americans," "Faith Community," the obligatory "Women," and a coterie of minority groups.[1] But as the saying goes, *Jack of all trades, master of none.* It's impossible to be all things to all people. These groups don't all have the same interests—and sometimes they're in direct conflict, as when the Dems frantically resist any kind of enforcement against illegal immigration to please their allies in La Raza (and to keep Hispanics voting for Democrats)—apparently with no concern about how illegals are contributing to the sky-high black unemployment rate.[2] Identity politics is great for Democrat politicians who sew up the votes of minorities and women by posing as their champions against the evil, racist, sexist, xenophobic Republicans. But it's not so great for the voters who are segregated into those identity categories, pitted against mainstream America, and expected to support the Democrats in lockstep fashion.

There is no better example of the Democrat Party's retail racism than their successful effort to segregate blacks from whites in nearly every aspect of society. Black History Month, black spokespeople, black media, and black studies departments are just a few of the ways Democrats work assiduously to put blacks back in the back of the bus—cut off from mainstream America and beholden to Democrats at the ballot box. The "post-racial America" we were promised if Barack Obama was elected looks more and more like a separate but equal nation rather than an integrated one.

Blacks don't seem to have advanced beyond segregation when it comes to the news media. Outlets such as *Ebony* and BET have been around for a long time, and the election of America's first black president has only seen a proliferation of "for blacks only" news sites. TheGrio and The Root are among the most notable. TheGrio is "devoted to providing African-Americans with stories and perspectives that appeal to them but are underrepresented in existing national news outlets."[3] Similarly, The Root describes itself as "the premier news, opinion and culture site for African-American influencers."[4] And not to be outdone, Politic365 is "the premier digital destination for politics and policy related to communities of color."[5] How remarkable it is that theGrio seems to know what appeals to every black person in America! I don't read theGrio, but as a black person I feel I'm very informed on issues impacting me by reading the *Washington Post* and the *Wall Street Journal* daily. Why do I need to be segregated from the newspapers white people read? What's next? Will modern-day Democrats bring back separate drinking fountains, restrooms, lunch counters, and schools for blacks to help us stay culturally in tune? Are white people allowed to visit these sites? Maybe the sites should ask visitors to verify their race before reading their content.

It's not only start-up websites that are devoted to "black only" content. Existing online news sites have also launched black versions of their websites, such as the Huffington Post's "Black Voices" channel and NBC's NBCBLK to help blacks get our "black only" news. Black people can get our news from the same sources as white people: TV, radio, and the Internet!

When a fellow black conservative asked me what I thought about NBC launching its black site, I responded, "Like Hollywood, I don't think news organizations should keep separating blacks from mainstream coverage. Why not just incorporate us in daily news?"

"AMEN!" he replied. "That's what I said! So we are just going to accept separate but equal? It's a dangerous slippery slope!" Some might say that black-operated and black-focused newspapers existed well before now and are nothing new. That's true, but before 1964, blacks needed black-owned newspapers because that was often the only way they could read about news affecting their lives, such as lynchings, murders of blacks, and the civil rights movement. But thankfully those days are over. Why are we being resegregated?

HOW THE TERM "AFRICAN AMERICAN" KEEPS BLACKS DOWN

Another condescending tactic employed by Democrats to treat blacks as "other" (that is, not part of the same America in which white people live) is the use of the term "African American." In 1989 the *New York Times* reported that thanks to "a movement led by Rev. Jesse Jackson" (the godfather of all race hustlers), more blacks wanted to change their name to "African-American." Noted the *Times*: "The term has already shown up in the newest grade-school textbooks, been adopted by several black-run radio stations and newspapers around the country, and appeared in the titles of popular books and in the conversations of many blacks as they warm to the idea and speak of visiting Africa one day."[6]

But not all blacks embraced the new term. "When did they take a vote on what blacks wanted to be called?" C. Hutherson, a black

Chicagoan, asked in a letter to the *Chicago Sun-Times*. "They must have done it while I was asleep. Jesse Jackson and other black leaders have a lot of nerve speaking for all blacks."[7] Why don't the politically correct Democrats have a hyphenated name for white Americans like "Caucasian-American" or "European-American"? Because white Americans would tell Democrats they're not changing their name, and because Democrats consider whites to be ordinary Americans—while they cast blacks as the perpetual outsiders and victims. I wonder how many blacks living in America today have ever been to Africa, much less have an immediate family member from any African nation. We should tell Democrats to shove this racist label back up the hyphenated hole it came from.

BLACK HISTORY MONTH: A GOOD IDEA TURNED INTO A SCAM

Black History Month has been pimped by Democrats to bring blacks down and brainwash us into believing we're living around the fringes of America, never fully participating in it equally. If it weren't for the Democrats, America wouldn't celebrate February as the blackness month that has become nothing more than a commercialized excuse for companies and organizations to make money off white guilt and black marginalization. Long before Black History Month was officially recognized and commercialized in 1976, Carter G. Woodson created Black History Week in 1926 to encourage black Americans to learn from their history in order to become empowered by it. Woodson, one of the first scholars to study black history, founded the Association for the Study of African American Life and History. Black History Week was first celebrated during the week in February in which both Abraham Lincoln and Frederick Douglass were born, because both men were champions of equal rights for black Americans. That made some sense because before 1964, schools didn't usually teach how blacks contributed to American history.[8] Sadly, they still don't really teach about most of those contributions. Today it seems the only black history students learn is footnotes on slavery and the civil rights movement. All the many other contributions of blacks throughout American history are omitted. Black history should be a part of American students' education and our national discourse 365 days a year, not relegated to a single month of meaningless propaganda. "If the Negro in the ghetto must eternally be fed by the hand that pushes him into the ghetto, he will never become strong enough to get out of the ghetto," observed Woodson.[9]

If more blacks were more knowledgeable about black American history, I doubt they would keep voting for Democrats with the intense herd mentality of the past fifty years. But when Black History Month rolls around each February, we see commemorations that more often than not demean rather than uplift blacks. For instance, Nike unveiled a series of "limited edition" high-priced black sneakers and sports apparel as a promotion for its 2015 Black History Month campaign. I couldn't make this up if I tried. Ranging in price from $120 to $300, the BHM Collection sneakers didn't come with any kind of special message about famous black Americans, just a high price tag. A portion of the proceeds was contributed by Nike to the Ever Higher Fund, a nonprofit that "leverages the power of sport to maximize the potential of underserved youth."[10] Whatever that means. Nike could have shown some better corporate responsibility by donating to historically black colleges and universities, many of which are in dire need of funds as they try to educate black kids. The last thing black teenage boys need is more expensive sneakers and encouragement to be professional athletes. What they need is more books and encouragement to finish high school. Nike shamelessly used Black History Month to sell more sneakers to black kids, who are buying sneakers at a greater rate than they're finishing high school.

Businesses use Black History Month as a "race shield" to prove they aren't racist—and to make money off blacks. Nike isn't the only company using Black History Month like it's Valentine's Day to pimp goods to blacks. Here, taken from their press releases, is a sampling of how some of America's other corporations "honored," "celebrated," or "saluted" Black History Month in 2015 with contests, TV shows, films, and dental care. Most black people aren't even aware of any of these purely symbolic commemorations:

Frito-Lay Celebrates Black History Month By "Calling All Artists" For A Chance To Win A Grand Prize Of $10,000

In celebration of Black History Month, PepsiCo's Frito-Lay North America division is asking consumers to submit an original piece of art online for a chance to win a grand prize of $10,000 through its "Create to Celebrate" Black History Month art contest.

American Airlines Proudly Celebrates Black History Month

American Airlines is celebrating Black History Month with numerous events and initiatives throughout February, including showcasing African-American aviation pioneers and paying tribute to notable African-American films and TV shows onboard daily flights.

Macy's Salutes the Culture-Defining Soul Era of Black Style in Celebration of Black History Month 2015

This February, culture-defining trends take center stage as Macy's examines the Soul Era of Black Style in celebration of Black History Month. From elegant high glamour to the hottest looks on the street, Black Style has influenced trends and designers that have shaped American and global culture.

Colgate-Palmolive And Family Dollar Partner To Celebrate Black History Month

Colgate-Palmolive Company ("Colgate") and Family Dollar have partnered to inspire African-American families during February's Black History Month to honor their past and treasure their future with a healthy smile.

Sony Movie Channel Celebrates Black History Month With A Special Programming Block Mondays At 10 P.M. ET In February

Sony Movie Chanel (SMC) celebrates Black History Month with a special programming block featuring African-American action heroes, Mondays in February at 10 p.m. ET.[11]

These platitudes are useless. What are these companies doing to really help "African Americans"? Certainly not putting them in their boardrooms. America's government has a black chief executive, "but 99% of the nation's largest businesses do not."[12] According to the Executive Leadership Council, a group of black executives working at major U.S. companies, in 2012 there were fewer than eight hundred black executives employed in the top positions of Fortune 500 companies.[13] McDonald's hired its first black CEO, Don Thompson, in 2012, then only two years later claimed to have accepted his resignation. While McDonald's said Thompson decided to step down, declining sales suggest the board of directors showed him the exit door. In 2012 America had six black CEOs leading Fortune 500 companies. In 2015 America had five: American Express's Kenneth Chenault, Delphi's Rodney O'Neal, Merck & Company's Kenneth Frazier, Carnival's Arnold W. Donald, and Xerox's Ursula Burns.[14]

All major corporations have "diversity programs," which are nothing more than cosmetic efforts to insulate themselves against lawsuits. I am not suggesting that any company should hire a black person just to fill a quota. But their candidate pools should be expanded to include more qualified blacks. It's beyond insulting for corporations to keep up this charade of Black History Month when they don't practice what they preach the other eleven months out of the year. As I wrote in the UK newspaper the *Guardian* in 2014, "It's hypocritical for businesses to honor Black History Month when the rest of the year they do little or nothing to mitigate the chronic double digit black unemployment or address the woefully low numbers of blacks in board rooms and executive positions."[15]

THE DEMOCRATS' PATRONIZING USE OF BLACK HISTORY MONTH

Instead of doing something about the numerous issues affecting black Americans—high crime, astronomical out-of-wedlock birthrates, or double-digit unemployment—the Obama White House decided to launch a Twitter campaign to honor Black History Month. Valerie Jarrett, the president's senior advisor and a member of his "brain trust," wrote, "There are countless men and women whose names may not appear prominently in our history books, but whose sweat, blood, and strength is woven into our national identity and continues to inform our sense of pride and dignity as Americans. Every day this month, I will be tweeting out their stories. To take part, follow me at @vj44 and tweet your suggestions of champions of Black history you think deserve to be highlighted. Make sure to use the hashtag #BlackHistoryMonth."[16]

The overwhelming number of black voters who voted for Obama should tweet Jarrett and Obama their displeasure with the state of black America. While Rome burns for black Americans, Obama gives blacks tweets for Black History Month. Blacks need to celebrate Black History Month by firing Democrats who've kept us economically oppressed for fifty years. The Democrat Party, whose logo is oddly enough the donkey or ass, wins the black vote by continuing to talk down to the black electorate like we're dummies.

THE RACE PIMPS

True!

There is no better example of Democrats playing blacks for idiots than the phenomenon of the race pimps, better known in polite liberal discourse as "black spokespeople" or "black leaders." No other race—white, Hispanic, or Asian—allows the Democrats to designate spokespeople to speak on behalf of their entire race except black people. Writing about the Senate's confirmation of Loretta Lynch in April 2015 as the nation's first black female U.S attorney general, *Politico* noted that "black leaders on and off Capitol Hill" had lobbied Republicans intensely to vote for her.[17] When I read this, I wondered who these black leaders were that publications like *Politico* refer to ad nauseam? The reporter, Seung Min Kim, didn't bother to name them.

As a black adult woman, I find her use of the term demeaning because it suggests that black adults are like children needing to be "led" or parented by other adult blacks. I wondered if white people have special leaders to tell them what to do. Liberal reporters like Kim never refer to white politicians as "white leaders" because dare I say that would be, well, insulting. Because (1) it would be considered racist, and (2) white people don't need "leaders."

You will never see Democrats like Obama convene a meeting of "white leaders" at the White House to discuss "white affairs." Democrats expect white people to think, act, and do things for themselves as individuals. According to the White House website, Obama met with "African American leaders" on November 9, 2011,[18] "African-American faith leaders" on August 26, 2013,[19] and "African American civil rights and faith leaders" on February 26, 2015.[20] Who are these black leaders American liberals keep telling us blacks about? As a black person, I don't ever remember voting for any black person to speak on my behalf—*ever!* Yet Democrats neuter individual thought among black Americans by anointing "black spokespeople" to speak on behalf of all of us.

You know them by name: Al Sharpton, Jesse Jackson, and the rest of the professional race-baiters. They are the self-appointed spokespeople for black America, and they're all Democrats. Whenever a crisis occurs affecting blacks, or a white cop kills an "unarmed black teen," the liberal news media trot out the "black spokespeople" to speak on behalf of every black person in America—because evidently black people can't think for ourselves. Have you ever heard a news anchor or TV host say, "Now we're going to talk to Mr. Jones, who's going to tell us what white America thinks"? No, because everyone views white people as individuals capable of critical thinking and possessing different opinions. In fact, blacks are no more or less similar to one another than whites are. We come from different socioeconomic backgrounds, but the Democrats are doing their best to make sure we're a monolithic group that all think, eat, sleep, and especially vote the same way, following the political orders of one party. They don't grant blacks permission to be freethinking individuals.

The Trayvon Martin trial was a good example of the liberal news media and Democrats talking down to blacks and viewing us as a group rather than individuals. For about a week following the verdict, there was a flood of news stories revolving around the theme of *What does black America think of the verdict?* or *What does this mean to black America?* The way media denigrated blacks was a tragedy. NBC's *Meet the Press* host David Gregory invited Reverend Al Sharpton as a guest on his July 14, 2013, show to tell white America what blacks thought about the verdict.[21] It demeans the intelligence of blacks for Gregory and other liberal journalists to continue to invite race hustlers like Sharpton on broadcasts to act as the spokesman for "black America," telling blacks what to think and then conveying our collective black thought to whites, as if blacks are deaf, dumb, and mute.

When the 2015 Oscar nominations were announced, Al Sharpton said he was going to protest their lack of diversity. His staged protests were intended to shake down Hollywood studios for money to line his pockets. Has Sharpton ever protested for something that actually helped black people instead of helping him? When was the last time Sharpton—

or any so-called black leader or advocate—organized a protest to address the chronic issues harming blacks, such as double-digit unemployment, high incarceration, and out-of-wedlock birthrates, or the violent crime issues plaguing blacks for decades?

Instead, Al protests to help Al grow his celebrity and bank account because Al is about the dollars—and lots of them. His nonprofit receives millions of dollars from corporations like Sony when he threatens to march. The man never met a protest he didn't like in the name of self-aggrandizement. Project Veritas, a conservative group founded by James O'Keefe, who is known for exposing Democrats' hypocrisy, produced an investigative video of blacks criticizing Sharpton for his hustle. "Sharpton's gonna be alright, he's been alright forever, he knows how to make money and get money," Jean Petrus, a Brooklyn businessman, told an undercover reporter with Project Veritas at a 2015 Trayvon Martin Foundation fund-raiser in Florida. "He knows how to make money and get money. They're shakedown guys to me. You know, let's call it what it is, they're shakedown," Petrus reiterated.[22] The narrator noted that Sharpton's National Action Network pays for the funerals of slain young black men like Trayvon Martin so he can be "the center of attention."[23]

Sharpton's National Action Network describes itself as "one of the leading civil rights organizations in the nation with chapters throughout the entire United States. Founded in 1991 by Reverend Al Sharpton, NAN works within the spirit and tradition of Dr. Martin Luther King, Jr. to promote a modern civil rights agenda that includes the fight for one standard of justice, decency and equal opportunities for all people regardless of race, religion, nationality or gender."[24] I'm fairly certain King would shudder at Sharpton's network of nonsense and self-promotion.

After the shooting death of Michael Brown in July 2014, Bishop Calvin Scott of Believers Temple in Ferguson complained that Sharpton had descended upon the majority-black town like a grenade: "I frankly was in one of his, more than one, several, a couple of meetings, two or three meetings that he was in. I think to some degree he sort of incites people for the wrong reason. You know, I'm in the gathering, he got 'em all fired up. But I just sense this is not the way you want to go. When you got a fuse that's already lit...you don't need to add no more fire to it."[25]

Adding fuel to the fire is exactly what Sharpton did. He got the black residents riled up, and riots ensued; black businesses were looted, burned, and destroyed. The Democrats foist race caricatures like Sharpton, Eric Michael Dyson, Jesse Jackson, and Cornel West on blacks to represent a skewed collective "black" point of view on America, whether blacks have cosigned to it or not.

When was the last time anyone heard the "Reverend" Al Sharpton give a sermon? I mean a real one, not a rant that incites racial unrest. Ever since Sharpton came to the defense of Tawana Brawley in 1987, knowing she HAD lied in accusing white men of raping her, he's been a professional race profiteer. Not only did Tawana lie, she lied big time: spreading dog feces on herself then hiding in a trash can to stage her rape. After Al "marched" in defense of Brawley, a grand jury concluded Brawley had concocted a "hoax" and the lawyers who represented her were disbarred. Steven Pagones, a Dutchess County assistant district attorney, was one of the men Brawley, Sharpton, and her advisors Alton H. Maddox Jr. and C. Vernon Mason accused of raping her. In 1998 Pagones won a defamation lawsuit against the three race-baiting stooges, who were ordered to pay Pagones $345,000 in damages.[26] Brawley was also sued by Pagones and ordered to pay over $400,000 in damages, which she only began paying in 2013.[27] In 1988 *People* magazine referred to Sharpton, pictured with Brawley on the cover its magazine, as "a belligerent black activist" whose actions were a "disgrace."[28] Today, a thinner, tailored-suit-wearing Sharpton works as a well-paid TV host of MSNBC's *PoliticsNation*.

The "Reverend" Al has also been quite successful in not paying over $4 million owed in federal and New York state taxes.[29] Obama's IRS was masterful at targeting conservative groups from 2010 through 2012 to silence their influence in elections by delaying or not approving their applications for tax-exempt nonprofit status. But you mean to tell me the IRS can't make Al Sharpton pay the $3 million in back taxes he owes the federal government? In spite of his lawlessness, Sharpton has visited the Obama White House about eighty times.[30] Apparently our Democrat president buys into Al's hustle. Or, like the Democrat Party in general, he finds it useful for winning elections. The first black president's embrace of Sharpton—enabling him to pose as a spokesman for us all—should show black Democrats how little Obama thinks of black people. Sharpton calls the president, governors, and congressmen his friends, just like Jesse Jackson, who pops up like a jack-in-the-box at every racial riot or protest alongside him.

But Al and Jesse aren't alone in belonging to the "black spokesperson" club. When "an unarmed black teen" is killed under America's first black president, the media also call upon Michael Eric Dyson and Cornel West to be the mouthpieces for black America.

As the Class of 1943 University Professor at Princeton University, West is best known for his book *Race Matters*. If he were intellectually honest, West would say race matters for keeping him employed, just like so many other black professors working in "Black Studies Departments" at colleges across the country. Dyson is another black professor, an "ordained Baptist minister" turned spokesperson for the black race. Like West, Dyson's only qualification for the job of speaking for an entire race seems to be his skin color.

As a professor of theology, English, and African American studies at Georgetown University, in 2011 Dyson taught a three-credit course on the black rap/hip-hop star Jay Z: "Sociology of Hip-Hop: Urban Theodicy of Jay-Z." "His body of work has proved to be powerful, effective and influential. And it's time to wrestle with it," Dyson recalled in an interview, as if he were analyzing the work of a great writer like William Shakespeare or James Baldwin.[31] Hip-hop lyrics, including Jay Z's, are notorious for glorifying gangsta behavior: crime, killing, and treating women like "bitches and hoes." Yet Dyson found Jay Z's song-writing talents were critical to the education of Georgetown students, who paid $40,000 in tuition that year.[32]

These are the credentials—race hustler, black preacher, or black studies professor—that catch the eye of liberal news organizations. Democrat-allied journalists further insult blacks when they class Sharpton in the company of true civil rights activists such as Martin Luther King Jr., Medgar Evers, and Rosa Parks. The news media and Democrat politicians know all too well that Sharpton and the rest of the black leaders are nothing more than liberal con artists. That's why they promote them, because they know blacks keep following the voice of these black Pied Pipers right to the Democrat ballot box without questioning their motives. The day blacks decide to question why black leaders are getting richer every election cycle while the black race wades deeper into an economic wasteland will be the day blacks own political power. "Still today, the best way to make a black leader mad is to say to him that black Americans are capable of being fully responsible for their own advancement," wrote Shelby Steele.[33] This is quite a revealing point that black Americans should spend some time thinking about. The livelihood of black leaders like Sharpton and others is based upon the Democrat precept that blacks are irresponsible degenerates, buried under a mountain of ignorance—and forever needing to be rescued by the Democrat Party.

BLACK STUDIES

Black Studies Departments, or African American Studies Departments, as they are now fondly referred to by Democrats, have spread across university and college campuses like a virus. Instead of educating students in subjects that might help them obtain a job, professors in these departments are cultivating either future race hustlers or clones of themselves—and in any case, blaming racism for all the black race's problems.

The overriding theme permeating all classes offered in these departments is that somebody or something else—never blacks themselves—is to blame for the disproportionate rates of crime, illegitimate births, and incarceration affecting the black race. Black Studies Departments are nothing more than "affirmative action departments"[34] to create jobs for black professors who wouldn't be qualified to teach in any other department. Wrote Dinesh D'Souza in his book *Letters to a Young Conservative*, "Consider Harvard's black studies program. Its spectrum of opinions ranges from liberal to radical-left.... Some of the liberals at Harvard are utterly mediocre figures who would be teaching at community colleges if they weren't liberal and they weren't black."[35]

Today Harvard has a faculty of over twenty professors and assistant professors teaching in the segregated African and African American Studies. Marcyliena Morgan is one of the professors in the department. She is a professor of African and African American studies and executive director of the Hiphop Archive at Harvard. Apparently, the art of hiphop is a subject worthy of study at one of America's oldest and most revered institutions of higher learning. And Harvard is by no means alone in teaching "blackness" as a college major. There are at least 361 four-year colleges in America that offer degrees in African American Studies, according to Peterson's, an authoritative website on higher education for parents and students. Based upon my own casual review of multiple schools' websites, it appears the faculty teaching these programs are overwhelmingly black, about 80 to 90 percent. Each of the nation's Ivy League schools, where more than 86 percent of the faculty's campaign donations go to the Democrats,[36] has a department of either African American Studies or Africana Studies, the new lingo for black. In the interest of equality, shouldn't Harvard, Yale, Brown, Cornell, Princeton, Penn, Dartmouth, and Columbia offer "white studies" majors? They don't, because that would be considered racist, but the Democrats in liberal academia are quite comfortable serving up "black studies" to black students.

When I majored in English literature at Georgetown, I studied writers of all races, nationalities, and eras, from Shakespeare, Chaucer, and Flannery O'Connor to Richard Wright, Tennessee Williams, and Moliere. As an honors English major my senior year, I was forced to take a feminist criticism class. It was taught by a lesbian professor who made her bias known in the selection of material we were required to read. The curriculum was virtually all lesbian writers like Kate Millet, who hated great works of literature like D. H. Lawrence's *Lady Chatterley's Lover* (one of my favorite books) and who denigrated *Madame Bovary* by Gustave Flaubert as exploitative of women. In reality these male writers gave women voices during a time when society silenced them. It was a shame the professor couldn't see that.

I hated the seminar and challenged the professor every opportunity I could. In spite of this one class, I was given an education on literature and the world that prepared me for a future career in writing, and more important, that gave me a wide knowledge of the world. I also spent my junior year of college studying French literature and art in Paris, taking classes at the Sorbonne Paris IV and Institut Catholique. Later I pursued a master's degree in acting and went on to a career in TV news and public relations, a field in which I've been working for over a decade.

One thing I realized during my academic career is that allowing black students to major in black studies is nothing short of exploitative. The departments are marketed as colleges offering a more "inclusive," "diverse" curriculum, when in reality they are very exclusive, encouraging black students to self-segregate from mainstream coursework. How many white students do you know who have majored in black studies? The name itself turns any white student away. Black history should be taught throughout public school history classes, not confined to a single month, and the same concept should be applied to higher learning. Black Studies Departments orchestrated by Democrat-dominated schools essentially banish black students to ghettos of inferior coursework, ironically, in the name of black empowerment. A degree in black studies certainly doesn't prepare blacks to advance up the economic ladder, but it does help keep blacks enshrined in their second-class status—and forever in need of the Democrat Party's patronage and help.

The curriculum in these classes is laughable. Perusing the various coursework offerings at the nation's Ivy Leagues, I couldn't believe students were earning credits toward degrees for these classes. As you can imagine, the courses are steeped in all things race and racist. Consider a sampling of the 2015 coursework from some of America's Ivy League schools.

Along with its Center for the Study of Race and Ethnicity in America, Brown University's Africana Studies Department offered courses including "Black Transnationalism" and "Black Lavender: Black Gay/Lesbian Plays/Dramatic Constructions in the American Theatre" and a class on what it means to be a black woman called "Narrating the Radical Self," which explores "how black women in the United States and elsewhere have written about their lives in autobiographies."[37]

Dartmouth College's African and African American Studies Program offered the obligatory "Race and Slavery in US History," which could be taught in an American history class, and "Constructing Black Womanhood," which examined the "status of black women in the United States." The school also served up some more ridiculous classes such as "The Black Sporting Experience," a course in which students were invited to "investigate the history of American sports through the Black experience." The course description further noted, "After providing a thorough historical background, the class will survey how race functions in the contemporary sporting landscape."[38] Students would have been better off skipping this class and reading the sports sections of national dailies or archived issues of *Sports Illustrated* magazine. But the most reprehensible black class Dartmouth offered was its ode to the "unarmed black teen" lie, "10 Weeks, 10 Professors: #BlackLivesMatter." The lengthy hyper-left-wing course description read:

Though the academy can never lay claim to social movements, this course seeks in part to answer the call of students and young activists around the country to take the opportunity to raise questions about, offer studied reflection upon, and allocate dedicated institutional space to the failures of democracy, capitalism, and leadership and to make #BlackLivesMatter. Developed through a group effort, this course brings to bear collective thinking, teaching, research, and focus on questions around race, structural inequality, and violence. Through this course, we examine the particular historical, geographical, cultural, social, and political ways in which race is configured and deployed in the United States and beyond in the past and present. We do so through using a number of different angles that stem from the various faculty of different disciplines who have come together to develop this course. The course is broken into three sections. Section One offers a context, both past and present, for the events in Ferguson, Missouri in 2014. Section Two places those events in a broader context of race and racism in the United States. And Section Three examines the entanglements of trauma and violence for individuals, communities, and society as a whole. By beginning our analysis in Ferguson and moving out from there, this course offers a way to place these very important present-day events in a broader national and international context.[39]

First, I'd bet my life savings that none of the faculty teaching the class held a "different" point of view. I'm certain they were all not only black but also most assuredly they were all liberal and ran with the "unarmed black teen" narrative on the shooting deaths of Trayvon Martin and Michael Brown. I'm sure professors teaching the class never discussed the facts that demonstrate how both teens contributed to their own tragic demise. Essentially, professors brainwashed students with this course, perpetuating the false Democrat narrative that black men are being gunned down by white men in America today—when in reality young black men are killing and being killed by each other. The course should have been titled "10 Weeks, 10 Professors Tell 10 Lies" and received lots of "Pinocchios" on the scale the *Washington Post* uses to rate public figures' exaggerations of facts. Dartmouth tuition in 2015 was $46,764. This is a steep price for students to pay to be a black studies major and be taught lies about trumped-up race wars in classes with intellectual rigor unworthy of middle school students.

Columbia University, like many of the other Ivies, appears obsessed with making sure students understand black women—because evidently black women are aliens. In 2015 Columbia's Institute for Research in African-American Studies offered a course entitled "Toward an Intellectual History of Black Women." Other bogus courses with loose definitions included "Black Intellectuals and Religion" and "Culture in Post-Civil Rights Black America."[40]

Cornell University's Africana Studies Program offered up core classes in 2015 for anyone who wanted to become an expert in the field. There was "Race and Racism/Law and Society," and "Women in Hip Hop," because I guess just listening to the misogynist music isn't enough to know what it's about. Making no attempt to hide its leftist agenda, Cornell also offered two classes in tribute to the Democrat black savior Barack Obama: "Being and Becoming Black: From DuBois to Obama," worth four credits, explored "What constitutes Blackness?"[41]

But the class that caught my eye for its sheer absurdity and unabashed politics was "Obama & the Meaning of Race." The course description read:

> The election of Barack Obama to the presidency has raised new questions in the American debate on race, politics, and social science. Has America entered a post-racial society in

which racism and inequality are things of the past? Or does Obama's post-Black, race-neutral approach to governing signal the end of Black politics, race-based activism and pre-scriptive policy? In this course, students will use the Obama presidency to think, talk, and write about how race works in America. We'll examine the symbolism of Obama's personal narrative and biracialism to analyze his race-neutral cam-paigns and governing within the context of history, politics, and policies. We'll look at the public image of Michelle Obama, especially how she is gendered as Black radical and fashionista.

I didn't know Obama represented every black person in America. I wonder, if Hillary Clinton gets elected the first woman president, will Cornell offer a course called "Hillary and the Meaning of Gender"? Of course not, because Hillary is white and liberals don't think one white woman represents the thoughts of all women. But in their mind, all blacks think alike. Again we see liberals sending blacks the subtle mes-sage that we must all think like Democrats. I hope the course gave stu-dents value for their yearly tuition cost of $31,146 (in-state residents) and $47,286 (nonresidents).

Princeton University's 2015 Center for African American Studies course offerings read like they came straight from Al Sharpton's racist mind, with heavy emphasis on Ferguson. Courses included "Race Riots and Revolution," about discrimination in housing in the 1960s, and "The New Jim Crow: US Crime Policy from Constitutional Formation to Ferguson," advertised to help students "understand the political con-struction of crime, colorblindness, and legitimate state violence."[42] I'm certain the professor didn't mention that black men are the ones com-mitting most of the violent crime in the country or the reason why: because the majority of young black boys are born into fatherless, unmar-ried households. The class that took the cake for absurdity was "Race Is

Socially Constructed: Now What?," which asked students "to develop a toolkit" to make sense of Ferguson:

> The truism that "race is socially constructed" hides more than it reveals. Have Irish Americans always been white? Are people of African descent all black? Is calling Asian Americans a "model minority" a compliment? Does race impact who we date or marry? In this course, students develop a sophisticated conceptual toolkit to make sense of such contentious cases of racial vision and division as the uprising in Ferguson. We learn to connect contemporary events to historical processes, and individual experiences to institutional policies, exercising a sociological imagination with the potential to not only analyze, but transform the status quo.[43]

It is hard to believe Princeton charged $43,450 in tuition in 2015 for professors to get paid teaching these courses. Liberal academia's proliferation of African American Studies Programs is tantamount to hostage taking. Our elite liberal-run schools of higher education are nothing more than incubators for Democrat Party voters and activists who see black Americans as a victimized underclass. Under the guise of African American Studies, liberal colleges in the United States are churning out students with degrees that won't help them get jobs and teaching black students they are victims never to be held accountable for their own actions in life. What expectation for success and achievement does that set?

Yale has the nerve to claim that its African American Studies program "prepares students considering careers in education, journalism, law, business management, city planning, international relations, politics, psychology, publishing, or social work."[44] Majoring in any of the humanities would better qualify students for jobs than a degree in black studies, which basically leaves you unqualified for 99 percent of jobs.

One thing is for certain: black students majoring in black studies may not graduate with widely marketable degrees, but they won't have an identity crisis. Graduates can compete for the few jobs available at black media outlets and organizations such as the National Association for the Advancement for Colored People, the United Negro College Fund, the Congressional Black Caucus Foundation, and Sharpton's National Action Network. A few graduates may even apply to work at the Office of African American Affairs, a new department created in 2015 by Washington, D.C., mayor Muriel Bowser. Bowser appointed a black named Rahman Branch, a former D.C. high school principal, to a full-time six-figure-salaried position as director of the office. Apparently, the only qualification for the director position was being black. So I suspect black college graduates with majors in black studies would be over-qualified to work in D.C.'s Office of African American Affairs.[45]

But "black only" jobs are few and far between. Identity-politics education creates an army of educated black fools, loaded with debt and unprepared for a fierce job market in which the black unemployment rate is in the double digits. But it does create jobs for black professors— and help keep up the racial resentments that benefit the Democrats. Giving blacks their black news sources, "black spokespeople," "black studies," and black movies and TV shows is a way to keep blacks in their black box of inferiority. Liberal academia, news media, Hollywood, education, and ultimately the Democrat Party control blacks by giving them just enough to believe they are emancipated and part of America. By remaining politically and intellectually "in the dark" (no pun intended), blacks allow themselves to be played for fools, used by politicians for votes and everyone else for profit. In the end the black race is continuously pushed to the back of the line. Every election cycle for the past five decades has found black Americans starting from the bottom, begging lawmakers to lift them up. How long will it take before blacks realize the Democrats' promised salvation is never coming?

how true.

CHAPTER ELEVEN

THE PARTY OF BIGOTRY AND LOW EXPECTATIONS

Ironically, the Democrat Party, which claims to be dedicated to equal rights, is really peddling an inferiority message of separate but equal. Democrats are constantly letting black Americans know that we're not capable of being treated as equal to whites or of taking personal responsibility for our actions. In nearly every aspect of our lives, from education to parenting to voting, the Democrats tell blacks we need to be rescued by the government to be able to achieve anything in life. This condescension further strains race relations between whites and blacks because whites think blacks are getting special treatment. Because we are.

Democrats create special government programs to "help" blacks, but all these programs really do is give blacks excuses not to take personal responsibility for our lives and help sustain low expectations for an entire race. Is this not racist at its core? If the Republicans were to talk to black voters this way, they would be accused of racism for treating blacks differently from whites. The Democrat Party's black voters should find this rhetoric insulting. Wasn't the whole point of the civil rights movement to give blacks equal access to our constitutional rights? Didn't Martin Luther King Jr. and other civil rights activists march, fight, and die so blacks could be treated as equals to whites and not be judged by the color of our skin but on merit?

The Democrats have worked tirelessly to take blacks back to the days of separate but equal. Democrats speak as if blacks are one monolithic group rather than individuals in charge of our own destiny. Since the days of Johnson's Great Society, black America's biggest problem has been Democrats helping us to fail with government program after government program and rhetoric telling blacks we can't stand on our own two feet like white Americans. That's why blacks on average have less wealth, less education, and greater poverty than whites. The endless excuse making the Democrats give for the shortcomings of blacks in post–civil rights era America is stunning—they must make whites of all political affiliations laugh. Democrats teach blacks that if you lose your job, fail to get promoted, don't get into college, get arrested, or get convicted of a crime, just cry racism.

VOTER ID CONDESCENSION

There is no better example of the inferiority complex that the Democrat Party has laid on black Americans than the debate over voter IDs. The Democrats have convinced blacks in America that it is blatantly racist to ask them to show an ID to vote. I guess it must be an insurmountable burden for blacks to get driver's licenses to drive or passports to travel overseas too. Despite the fact that every state with a voter ID law provides free IDs, Democrats scream that the laws are modern-day Jim Crow poll taxes.

If no voter fraud is occurring, as Democrats allege, why do Democrats have such a problem with voter ID laws? In the twenty-first century, for Democrats to suggest to blacks they are incapable of getting a voter ID—merely because of the color of their skin—is ludicrous. There is no comparison between today's voter ID laws and the barriers to voting instituted by racist Southern Democrats before 1965. Dixie-crats, as these Southerners were called, imposed black-only voter literacy tests and poll taxes to stop blacks from registering to vote. Democrat Governor George Wallace of Alabama was one of the worst offenders, allowing black voter suppression and police murders of blacks. According to a report by the U.S. Commission on Civil Rights, Lowndes County, an area between the south of Montgomery and Selma, Alabama, had no blacks registered to vote despite blacks outnumbering whites there by four to one.[1] Blacks seeking to register to vote in Selma were required to go to the courthouse, where they were assigned numbers. In *Shocking the Conscience*, his book about covering the civil rights movement as a reporter for *Jet* and *Ebony*, Simeon Booker wrote, "The voter registration test included 300 questions, taking an average of one hour per person. With whites in line as well (and not required to take the test), few blacks got into the courthouse in any given day. It took six weeks to six months to learn if you had passed. The process was humiliating, but nobody except the blacks excluded from the polls seemed to care."[2]

The 1965 Voting Rights Act ended racist practices such as literacy tests and poll taxes that had been used to disenfranchise blacks. Today there are no such tests. Voter ID laws are designed to prevent voter fraud, which does occur. Here are a few examples of the voter fraud that Democrats like to pretend doesn't exist:

- According to a February 2012 report by the Pew Research Center, nationwide there were 1.8 million dead people registered to vote and another 2.75 million people registered to vote in more than one state.[3]
- When government officials in Virginia cross-referenced the state's voter database against those of twenty-one other

states, they found that seventeen thousand voters were registered in three or more states.[4]

■ In Minnesota's tight 2008 Senate race, Democrat Al Franken was declared the winner over Republican Senator Norm Coleman by a slim margin of 312 votes, after eight months of litigation. An investigation by a conservative organization, Minnesota Majority, found that 1,099 felons voted illegally in the race. In *Who's Counting*, Hans von Spakovsky and John Fund noted that 177 people were convicted of voter fraud in that Senate race. Franken was the sixtieth vote Senate Democrats needed to stop a Republican filibuster and pass Obamacare. "If Coleman had kept his seat, there would have been no 60th vote, and no Obamacare," wrote Byron York in the *Washington Examiner*.[5]

■ Using data from the Cooperative Congressional Election study, professors from Old Dominion University found that 6.4 percent of noncitizens voted in 2008 and 2.2 percent of noncitizens voted in 2010. "Because non-citizens tended to favor Democrats (Obama won more than 80 percent of the votes of non-citizens in the 2008 CCES sample), we find that this participation was large enough to plausibly account for Democratic victories in a few close elections," they wrote.[6]

Democrats' contention that voter ID laws are racially motivated barriers to prevent blacks from voting defies comprehension and common sense. As the nation's first black attorney general, serving under the nation's first black president, Eric Holder made it one of his top priorities to assail voter ID laws as discrimination tools of the Right. In the June 2013 case *Shelby County v. Holder*, the Supreme Court struck down the "coverage formula" of Section 4 of the Voting Rights

Act of 1965, which had determined the states and localities that needed to get approval, or "preclearance," from the federal government to change their voting laws. Following the ruling, Holder sued North Carolina and Texas over their voter ID laws. In *Shelby County v. Holder*, the court had concluded that the Section 4 provisions in question were outdated and an unconstitutional restriction on states' powers to regulate elections. Nine Southern states no longer needed to apply to the Justice Department to change their voting laws because blacks now voted at rates equal to or higher than whites.[7] During oral arguments, Chief Justice John Roberts exposed how outdated the preclearance provision was when he grilled Solicitor General Donald Verrilli on current voting statistics.

> CHIEF JUSTICE ROBERTS: Just to get the—do you know which State has the worst ratio of white voter turnout to African American voter turnout?
> GENERAL VERRILLI: I do not.
> CHIEF JUSTICE ROBERTS: Massachusetts. Do you know what has the best, where African American turnout actually exceeds white turnout? Mississippi.
> GENERAL VERRILLI: Yes, Mr. Chief Justice. But Congress recognized that expressly in the findings when it reauthorized the act in 2006. It said that the first generation problems had been largely dealt with, but there persisted significant—
> CHIEF JUSTICE ROBERTS: Which State has the greatest disparity in registration between white and African American?
> GENERAL VERRILLI: I do not know that.
> CHIEF JUSTICE ROBERTS: Massachusetts. Third is Mississippi, where again the African American registration rate is higher than the white registration rate.[8]

In 1965 Mississippi was one of the worst voter suppression offenders, but not anymore. As Roberts suggested, perhaps Massachusetts should have been required to get preclearance for changes to its voter laws because it has proportionately more whites registered to vote than blacks. Why didn't Democrats accuse that state of suppressing the black vote? Could it be because Massachusetts was led by Democrat governor Deval Patrick from 2010 to 2014? Or that Massachusetts is generally known as a Democrat stronghold? Once again, government by Democrats doesn't seem to be improving blacks' lives.

But blowing right past the Supreme Court's decision, Holder continued his preposterous crusade against voter ID laws, filing his lawsuits against Tennessee and North Carolina. It is not just ironic but reprehensible that our first black attorney general and our first black president will fight for blacks not to be treated as equals at the ballot box. Pretending that blacks are not as capable as whites of getting driver's licenses (or, if for any reason they don't drive, free voter IDs from their states) makes us out to be complete incompetents. Martin Luther King Jr., the man who led a march on Selma to end real voter suppression, would be aghast to witness Holder's tactics. Blacks don't seem to have problems getting driver's licenses to drive cars or obtaining photo IDs to board planes, buy a prescription, purchase alcohol, or even attend the 2012 Democratic National Convention—where photo IDs were required of attendees. But to ask a black person to produce an ID to vote is, in the mind of Democrats, discrimination cooked up by Republicans to prevent blacks from voting. Even President Obama admitted that the laws aren't really stopping blacks from voting. In a 2014 radio interview with his buddy Al Sharpton, Obama said, "Keep in mind most of these laws are not preventing the overwhelming majority of folks who don't vote from voting. Most people do have ID. Most people do have a driver's license. Most people can get to the polls. But the bottom line is, if less than half of our folks vote, these laws aren't preventing the other half from not voting."[9] What Obama seems to be saying here is that black Americans are too lazy, stupid, or generally not responsible enough to get IDs to vote. It's the mirror image of Eric Holder's contention that voter ID laws discriminate against blacks because somehow we're not capable of getting IDs. Apparently government must treat blacks as victims and not hold us accountable to the same standards of voting as whites. Do Democrats view blacks as mindless children to be coddled? It seems so. I'll bet our first black president, Barack Obama, and Attorney General Eric Holder have had photo IDs for a very long time. I'm certain neither found it "a burden" to acquire them. Obama all but admitted that it's not a problem for most blacks. But howling that the laws are racist makes a better narrative—one that keeps blacks dumb and Democrat.

At a 2013 American Bar Association speech, former secretary of state Hillary Clinton declared, "Not every obstacle is related to race, but anyone who says that racial discrimination is no longer a problem in American elections must not be paying attention."[10] Hillary Clinton is entitled to her own opinion, but not her own facts. And the facts indicate blacks aren't suffering one iota of burden when it comes to voter ID laws. Blacks aren't being blocked from the ballot box because of their race as they were in the pre-1964, racist, Democrat-governed, segregated South. The truth is just the opposite—as we now know from the actual data since the passage of voter ID laws, which have been enacted in about thirty-four states.[11]

Voter ID laws have increased black voter participation, not deterred it. In 2012, for the first time in history, blacks voted at a higher rate (66.2 percent) than whites (64.1 percent) in America according to a May 2013 Census Bureau study.[12] If voter ID laws were passed to prevent blacks from accessing the polls in order to reelect Obama, it didn't work in 2012. Surprise! It turns out there's nothing innately wrong with blacks to prevent us from getting driver's licenses and voting at the same or higher rates than whites. Chew on that for a moment. The NAACP swears that 25 percent of black adults lack a government-issued photo ID—which "would mean," as former U.S. attorney general Edwin Meese and former Cincinnati mayor J. Kenneth Blackwell have pointed out, that "millions of African-American men and women are unable to legally drive, cash a check, board an airplane or participate in everyday activities of modern life enabled by a photo ID such as a driver's license."[13]

If voter ID laws are racist, as Democrats claim with such authority, how is it that black voter participation increased when ID laws were passed in Georgia and Indiana? In 2007 when Georgia's voter ID was passed, it allowed six different forms of ID and in no way stopped blacks from voting. A year later, in 2008, the black vote had increased by 42 percent, with 366,000 more blacks voting than had voted in 2004. Blacks in Georgia voted at a higher rate again in the 2010 congressional midterm elections, increasing their votes by 44.2 percent compared to the previous midterm election, in 2006.[14] If Republicans are backing voter ID laws to suppress the black vote, it's not working. This isn't 1964, when voter suppression was indeed occurring—under the orchestration of racist Southern Democrats.

When Republicans assert voter fraud *does* happen, Democrats run a laugh track. Here's how our first black president joked about voter fraud in an April 11, 2014, speech to Al Sharpton's National Action Network:

> So let's be clear—the real voter fraud is people who try to deny our rights by making bogus arguments about voter fraud.
>
> And I have to say, there have been—some of these officials who have been passing these laws have been more blunt. They said this is going to be good for the Republican Party. Some of them have not been shy about saying that they're doing this for partisan reasons.[15]

I guess Obama overlooked how black voter participation surged beyond white for the first time in history during the 2012 election, winning him a second term. So I'm not sure how voter ID laws helped Republicans, but they do combat voter fraud, which is more than minuscule.

No wonder Obama and his cohorts are so vehemently opposed to voter ID laws. Voter fraud helps Democrats win! "If the available evidence suggests that the amount of voter fraud is understated, the evidence that voter ID laws suppress voting is nonexistent," commented Robert Popper, former deputy chief of the DOJ Civil Rights Division's voting section.[16]

In his National Action Network speech, President Obama proclaimed, "America did not stand up and did not march and did not sacrifice to gain the right to vote for themselves and for others only to see it denied to their kids and their grandchildren." But hang on a second, Mr. President. Dr. King and the others didn't die so Democrats like you could lie to blacks and tell us we are so inferior to other races that we can't get a driver's license. How is this empowering or realizing King's dream of equality? The real shame is that the majority of black Americans who vote Democrat don't know how insulting the Democrats' voter ID rhetoric is.

EDUCATION PANDERING

Along with Democrats telling blacks we're too incompetent to get an ID to vote, they also treat blacks like dummies when it comes to education. Instead of expecting blacks to compete at the same educational levels as whites, Democrats always lower standards for blacks. We've already seen how affirmative action hurts the very people it pretends to help. Let's look at another Democrat-backed initiative that's even more ridiculous and damaging: Ebonics. In December 1996, the Democrat-dominated Oakland, California, school board voted to teach broken English in its public schools to help black students learn standard English. The idea would be funny if it weren't so utterly idiotic. At the time blacks accounted for 53 percent of the district's fifty-two thousand students and on average had the lowest grades.[17] According to school officials, most of the black students spoke black English or, as I call it, "ghetto"—because, let's face it, that's what it is. Apparently the school board didn't grasp the fact that encouraging black students to speak Ebonics was going to make it harder for them to succeed. Try graduating from high school or getting a job being proficient in Ebonics. It won't happen. It defies common sense.

The school board even sought federal funding to teach black English—which was immediately denied by President Bill Clinton's secretary of education Richard Riley. Republican California governor Pete Wilson opposed the idea also. Can anyone imagine a school board declaring that poor white trash slang would be taught in a majority-white public school district? Absolutely, unequivocally, no, because liberals expect white people to rise up to standards while they expect blacks to fall down on them! Jesse Jackson, the washed-up civil rights activist, first opposed the idea, then supported it—by talking in Ebonics.

> Just as you go from Spanish to English, you must go from improper grammar [ebonics] to English.
>
> The bottom line is, make our youth efficient English speakers so they can be competitive—ain't that the real point?[18]

How could a person who stood alongside Dr. King and claims to be an advocate for black Americans utter such nonsense? And Jackson was by no means the only one advocating Ebonics be taught to black kids in Oakland public schools, many of whom were already far from proficient in reading. Ebonics, also referred to as African American Vernacular English (AAVE) or black English, is studied and praised by liberal academics as "nonstandard English" (not slang or ghetto talk, mind you). In an academic paper published on the University of Hawaii website, linguistic anthropologist Jack Sidnell wrote that some of the negative reaction to the Oakland School Board's Ebonics effort demonstrated the public's "prejudiced understandings of what AAVE is and what it says about the people who speak it."[19]

Praising new words in Ebonics as "innovations" in vocabulary, Sidnell gave Ebonics grammar examples as if he were teaching a foreign language (all bold in original).

> Standard English uses a conjugated **be** verb (called a copula) in a number of different sentences. (This may occur as **is, 's, are, 're,** etc.) In AAVE this verb is often not included. The frequency of inclusion has been shown to depend on a variety of factors. Here are some examples:
>
> In future sentences with **gonna** or **gon** (see below):
>
> **I don't care what he say, you __ gon laugh.**
>
> **…as long as i's kids around he's gon play rough or however they're playing.**[20]

Sidnell also explained the use of negatives in Ebonics:

> AAVE has a number of ways of marking negation. Like a number of other varieties of English, AAVE uses **ain't** to negate the verb in a simple sentence. In common with other nonstandard dialects of English, AAVE uses **ain't** in standard English sentences which use "haven't". For example standard "I haven't seen him." is equivalent to AAVE **I ain't seen him.** Unlike most other nonstandard varieties of English, AAVE speakers also sometimes use **ain't** for standard "didn't" as in the following examples:
>
> **I ain't step on no line.**
>
> **I said, "I ain't run the stop sign," and he said, "you ran it!"**

I ain't believe you that day, man.[21]

As the Ebonics debate intensified in 1996, Stanford University offered a four-credit linguistics course on African American Vernacular English during its fall semester. Appropriately taught by black professor John Rickford (who knows better about black English than a black man?), the course explored "the distinctive varieties of English used by and among African Americans, particularly in big-city settings, and their parallels elsewhere in Africa and the New World (especially in the Caribbean)." Part of the coursework required students to visit black churches to hear Ebonics live, being blurted out of the mouths of black preachers.[22] In a 1996 op-ed published in the *San Jose Mercury News*, Rickford praised the Oakland school's decision to teach Ebonics to black kids because "while existing methods of teaching English work superbly for white and middle class children, they fail miserably for working class African American children." Noting that a 1990 California Assessment Program study of third graders found whites more proficient in writing than blacks, Rickford seemed to be arguing that lowering learning standards for black students by teaching Ebonics, as Oakland had, would help blacks learn.[23]

By offering college courses on black English, schools like Stanford not only legitimatized an inferior form of English as standard for blacks but reinforced our position in society as perpetual victims. Democrats' passion for Ebonics is another example of keeping blacks dumber, not smarter. The liberal movement to acknowledge Ebonics in the 1990s as an "initial literacy teaching tool" played into Democrats' view of blacks as helpless victims, incapable of the most basic skill of learning to speak and write proper English. The Democrat Party never has nor ever will encourage whites to put themselves at a disadvantage in life by not learning proper English. But the Democrats' rules for blacks are always different; to them, substandard benchmarks of achievement are standard for black people.

Ebonics is not the language of the smart and the successful. It is often the language of black criminals. I wish I were kidding. Under Obama's presidency, the Drug Enforcement Agency issued a solicitation to contractors in August of 2010 explaining it was in dire need of Ebonics translators to help it arrest drug dealers.[24] The DEA indicated that it needed nine "Ebonics experts" (eye roll) to work in its Atlanta field office helping investigators translate phone calls and other communications with Ebonics-speaking drug dealers.[25] Ebonics was and is the classic example of Democrats' peddling the politics of low expectations to black people. Those liberals who support teaching black English to black children should be a little more honest about their bigotry and admit how little they think of blacks and our ability to achieve.

In *A Dream Deferred,* Shelby Steele explores how post–civil rights era liberalism has produced policies that hold whites to high standards of achievement, but preferential treatment for blacks that trap them in mediocrity. Steele makes clear that there is something very screwed up in the Democrats' mindset, which accepts as normal the idea of blacks dominating professional basketball, football, and music but not academics: "American inner cities have the poorest facilities for basketball in the country, yet produce the greatest basketball players in the world. This is because the people there have internalized a commitment to excellence in basketball that supersedes what others do for them."[26]

If blacks applied the same tenacity to learning as we do to the above-mentioned sport, our academic performance would have improved over the past fifty years. But the opposite is true. Despite affirmative action admission programs in virtually every college or university in the nation, blacks have the "highest dropout rate and lowest grade point average of any group."[27]

If Democrats were serious about holding blacks to high standards of personal responsibility and meritocracy, maybe we wouldn't be in such bad shape. Over and over again, the Democrat Party continues to play a big joke on blacks, conning us into voting for candidates who

do everything to keep blacks down and beholden to the Democrat Party
and big government to fix our problems. Obviously, black minds, like
black lives, don't matter to Democrats. There's political power for
Democrats in keeping blacks blinded to the reality that they are indeed
created equal to whites. Whether it's pretending voter ID laws are racist, taking the side of black criminals against the police, or teaching
Ebonics, the victim message from Democrats to blacks is clear. *You are
an inferior race. You need us—the Democrat Party—and the government to prop you up to achieve anything in life.*

CHAPTER TWELVE

THE PARTY OF CORRUPTION AND NEVER-ENDING EXCUSES

The Democrat Party is running a con job on its black constituents, inflaming racial divisions to hold onto the black vote while doing nothing for blacks once in office. But there's one group of Democrat con artists and race hustlers who outdo all the others. Let me introduce you to the Congressional Black Caucus.

According to the Congressional Black Caucus, the Democrat-dominated club for black members of Congress, the white man is to blame for all the problems keeping blacks down. The CBC is open to any black member of Congress, but it is 99 percent Democrat. Membership in the CBC hovers around forty members in any given Congress. In 2013 there were forty-two members, and in 2015 the CBC had its largest membership in history with forty-six members from twenty-two states in the House of Representatives—only one of them a Republican. Since its creation forty-four years ago, you can count on one hand the number of black Republicans who've been members of the Congressional Black Caucus (former congressman Allen West and current congresswoman

Mia Love among them). Thus Democrats who all share the same political views dominate the CBC.

And naturally the Democrat-dominated group has a myopic obsession with stoking racism rather than helping blacks. In fact, CBC members do more to help themselves than to help "their people," who are withering as a race under decades of missed opportunity due to the Democrats' misguided policies. In his speech as incoming 2015 chairman of the CBC for the 114th Congress, G. K. Butterfield proclaimed, "The CBC was formed in 1971 because its founders understood that Black lives matter. Black boys matter. Black girls matter. The Black family matters." If this is the case, then why haven't the members of the CBC, many of whom have served in Congress for decades, made any progress in moving the needle on black America's prosperity? As we've already seen, Butterfield claimed the current condition of black Americans is a "state of emergency." Yes, and it happened on the Congressional Black Caucus's watch.

"Every day, members of this Caucus go beyond their constitutional duties to lead in their communities. They are making a difference in the lives of millions of people," Butterfield insisted.[1] The reality is quite the opposite. CBC members are making some blacks' lives much better— their own. The improvements in the personal fortunes of many black members of Congress, who also happen to be overwhelmingly DEMO-CRAT, have come through criminal or near criminal behavior—Representative Charlie Rangel, Representative Maxine Waters, and former representative Jesse Jackson Jr., to name a few.[2]

"If you are a member of the Congressional Black Caucus, chances that you will eventually face an ethics probe are better than your chances of becoming President, a senator or a Nobel Prize winner," wrote Daniel Greenfield of FrontPage Magazine.[3] Greenfield was referring to a 2012 National Journal report that found that one-third of elected black members of Congress were targets of ethics investigations during their careers.

In 2008, then–House Speaker Nancy Pelosi created the Office of Congressional Ethics (OCE) as a watchdog to oversee her colleagues' behavior. While it lacks the power to punish lawmakers, the OCE makes its findings public and has the power to recommend that the House Ethics Committee conduct further investigations into House members.[4] The *National Journal* found that of the twenty-six cases the OCE referred to the House Ethics Committee since 2008, a dozen—46 percent of the total—were Congressional Black Caucus members. Not a flattering statistic when you consider that black lawmakers make up only about 10 percent of the House of Representatives. The year 2009 looked like a reality show called *Congressional Black Caucus's Most Wanted* because every single one of the active investigations conducted by the House Ethics Committee was against black Democrats—seven of them: Representatives Charles Rangel of New York, Maxine Waters of California, Carolyn Cheeks Kilpatrick of Michigan, Bennie Thompson of Mississippi, Donald Payne of New Jersey, and Laura Richardson of California and Delegate Donna M. Christian-Christensen of the U.S. Virgin Islands. Representative Jesse Jackson Jr. would have increased that number to eight if the committee hadn't dropped its probe of Jackson when the Justice Department began its criminal investigation of him.[5] Democrat Representative Emanuel Cleaver of Missouri, a black member of the House and a former chair of the CBC, told the *Hill* that Pelosi's creation of the OCE "was a mistake."[6] Cleaver was just saying what most of his colleagues believe. Many CBC members, like Waters, Cleaver, and Missouri Democrat Representative Lacy Clay, voted against the resolution to form the Office of Congressional Ethics in the first place.[7]

As investigations against black members heated up in June of 2010, Democrat Representative Marcia Fudge of Ohio and nineteen other members of the Congressional Black Caucus introduced a bill to neuter the Office of Congressional Ethics.[8] CBC members like Waters pull the race card when they become targets of the OCE's investigations. No wonder they think the OCE was a "mistake" in the first place.

But the real mistake is for black members of Congress to think they can commit egregious acts of ethical lapses and get away with it. Sounds like they're standing on the moral high ground of quicksand.

A CBC member even told *Politico* that black lawmakers were being targeted for investigations because they make less money and have smaller campaign accounts than white members of Congress.[9] Seriously? When black legislators are caught red-handed with their hands in the cookie jar, members of the CBC pull the race card—blame "whitey"—and say they're being "set up" because they're black. But racial profiling cannot explain these black Democrats' ethics woes. Black members of Congress are being investigated because of their own corruption and arrogance.

From the time of its founding in 1971, the Congressional Black Caucus was supposed to exist to advocate on behalf of black Americans and hold lawmakers and the president of the United States accountable for policies adversely impacting blacks. Today, it is virtually a Democrat club. Sometimes referred to as "the conscience of the Congress," the CBC should change its slogan to "corrupted by the Congress." Instead of garnering a reputation for advancing policies to help their black constituents, the members of the CBC have earned a reputation for putting themselves first. Many Democrat members of the Congressional Black Caucus seem to think getting elected to Congress gives them a license to break the law or act unethically.

PROFILES IN THIEVERY

In December 2010 Charlie Rangel, then chairman of the powerful House Ways and Means Committee, which writes the nation's tax laws, was censured, humiliated, and stripped of his chairmanship for evading taxes and breaking ten other House rules. At the time, the House was controlled by Democrats, who voted overwhelmingly—170 of them—to censure their colleague Rangel. That is, except for 97 percent of the Congressional Black Caucus, thirty-six of thirty-seven members, who voted against censuring Rangel—including Rangel himself. The benefits of being black and a corrupt member of Congress is that your black buddies will defend you even when you're wrong, because race always trumps criminal behavior. Representatives Alcee Hastings and Kendrick Meek of Florida did not vote. The only CBC member who had the guts to do the right thing was Representative Artur Davis of Alabama.[10]

As chairman of the committee that oversees the Internal Revenue Service, Rangel said he simply forgot to pay seventeen years' worth of taxes on $600,000 he had earned from renting out his Dominican Republic beach house. But clearly taxman Charlie just wanted to avoid paying taxes.

And things didn't stop there for Charlie. He used his official House of Representatives stationery to solicit millions of dollars in contributions from corporations for the Charles B. Rangel Center for Public Service at the City College of New York. Coincidentally, many of the corporations Rangel sent letters to, such as insurance company American International Group, had "business interests before the committee."[11] Thinking again how he could enrich himself, Rangel also leased *four* rent-controlled apartments in a "luxury building" in Harlem, his congressional district. He used one apartment as a campaign office, violating New York City and state laws that require occupants to live in apartments with below-market rents as their primary residence. The rules simply didn't apply to Charlie. After serving in Congress for over forty years, Rangel wanted his colleagues, the media, and his constituents to seriously believe he was oblivious to the House rules of conduct for members. And apparently his constituents believed him. Rangel's breaking the law didn't matter; blacks helped vote their Democrat representative back into office in 2012—for a *twenty-second* term. "No one has been through the fire more so than our congressperson and we in the district have sent him back because we have faith in him, and that he has our interests in mind, and quite frankly he's one of us," said New York state assemblyman Keith L. T. Wright.[12]

It doesn't say much for black Democrat voters like Wright if all Rangel has to do is be "one of us"—that is, black—to be worthy of their vote. What happened to judging a candidate on his record? I don't know how Rangel's breaking the law and evading taxes is an example of having his constituents' "interests in mind." On his day of reckoning on the House floor, Rangel shed a tear or two but was not contrite or apologetic for his lawless behavior. "I know in my heart I'm not going to be judged by this Congress," he crowed.[13] This was more than ironic, considering that in 2008 Rangel asked the House Ethics Committee, almost dared it, to conduct an investigation of his apartment rentals and fund-raising activity. In her formal rebuke of Rangel, Pelosi said, "He violated regulations. He violated the rules of this House."[14]

Shame on you, Charlie. But at least Rangel didn't serve prison time like Representative Jesse Jackson Jr., now not only a disgraced member of the CBC but a convicted felon. Representing a majority-black district of South Side Chicago since 1995, Jackson was well on his way to becoming a politician for life. But in 2013 he pled guilty to campaign fraud and was sentenced to two and half years in prison by a federal judge in D.C. Jackson became blinded by the bling. He illegally spent $750,000 of campaign money to live the lush life straight out of an episode of *Lifestyles of the Rich and Famous: Members of the CBC*. From 2007 to 2011, Jackson and his wife, Sandi, bought everything he thought a black Democrat member of Congress was entitled to. The list of goods and services the Jacksons purchased looks like an adult's wish list for Santa Claus. From news reports, here are a few of Congressman Jackson's favorite things—all paid for illegally from his campaign fund:

- $43,000 Rolex *(every professional man should have one)*
- $7,000 elk heads from Montana *(because every congressman needs one)*
- $10,977.74 of flat screen TVs, "DVD players and DVDs from Best Buy" *(a necessity now, why not?)*

- "$466.30 dinner at CityZen restaurant in the Mandarin Oriental in D.C." *(gotta eat well)*
- "$5,587.75 vacation at the Martha's Vineyard Holistic Retreat" *(hard work deserves rewards)*
- $313.89 on "stuffed animals and accessories for stuffed animals" from Build-A-Bear Workshop *(had to buy something for the two small kids)*
- "$5,000 football signed by American presidents" *(honoring America's favorite pastime)*
- $4,600 hat of Michael Jackson's *(he was the King of Pop)*
- "$2,306.08 at Walt Disney World" *(again, why not?)*
- $5,150 of furs *(Chicago winters are frigid!)*[15]

It wasn't as if Jackson and his wife weren't making a good living. The couple reported income of about $350,000 in 2011, but that wasn't enough. They felt entitled to live beyond their means. This wasn't even the first time Jackson had been suspected of violating ethics rules. Before Jackson became a convicted felon, in 2013, he was the subject of an investigation by the Office of Congressional Ethics. In 2011 the OCE found Jackson likely violated House rules when he tried to bribe Governor Rod Blagojevich to appoint him to serve out the rest of Barack Obama's term in the U.S. Senate after Obama won the 2008 presidential election. Jackson denied the allegations. The Democrat-allied news media of course characterized Jackson as "an advocate for the less fortunate."[16] But these CBC members look very much like advocates for themselves.

Jackson's spending spree was reminiscent of the career of a Congressional Black Caucus trailblazer in corruption and denial, former Congressman William Jefferson, Democrat of Louisiana. Serving in the House from 1991, this distinguished Democrat member of the CBC was caught red-handed by the FBI in 2005 stashing $100,000 of bribe money in his freezer. You can't make this stuff up. Here's how it went down: A source tipped off the FBI that a U.S. congressman had taken money in exchange for helping companies interested in doing business in Africa get approval from U.S. and West African government agencies. The congressman was Jefferson, and from 2000 to 2005 he had received over $478,000 in bribes. In 2005 the FBI videotaped Jefferson accepting $100,000 in cash from an FBI witness to pay off an African government official. And then, "a few days later, the FBI—while serving a search warrant on his residence—found $90,000 of that same cash in Jefferson's freezer."[17] House Speaker Nancy Pelosi removed Jefferson from the powerful House Ways and Means Committee, and in August 2009 Jefferson was sentenced to thirteen years in prison. All this happened not because Jefferson is black but because he was greedy, dishonest, stupid, and arrogant, like many of the other Democrats in the CBC club.

In 2009 Democrat Representative Maxine Waters of California was part of the CBC gang of seven investigated by the House Ethics Committee for helping to arrange a 2008 meeting with the Treasury Department for OneUnited, a minority-owned bank. This wouldn't have been a problem if her husband, Sidney Williams, hadn't been a member of the bank's board of directors and, oops, owned $250,000 in stock.[18] After the meeting, the bank ended up receiving $12 million in bailout money from Treasury's Troubled Asset Relief Program, or TARP. Another black Democrat career politician who has served in the House since 1990 said Maxine was "hopping mad" about the investigation.[19] That response is very believable, since Waters was one of the CBC members who voted against the creation of the Office of Congressional Ethics, which referred the case to the Ethics Committee, in the first place. It's hard to believe that Waters, who was the third-ranking Democrat member of the House Financial Services Committee, didn't know better, and didn't gain personally from phoning Treasury to help schedule the meeting. But in 2010, Waters prevailed. Astonishingly, the Ethics Committee found no evidence she had violated any rules.

Not to be outdone by Waters, Representative Laura Richardson, another Democrat from California and CBC member, was investigated by the House Ethics Committee in 2009 for receiving preferential treatment from her bank when her home went into foreclosure. After selling the foreclosed home to someone else, the bank had a change of heart, restructured the loan, and gave the home back to Richardson. In 2010 the Ethics Committee bizarrely concluded that Richardson hadn't violated any House rules or laws in that case. But in a separate investigation, the Ethics Committee concluded Richardson had violated the law and House rules "by improperly using House resources for campaign, personal, and nonofficial purposes; by requiring or compelling her official staff to perform campaign work; and by obstructing the investigation of the Committee and the Investigative Subcommittee through the alteration or destruction of evidence, the deliberate failure to produce documents responsive to requests for information and a subpoena, and attempting to influence the testimony of witnesses."[20] Richardson was officially reprimanded by the House and fined $10,000. Her defense was that she didn't "intend" to break the law. Unlike most of her CBC colleagues, who hold their seats for life, Richardson, who had served in Congress since 2007, didn't win her reelection in 2012.

Every year, each member of the CBC receives $10,000 in scholarship money from the Congressional Black Caucus Foundation (CBCF) to award to constituents. The CBCF prohibits relatives of members from receiving scholarships from the foundation, but in 2010, CBC member Democrat Representative Eddie Bernice Johnson of Texas doled out an estimated $20,000 in scholarships from the Congressional Black Caucus Foundation to relatives and children of her staff. From 2005 to 2008, Johnson enjoyed showering twenty-three scholarships on two grandsons, two grandnephews, and a son of one of her Dallas-based staffers. Formed in 1976, the Congressional Black Caucus Foundation purports to be the arm of the CBC dedicated to "advancing the global black community" by funding things like scholarships and internships, public health, and economic empowerment programs."[21] In reality, it's a "nonprofit" that shakes down corporations for donations they have to pay to insulate themselves against allegations of racism from the CBC. Like its parent the CBC, the foundation pretends to advocate for blacks. It is best known for hosting the Annual Legislative Conference, which it markets as a "premier gathering of African Americans, cultivating engaging policy discussions on issues that impact black communities around the world," but which is really nothing more than four days of partying by black Democrats and politicians in D.C. In 2014 the foundation estimated that ten thousand people had descended on Washington to enjoy corporate-sponsored parties, dinners, and breakfasts.[22]

Neither the parties for politicians nor the scholarship money for staffers' family members has done much to advance the global black community. Johnson claimed she was "unaware of being in any type of violation and never intentionally violated the CBCF's rules."[23] It is hard to believe that a career politician such as Johnson, who at the time had served nine terms and was running for her tenth, wasn't aware of the foundation's rules against nepotism. Once she was caught, she agreed to repay the foundation the money.

Less egregious in comparison with these other cases was the 2009 Ethics Committee investigation of a trip members took to St. Maarten in 2008. They included Rangel, Representatives Carolyn Cheeks Kilpatrick of Michigan, Yvette Clarke of New York, Donald M. Payne of New Jersey, and Bennie Thompson of Mississippi and Delegate Donna M. Christian-Christensen of the U.S. Virgin Islands. Their disclosure forms indicated the event was sponsored by a nonprofit group. But the watchdog group the National Legal and Policy Center gathered evidence showing that for-profit corporations may actually have sponsored the event—which would violate House ethics rules. Members of Congress cannot accept trips paid for by corporations. But the committee found Representatives Thompson, Clarke, Payne, and Kilpatrick and Delegate Christian-Christensen "did not knowingly violate any provision of the Code of Official Conduct or any law, rule, regulation, or standard of conduct...." All these representatives' actions were bad, but once again

Charlie Rangel distinguished himself for his corruption. The committee found that "Representative Charles B. Rangel violated the House gift rule by accepting payment or reimbursement for travel to the 2007 and 2008 conferences."[24] Greedy Charlie Rangel was admonished and asked to repay the costs of the trips. Yet he is still one of the longest-serving members in Congress today. No matter what bad acts Democrat members of the CBC commit, they manage to remain in office for decades.

CAMPAIGNING ON RACE

Virtually every black Democrat member of Congress represents a majority-minority district thanks to gerrymandering, another institution that helps blacks get elected to office. Black voters reward these Democrat politicians for merely being black, rather than holding them accountable for a record of helping their constituents. They have "unyielding support of their black voters. It most cases, it takes nothing short of an act of God to remove them from office," wrote Javier David for theGrio in 2010.[25] David described black voters as sheeplike and ignorant, going to the polls each election cycle, voting for black congressional Democrats like they're "Third World dictators." Scandal-plagued CBC members are entitled politicians who are living above the law—and their people, helping only themselves—acting a lot more like Fidel Castro, Hugo Chavez, and the mullahs of Iran than genuine representatives of the people who put them in office.

In 2014 the Congressional Black Caucus played the race card yet again. After the November midterm elections—always thinking of themselves first—CBC members complained that congressional Democrats' process of picking committee chair and ranking positions should continue to be based on "seniority," not merit. Then–CBC chairman Marcia Fudge wrote this in a letter to her fellow Democrats: "The seniority system has worked well and should be honored. This has been the historic position of the CBC and we fully support its continuation."[26] Being judged on their merits won't bode well for the entrenched members of the CBC. So they cry racism. Rangel, arguably one of the most disgraced black members of Congress, was the most vocal. "It's terrible to break a tradition like this without discussing it with the members. Especially members who believe that Congress, as well as other institutions, still have prejudices that run against color and minorities."[27] What's really "terrible" is that Rangel, like many of his colleagues, thinks he's entitled to things just because he's a black and a member of Congress.

The impetus for the creation of the Congressional Black Caucus was the 1970 election of Republican President Richard M. Nixon. In 1970, when Nixon was elected, the CBC, originally called the Democratic Select Committee, requested to meet with him to discuss issues impacting blacks. In 1971 the group changed its name to the CBC and boycotted Nixon's State of the Union because he refused to meet with them. The organization vowed to hold Nixon and every other president accountable. Well, all except Obama—our first black president. Obama got a free pass because he was one of them.

Obama refused to meet with the CBC until after his first full year in office, even though 95 percent of blacks voted for him in 2008. With this refusal, Obama acted like Nixon, ignoring black Democrat members of Congress. That's not a nice way to thank your most loyal voting bloc. After the president had basically ignored blacks, CBC chairman Emanuel Cleaver joked in a September 2012 interview with The Root that Obama's blackness trumped holding him accountable for his record like white presidents. Regardless of the dire straits blacks found themselves in under Obama, Cleaver and every other CBC member except Allen West told blacks to vote for Obama a second time, not because he had done anything for blacks but because Obama needed more time to get things done. Really he needed more time to collect the black vote and continue ignoring blacks' concerns—just as Democrats have done for decades.

Our first black president hadn't had time to do anything for blacks— he was busy spending his political capital on illegal immigrants. Obama promised during his 2012 campaign to grant amnesty to illegal aliens if he got reelected—though amnesty will only exacerbate double-digit black unemployment. This is how little the country's black Democrat president thinks of his most loyal constituents. Illegal immigration is no friend of blacks in America. Many studies show blacks are harmed more than any other racial group by illegal aliens, mostly Hispanics and Latinos who broke the law to come here. When illegals began arriving in droves in the 1990s as a result of President Ronald Reagan's signing the amnesty-like Immigration Control and Reform Act into law in 1986, they took jobs in hospitality, restaurants, construction, cleaning, and lawn care that black Americans used to have.

For decades blacks have suffered higher unemployment rates than other racial groups. So what does the Congressional Black Caucus do when "immigration reform" heats up in Congress in 2014? Support it, of course. Representative Marcia Fudge, the CBC chairman at the time, along with her colleagues, voted for HR 15, the Border Security, Economic Opportunity, and Immigration Modernization Act that would have granted amnesty to over 11 million illegals living and working in America against the law.[28] At the time the debate on the amnesty bill was occurring, Fudge noted that the CBC was actively lobbying for an increase in "diversity" visas for African and Caribbean immigrants trying to come to the United States. Instead of trying to reduce the number of people, legal or illegal, competing for jobs against blacks, the CBC worked to increase the already tight labor pool. "We are concerned that the Diversity Visa Program has been eliminated. Members of the Congressional Black Caucus's Taskforce on Immigration Reform are currently reviewing the bill to make sure it addresses the unique concerns of the Black Immigrant and African American communities, particularly in ensuring diversity of immigrants, justice reform, and efforts to invest in STEM programs at minority-serving institutions remain top priorities," Fudge said in a 2013 statement.[29]

Think about this: the CBC supported legislation to take jobs away from blacks rather than create jobs for them. CBC's support of amnesty makes no sense unless you consider that Obama supported granting amnesty—and eventually did it through executive order, in 2014. Then it makes perfect sense because, as Representative Cleaver said, CBC members show Obama "deference" because he's black. For the CBC, what Obama wants trumps anything—even what's in the best interests of their black constituents. That only makes sense if the Democrats are in the game to help one another gain power and profit, rather than to help their most loyal, black constituents—and they are.

Representative Sheila Jackson Lee of Texas, a black Democrat CBC member, praised Obama's November 2014 amnesty proposal in an impassioned speech on the House floor. Mentioning that Texas has 1.3 million "undocumented individuals," Lee said, "This is not amnesty. This is prioritization," praising a policy that effectively robs her black constituents, American citizens, of jobs.[30] Of course this is the same congresswoman who handed out lollipops to illegal children held at detention centers in Texas. They crossed the border illegally like herds of cattle at the behest of their lawless parents.

Before the CBC was for Obama's amnesty program, it was against black unemployment. In 2011 the Congressional Black Caucus launched a jobs tour, wheeling through cities across the country to connect blacks with jobs. At the time, the black jobless rate was over 16 percent, double the national average. In an interview with NPR about the jobs tour in August 2011, Representative John Lewis, a Democrat member of the CBC, sounded like a fighter for blacks: "As representatives of people, we have a moral obligation to stand up, to speak up, to speak out and do what I call get in the way. Sometimes, you have to make some noise. You have to disturb the order of things."[31] How soon Lewis and his colleagues forgot about black Americans, the Democrat party's most loyal constituents, and put Obama, politics, and their own advantage above priorities for "their people."

Instead of making noise about important issues that actually impact black Americans, the CBC and its members also routinely take stands on issues irrelevant to those constituents' real problems. In February 2015 CBC chairman Butterfield and civil rights activist Representative John Lewis planned to boycott Israeli prime minister Benjamin Netanyahu's March speech to the U.S. Congress because House Speaker John Boehner did not ask Obama's permission before inviting Netanyahu. Butterfield told the *Hill* newspaper, "The United States is and will remain Israel's strongest ally. However, I refuse to be a part of a political stunt aimed at undercutting President Obama."[32] Yet Butterfield was okay with being part of Obama's amnesty stunt to rob blacks of jobs, who he himself claimed were in a state of economic emergency.

Lewis told the Associated Press, "I think it's an affront to the president and the State Department what the speaker did."[33] I don't remember Lewis saying it was an affront to him and other members of the CBC when Obama ignored black lawmakers during his first year in office. Nor do I recall Lewis expressing outrage that Obama's agenda has done nothing to address the double-digit unemployment weighing down blacks during Obama's two-term presidency. Blacks are suffering economic malaise, and CBC members focused on the vital issue—not!—of skipping Netanyahu's speech.

At least white Democrat politicians do a pretty good job of faking concern about blacks to win their votes. The black Democrats in the CBC seemingly don't even bother anymore. "Running for office while black" is the extent of their campaigns waged to win the black vote. Yet too many of us faithfully keep punching the race card at the ballot box—then complain when the black politicians don't address our concerns. Maybe it's time for black Americans to look beyond these skin-deep campaigns and vote for politicians who have ideas to help blacks succeed, and don't just focus on their own reelection.

These Democrat con artists know black America is in a "state of emergency"—after all, that's a direct quotation from the head of the

Congressional Black Caucus. They just don't care. Remind me again why this is the political party that gets more than 80 percent of the black vote in every election? What a con job!

A PERSONAL STORY

The Democrat Party's con job depends on convincing us to believe in a lot of fictional racism—especially the fantasy that 2015 America is full of cops who are shooting "unarmed black teens" for no reason but the bigotry and hatred in their ugly hearts. So am I saying there's no such thing as racism? That's the Democrats' stereotype of black Republicans: that we're in denial about the very real sufferings of our own people.

People ask me all the time why I named my blog *Conservative Black Chick*. Because all those things define me—I am a woman, a black person, and a Republican. And the fact that I'm a Republican doesn't mean that I don't recognize racial hatred when I see it. As a matter fact, like a lot of black Americans, I've been a victim of racism in the course of my life, and that too has defined who I am—it has given me strength. I don't fit in the black box the Democrats would confine me to. I'm an individual just like my white peers: I am to be whomever I decide to be.

"Conservative Black Chick" defies the stereotype of what kind of black woman people think I'm supposed to be. In most people's mind, I'm supposed to be a Democrat because I was born black. And according to liberals in America, that only gives me the right to punch the donkey card when it comes to politics. Sorry folks, my parents didn't raise me to be an "ass." They raised me to be an independent thinker, and if that meant choosing the elephant party (the symbol for the GOP), so be it. Just the name of my blog often offends people by defying their stereotype of who they think I should be, and no group is more offended than black Democrats. Black liberals are beyond offended by me; they get downright angry with me for not assimilating into their monolithic black mentality. Daily I receive nasty e-mails or taunting tweets calling me "bitch," "cunt," "sellout," or "Uncle Tom," and lots of other unsavory words. Why? Simply, because I have the audacity to vote Republican.

When liberals, particularly blacks, encounter a black conservative chick like me, their reaction is hostile: "How dare you buck the tide? How dare you have an independent opinion on the problems plaguing the black race?" Like our 73 percent out-of-wedlock birthrate or dramatic number of homicides? Some liberals even accuse me of using my blog name just to get attention because there are so few black Republicans. And they are partly right: the name seeks to embolden more black Republicans to come out of the closet into the light. We exist. We date back to before the Civil War, when President Abraham Lincoln helped found the Grand Old Party. The GOP was formed to combat slavery, specifically the expansion of more slave states in the Union out West. That's one reason I'm a Republican today.

Another reason is because of a heartbreaking incident in my child-hood.

THE COUNTRY CLUB

As a child, I never remember my parents belonging to any one social group or herd. To this day they socialize in both the white and black circles in Richmond, Virginia, where I grew up and they still live. My parents lived their lives on their terms and did what was right for them. No better example of independence and strength of character did my mother, Barbara, and father, Thomas, give me and my two brothers, Thomas Wright III (Trey) and Arthur Baker Wright (Art), than when they sued the Salisbury Country Club for discrimination in 1979 after the club twice rejected my parents' application for membership just because they were black. Not pretty to think about, is it? And it wasn't that long ago.

Recently I decided to go back through the documents of the case as an adult. Dredging up this family history and reading through the court filings, press clips, and letters my parents received about the case made me sick to my stomach. I came across language like the kind I found in the Salisbury Country Club's booklet *Policies Governing the Use of the Club*, which stated, "From its inception, the Club was established for the exclusive use and enjoyment by members and guests of the Caucasian Race. Rules and customs in this regard long observed will continue. Reasonable variance in special appropriate instances by the proper Committee may be made to accommodate non-Caucasian guests."[1]

Ouch.

Let's go back in time a bit. My mother recalls the summer of 1979 as "such a happy time in our lives." My mother, who was an elementary school teacher for kindergarten through second grade students, had stopped teaching to be a stay-at-home mom. My father's dental practice was thriving. We were living in a nice home in the city of Richmond, but we were all excited because the new house located in Chesterfield County, a suburb of Richmond, was going to be bigger and we kids were going to have our own playroom. Actually, we would have several rooms in the new house to play in, to my mother's chagrin. Building her "dream home" as my mom said, was like "giving birth to my last child because it took nine months to construct." Every weekend my parents would take me and my two younger brothers to see the progress on the house. I was ten years old, Trey was six, and Art was three. My youngest brother was just getting potty trained, and my mom said he always had to pee when we went to see the new house. During the week, my mom would take him with her to the house to meet up with my dad and the builder to inspect things or approve materials. The woods became his port-a-potty.

We moved into the English Tudor at 2801 East Brigstock Road, Midlothian, Virginia, in May 1977. It was a month before my eleventh birthday, and boy we were excited! We had a pool where I enjoyed many birthdays and challenged my brother Trey to see how many laps we could swim under water without coming up for air. I think we got up to four. We kids had a playroom upstairs, called the Blue Room because the room had blue carpet and the walls were painted blue. There we battled each other in Atari video games like *Pac-Man* and *Asteroids*, watched TV, and wrestled. Another favorite pastime was jumping off my brothers' bunk beds. As she heard the KA-BOOM! from downstairs, my mother would shout, "Crystal, Trey, and Art, I know you're not jumping off those beds!" "No!" we would shout back in unison.

But our favorite room to romp in was the Great Room. It was a big room with wood parquet floors that led into the dining room. It had a fireplace and a spiral staircase that led up to a second-level loft where you could read and listen to music. My mom loved to use the room for entertaining. We kids, on the other hand, loved using it for sleepovers, playing, and mischief. When my parents were out of town or left us with the babysitter, Trey and I used to tie Art's hands to the columns in the Great Room, turn off the lights, and leave him there for a few minutes. He was afraid of the dark and we thought it was funny. As adults, it doesn't sound too nice now, and we have apologized to him. Of course, like most siblings my brothers and I didn't always get along. Knowing I hated him to come into my room, my little brother Trey would just stand in the doorway and refuse to leave. He would flash a huge grin and laugh as I shouted, "Mom, Trey's in my room. Make him get out!"

The Salisbury neighborhood was our little oasis. My brothers and I would ride on our bicycles for hours with friends well into the summer evenings. We would ride trails through the neighborhood to Sycamore Square, a shopping center with a grocery store and a Benjamin Franklin arts and crafts store where we would buy candy for a nickel or dime. The "Hill Climbs," hills of red clay buried in the woods, were fantastic fun too. My brothers, with their BMX bikes, were more daring on the Hill Climbs than I was with my five-speed. Ironically, my brother Trey recently reminded me, one of the entrances to the Hill Climbs bordered the Salisbury Country Club's property.

For my family, all our memories of the Salisbury neighborhood always come back to the Salisbury Country Club. After unpacking boxes and settling into our new home, in June of 1977 my parents turned their attention to applying for membership to the "club" located in the neighborhood. They had already been there as guests—in 1976, before their membership application, my father had attended a meeting held at the club by the Richmond Dental Society Study Club and the Southside Dental Study Club, of which he was a member, and that same year he and my mother were invited to the Salisbury Country Club for a cocktail party hosted by Dr. Black and Dr. Spiller, Ltd.[2]—and it never occurred to them that there would be any problem with their membership application. Having a club in their neighborhood that they and their kids could enjoy was a huge reason why they had chosen to build a home in the subdivision. The abundant promotions for the Salisbury Country Club gave the impression that if a family lived in the neighborhood, they would automatically become members of the club. Real estate developers and realtors promoted access to the club to encourage people to buy or build homes in Salisbury. The Salisbury Home Owners Association welcomed in new owners to the neighborhood and acquainted them with the club and its facilities through the "Welcome Wagon" hospitality program. The *Salisbury Village Crier*, the neighborhood's monthly newsletter, also promoted the club. Although the Salisbury subdivision was a predominately white neighborhood, my parents assumed their application to the Salisbury Country Club would be routine. After the club's relentless marketing campaign, how could anyone living in the Salisbury subdivision not apply for membership? All the process required was the recommendation of two members and the submission of an application to the membership committee, which referred the application to the board of directors for a vote. The Salisbury Country Club had even conducted a survey asking members if they approved of admitting blacks. Only about 13 percent objected, while 87 percent supported blacks joining or didn't care. Seemingly, the membership was fine with blacks joining. Yet shortly after submitting their application, my parents were shocked to learn that the club's board of directors had voted seven to four against their application, on June 28, 1977, along with that of Willie Lanier, a black former linebacker for the Kansas City Chiefs.

The rejection was insulting enough, but making things even worse was that at the time of my parents' application, the club was in the process of conducting an aggressive membership drive to residents in the neighborhood and the surrounding area. The Salisbury Corporation, owned by J. Kenneth Timmons and C. Porter Vaughan, developers of the subdivision, frequently ran ads in the *Richmond Times-Dispatch*, such as this one from November 13, 1977: "Spacious home sites of one to seven acres are scattered among woods, lakes and fairways. Salisbury Country Club just a brief walk or bike ride from your Salisbury home offers a championship golf course, tennis courts, an Olympic pool and abundant social life."[3]

Prior to the Wrights and the Laniers applying for membership to the club, no one living in the Salisbury neighborhood had ever been rejected. Samuel H. Dibert, a former club president who supported both families' applications, said that "acceptance of previous applicants had been almost routine." Only if an applicant had "a bad reputation or couldn't pay club dues" would he be rejected, Dibert added.[4]

The club wanted new members, just not any black ones. Over a decade after the 1964 Civil Rights Act was passed, racism was alive and well in the heart of the former Democrat Confederacy.

A few weeks later, in early July, the news media got wind of an all-white country club in Richmond rejecting black members. My mother suspects my dear departed uncle, her brother Dr. Stanley E. Baker, tipped off the local *Richmond Times-Dispatch* about the club rejecting my parents' application. My uncle was a professor at Virginia Commonwealth University and fiercely protective of his baby sister. He was like a grandfather to us after his father, my grandfather, was killed in 1970, when I was only four. My Uncle Buddy, as we called him, also loved stirring up trouble.

News of the Salisbury Country Club's racist ways made its way into the *New York Times*, *New York Post*, *Richmond News Leader*, and other news outlets. What did the Salisbury Country Club have to say in response to questions from the media? "Thomas J. Hampton, club president, refused to answer any [*Richmond Afro-American*] questions concerning the board's rejection of the Wrights and Laniers. Speaking like a voice from a tape recorder, he answered each question by saying, The Salisbury Country Club is a private club. This is a private club matter. I have no comment."[5]

That would be the club's defense when my parents took the case to court. Interestingly, Hampton worked as a field maintenance supervisor for E. I. DuPont de Nemours and Co. in Richmond and managed a two-hundred-worker crew, of whom thirty-five were black.

As articles on the club's dirty little racist secret began pouring out in the press, many members of the club learned of the club's whites-only policy for the first time. "When there were no black applicants, the club could hide behind the fact that no blacks applied. Now that they have applied, everybody can see problems they didn't have to face before," attested club member Jan Gabler.[6]

My parents, of course, were very hurt. "We had hopes. It was the American dream to build a house in the suburbs and join the country club. But now it's as if our bubble has burst. There is no American dream," said my mother to the *Richmond Afro-American*.[7] "This is a big slap in the face. I'm shocked that these people would be so insecure. I am deeply hurt. To think that because of my color, they would reject us in 1977. This tells me I'm not a first-class citizen."

In response to the rejection of two black families, members of the club began a letter-writing campaign to protest the board's vote. "Those who think the club has made a big mistake are writing to tell them so…it may be a majority," said Mrs. Robert Boclair, a club member.[8]

"I'm very, very upset, and I feel the majority of members are very upset. But I would not resign. I think there are other things we can do. Eventually, if I felt they would never allow blacks to join, then my conscience would force me to quit," said Mrs. Eugene V. Freund.[9] I wonder if Mrs. Freund felt compelled to quit the club when my parents' application was denied a second time?

Another member, Cuyler M. Gibbons, wasn't as gracious. "I think it's no one's business but the members of the club," Gibbons snipped.[10]

Looking at all the press clippings and legal documents from the case, what surprised and touched me was reading quotations from two members of the club: Virginia attorney general Anthony F. Troy and former Republican National Committee cochairman Richard D. Obenshain, who both condemned the club's blatant racism. In a letter to club president Thomas Hampton, Troy wrote, "As a member of the club, I do not believe the decision reflects the thinking of the majority of the club members; as attorney general of Virginia, I know that the decision is contra to the present thinking of a vast majority of modern-day Virginians."[11] Troy added that if both families weren't admitted, he doubted he would remain a member,[12] and he did eventually resign from the club because of its rejection of my parents' application. Obenshain, a lawyer who had been a member of the Salisbury Country Club for a year, wrote a letter to "voice his objection and ask the board of directors to reconsider their decision."[13]

A few years ago, I ran into Kate Obenshain, one of his daughters, at a political panel discussion we both participated in hosted by the

Conservative Political Action Committee (CPAC) in September 2012 in Denver, Colorado. The two of us hadn't seen each other since we were kids attending Collegiate School in Richmond, Virginia. The minute I saw her, I recognized her from Collegiate and said, "You went to Collegiate. I think I know you. I'm Crystal Wright." Kate recognized me too, and we quickly began to reminisce about our days at Collegiate. At some point during our discussion, I reminded her of what her father had done and told her that meant so much to my family. My mother told me, "It took courage for a white person in his position to take that stand, and I will be forever grateful." (Unfortunately, Richard Obenshain died tragically in a plane crash in 1978 after he won the Republican Party's nomination for a Virginia U.S. Senate seat.)

And the goodness in people didn't end there. On Sunday, July 10, 1977, the Reverend James A. Burge, associate pastor of St. Edward's Catholic Church, to which about 30 percent of Salisbury Country Club members belonged at the time, condemned the club's action during five masses. The Reverend Burge said the action was "against the Gospel of Jesus Christ" and asked parishioners to stand together and get in touch with their membership committee.[14] Learning about the Salisbury Club's racist actions, an employee from the Briarwood Club, located a few miles down the road, phoned my parents and told them they were welcome to join their club anytime. Eventually my parents would join the Briarwood Club, where my brothers and I would spend many years swimming, taking tennis lessons, and enjoying the company of our friends. But my parents' fight wasn't over.

THE FIGHT CONTINUES

My parents resubmitted their application again, in August 1977, and again it was rejected. The club's actions gnawed away at my mother night and day: "I'm trying not to be bitter, but I have to admit that this incident is the first thing I think of in the morning and the last thing I think of at night. I pass that country club when I drop off the children for their bus to camp. Tell me, how do you explain to your children, they can't go swimming there?" my mother said.[15] Eventually, my mother felt the rejection was so wrong, racist, and dismissive of the civil rights she had fought for as a young adult that she told my father they had to file a lawsuit. "You will not put me in the back of the bus again is what I thought. It wasn't just about me but this time, it was about my children. I came out roaring like a mother lion," she recalled.

My mother's own refusal to back down started young. When she was thirteen years old, living in the segregated south of Richmond, Virginia, she was riding in the back of a public bus on her way home from ballet class. The bus was full, and a white man getting on the bus told her to move. This skinny little girl calmly looked at him, said, "I'm already in the back of the bus," and refused to leave her seat. The man yelled at the bus driver, "Make this woman move!" Since when did a thirteen-year-old girl become a woman? Glancing back, the driver saw my mother, closed the bus door, and drove off without responding to the man.

So as you can imagine, my mother wasn't going to take this bigoted crap lying down. Some time passed. My father was angry but a little less willing to fight. He worried about how a lawsuit in a close-knit city like Richmond, which was socially segregated, would affect his growing dental practice. Ever the optimist and fighter, my mom explained to my dad, "This won't affect the respect your patients have for you because you put them first. They will admire you for putting your family first."

At some point following the club's rejection of our family, my parents were contacted about filing a lawsuit by the Washington, D.C., office of the Anti-Defamation League (ADL), a nonprofit legal organization dedicated to fighting discrimination. The ADL recommended they contact Richmond lawyer Arthur Samuel with the law firm of Samuel & Pustilnik. Samuel formally filed the lawsuit against the Salisbury Club's board of directors in the U.S. District Court, Richmond Division, on July 2, 1979. The accusation was that the club had violated the 1964 Civil Rights Act by denying my parents membership to the club solely because they were black. While the Salisbury Country Club believed it qualified for the act's exemption clause, which allowed private clubs or organizations to discriminate, Samuel argued that the club didn't qualify for the private exemption because the club was "not a private social club or fraternal organization, but rather is a recreational facility, which has no purpose of exclusiveness other than race." In other words, they argued that Salisbury failed the test of being a private club because there was no selectivity standard or process for exclusion *except* race. "No one applying from Salisbury ever has been turned down," stated the brief. "Anyone can join if he is financially able, and is not a troublemaker. All he needs is the recommendation of two members, and the board will approve him if he is white."

As the case got going and all this racist drama was unfolding in Richmond, my parents had to explain to their children why we couldn't go to the neighborhood club with their friends to swim or learn to play tennis. Although my parents largely shielded us from the litigation, my mother was very frank with us. As an extrovert, she has always been unafraid of having those tough conversations with us. Having been a grade school teacher, my mom was good at spelling things out to kids calmly and clearly. She told her three children we couldn't *ever* go to the club because they didn't want black people there. I don't know if she ever used the words "white friends," but we knew what she meant when she told us to tell our friends, "No, thank you," and nothing more, when they invited us there.

I remember being pretty crushed about it and looking at some of the girls I played with, thinking, "Why are their parents racist? Why do they belong to a club that doesn't like black people?" At eleven, twelve, and thirteen years old, it made me feel bad every time I either saw or thought of "the club." To add insult to injury, for the first few years we lived in Salisbury, our bus stop for school was in the Salisbury Country Club's parking lot! I remember getting on the bus in the morning, looking out of the window at the club's long colonial red-brick building and feeling excluded, thinking, "What's wrong with those people?" One afternoon, my mom was late picking me up from the bus stop and for whatever reason my brother Trey wasn't with me that day. I waited in the parking lot and decided to walk home. It was about a fifteen-minute walk, but it felt like an eternity, particularly when I walked along the stretch of road in front of the club. As I passed the club with every step, I looked straight in front of me and wondered if people were staring at me because I was black. My mother made a point of not driving by the club but taking the subdivision's longer second entrance to avoid seeing that painful icon of racism. I too developed a disdain for the building, and when I learned to drive I avoided the front entrance of the neighborhood. As we got older, my parents told us about other all-white clubs in Richmond, including the Country Club of Virginia and Willow Oaks Country Club, and reminded us if we were ever invited to any of them we had to decline those invitations too. Black friends of my parents weren't very supportive of the lawsuit, telling my parents, "Well, it's a private club. Why would you apply?" or "Why didn't you apply to one of the black clubs?" One day, my mother recalled shopping at a local drug store and Willie Lanier, whose application had also been denied, but who declined to pursue things further, approached her and said, "Why don't y'all just let that stuff go?" She coolly replied, "We have to do what's right for us and our family." She told me no one had done anything like that in Richmond, suing a white country club. Many blacks "weren't ready for change," she said. "We wanted more. We didn't want to drive across town for a social club. Black clubs in Richmond didn't offer tennis and swimming for kids. We wanted our kids to take advantage of the same things that other kids did."

There were even blacks in my own family who weren't supportive of us. One of my mother's aunts began making heckling calls to our house once a week. At first my mother didn't know who it was. The woman would say, "Why don't you give it up? Stop suing that club," and hang up the phone. After a few calls, my mom recognized the voice as that of one of her father's four sisters. The next time her aunt called, she said

her name and added, "Don't call my house again. You may not agree
with what I'm doing but I have to do what's right for my family." That
was the end of the calls. When I asked why my great-aunt would do such
a thing, my mother said it was her way of trying to protect us because
she didn't want harm to come to us. "She was one of those black people
who was still afraid of white people," my mom said.

Some white neighbors who had supported my parents' membership
remained members of Salisbury after my parents' application was rejected
and the lawsuit was filed. One family that lived in the neighborhood, whose
sons my brothers played with, explained to my parents that they continued
to belong to the Salisbury Country Club so their kids could take swimming
and tennis lessons. "We think it's just terrible," they would say. Evidently
not terrible enough to resign their membership at an all-white club.

On October 18, 1979, five days after my mother's birthday, U.S.
District Judge D. Dortch Warriner of Richmond ruled that Salisbury was
"a truly private social club" and as such qualified for exemption under
the 1964 Civil Rights Act. "The government has no business telling
anyone who he must invite into his home; nor has the government the
right to tell Salisbury, a private country club, who it must admit to membership," wrote Warriner. He further added that the Ninth Amendment
gives private club members rights that protect the club from governmen-
tal intrusion into its membership policies: "The enumeration in the
Constitution of certain rights shall not be construed to deny or disparage
others retained by the people." While Warriner wrote that his decision
"neither endorses nor approves of racially discriminatory membership
policies," his opinion looked like it gave the stamp of approval to the
Salisbury Country Club to discriminate based on race.

THE FINAL BATTLE

This decision wasn't the end of the road for my parents' journey to
justice. In January 1980 my parents appealed the decision. Samuel &

Pustilnik brought in lawyer Allison W. Brown Jr., an expert in civil rights cases who had argued before the Supreme Court. Brown's experience was critical to my parents' case. In 1976 he had won *Runyon v. McCrary* before the Supreme Court, forcing private schools to accept blacks. Previously, in 1968, he had argued successfully before the Supreme Court in *Sullivan v. Little Hunting Park* that private swimming pools couldn't deny people membership based upon race.

About two weeks before my fourteenth birthday, on June 4, 1980, Brown and Arthur Samuel, the lawyers for my father, gave oral arguments in his appeal with the U.S. Court of Appeals for the Fourth Circuit. "By the way, the United States Government has filed a brief in our favor and has asked to argue the case orally also," Samuel had written in a May 13, 1980, letter to my father. "I'm enclosing a photocopy of their motion for leave to participate in oral argument, thought you and your wife would like to see it," he added. Reading that letter in the file my father gave me about this case gave me goose bumps. To think my parents' three-year battle against bigotry inspired the U.S. Justice Department to fight with them in a friend-of-the-court brief (*amicus curiae*). What an awesome legacy. That is a big part of what has given me the guts to bust stereotypes and call myself Conservative Black Chick!

During the oral argument, Brown gave three reasons why the appeals court must overturn Warriner's decision. First, the club was created for a commercial purpose, to develop the Salisbury subdivision, "and not for a valid plan of exclusiveness."[16] The brief notes that the Salisbury Corporation, owned by Vaughan and Timmons, had used the guarantee of club membership to subdivision residents to sell homes in Salisbury. Under the law, commercial entities offering a public good cannot discriminate on the basis of race. Second, Brown said the club advertised for members in the *Salisbury Village Crier* newsletter and elsewhere, including the "Property Buyers Guide" and the "Salisbury Hospitality Program."[17] Third, Brown concluded the club's membership wasn't exclusive because "it had admitted everyone from the subdivision who has ever applied for 15 years."[18]

A three-judge federal appeals panel composed of Judge Harrison L. Winter and Judge Kenneth K. Hall, both of the Fourth District, and Judge Edward M. Kidd of Bluefield, West Virginia, heard the arguments. During the oral arguments, Judge Winter asked James M. Minor, of Minor, Forb & Batzli, who represented the Salisbury Country Club, if my father "could reasonably believe that his application would be favorably entertained." Minor answered no, that my father should have known his application would be open to "subjective criteria." Minor continued, "The Salisbury Club is perhaps the most private organization ever to be reviewed by this court. The Constitution requires that its privacy be respected."[19]

After my parents argued their case a second time, my brothers and I enjoyed the summer of 1980 with the usual fun of camp, bike rides in the neighborhood, swimming with friends in our backyard pool, and a family vacation. As school got under way, on September 30, 1980, the court announced its unanimous ruling that the Salisbury Country Club wasn't "a truly private club" and couldn't deny membership to blacks who lived in the subdivision, for three reasons. First, the court concluded that the Salisbury Club did "not follow a selective membership policy other than race...the only residents of the subdivision who have been denied membership are the plaintiffs and another black family who applied for membership at about the same time. They were admittedly refused membership because of their race." Second, Winter ruled the club didn't qualify for the Civil Rights Act exemption because it sought new members through public advertising in the subdivision newsletter and throughout the Richmond area. Lastly, since 1963, when the club was founded, it was used to serve the commercial interests of the developer to help him sell homes in the subdivision. "Singly, any one of these characteristic belies the club's claim that it is a genuinely private organization. In combination, they demolish the club's 'truly private' defense," the court wrote.

The court's decision made the front page of the September 30, 1980, *Richmond-Times Dispatch*. The story's headline read, "Salisbury Club Held Not Private; Court Says Blacks Cannot Be Excluded," and it appeared above the fold next to the other top story, "Iran Attacks Baghdad, Refinery." Reagan was the Republican presidential nominee running against the incumbent president Jimmy Carter, and after the first debate an ABC News–Harris Survey poll found Reagan ahead of Carter 42 to 36 percent. The *Times-Dispatch*'s editorial page on October 1, 1980, opined, "Yesterday's unanimous ruling whereby Salisbury Country Club was found to have excluded blacks from membership illegally strikes us as eminently correct." But the paper reminded readers it had no problem with private clubs discriminating. "Private clubs are one thing. They ought to be able to reject for membership any applicant for any reason from the color of his tie to the cut of his jib. As former Supreme Court Justice Arthur Goldberg wrote in a case, 'Prejudice and bigotry in any form are regrettable, but it is the constitutional right of every person to close his home or club to any person...solely on the basis of personal prejudices including race.'"[20]

My father declined to comment and was prohibited by the court from revealing the settlement for damages my parents received. My mother was emotional. "We did it for our children, so they can hold their heads high and not be second-class citizens," she tearfully told a reporter upon learning of the appeals court ruling. I was fourteen years old, my brother Trey was ten, and my little brother Art was seven.

Needless to say, even though my parents won the right to join the Salisbury Country Club, they never joined because the lawsuit was never about the club accepting us. My parents would not be treated like second-class citizens, like slaves, like we weren't good enough because we were black. My parents never stepped inside the club again, and my brothers and I never walked inside its red-brick walls. To all of us it was a painful reminder that some people didn't like us because we were black. Founded in 1963, the Salisbury Country Club still exists today. I don't know how many black families belong to the club.

In 1983, three years after the appeals court decision, my parents would leave their dream home and move into another great home in another Chesterfield County subdivision, named Bexley. Both my father and mother said they just couldn't continue to live in Salisbury and be reminded every day of that racism and know their kids couldn't freely enjoy the club's facilities without forever feeling unwanted. "It still leaves a cloud over us. We don't feel as if we're wholesome residents," my dad told the newspaper.[21] While my mother loves the house in Bexley, she always talks about how special the house in Salisbury was and how hard it was to leave it. "We had such happy times there and memories I will forever cherish," she said. Me too!

Decades after my parents won this battle, I referenced the case in an article that I wrote for CNN.com in 2014, "When Is It Ever OK to Call the President the N-Word?" In response to the story, I received this e-mail from the grandson of Samuel Dibert, who was the club's president at the time and supported my parents.

Crystal,

Just want to say that I really enjoyed your CNN article last month: "When is it ever OK to call the president the n-word?"

My grandfather was a member of the Salisbury Country Club board and a neighbor of your dad's. He spoke out publicly against the decision and ended up resigning from the club in protest. Shortly thereafter he sold his house and moved out of the neighborhood.

I had been looking for more information about the controversy, so it was fascinating to come across an article written by Dr. Wright's daughter. I'd heard stories, but didn't know many of the details.

Anyway, just wanted to say thanks. Keep up the good fight.

Sam Dibert, Jr.

I cry whenever I read this letter. Real racism still exists in modern America, and it hurts real people. But when hustlers like Al Sharpton and other liberals are quick to label every incident in America racist, from voter ID laws to the shootings of black teens, it diminishes the rightful attention that true racism should receive. As the letter above shows, almost thirty years after my parents stood up to the Salisbury Country Club, a young white man takes pride in what his grandparents and my parents did. He is proud because they did the right thing, not because they were white or black.

To this day the whole case still leaves a dark cloud over my family, but one from which we gain strength to stand up for who we are and what we feel is right. Through fighting the Salisbury Country Club's racism, my parents gave me the gift of individualism. Growing up, I was teased by my classmates at Collegiate School for being different. Many afternoons in sixth grade, I remember coming home crying and begging my mother to let me attend another school. She would not yield to my tears. Instead she would always tell me, "It's difficult sometimes being an individual, but it's worth it. You'll see one day." Now I see.

ACKNOWLEDGMENTS

F amily and friends too many to count helped me in numerous ways to write this book. I'm grateful to my brothers, Trey and Art, for sharing my politics and putting up with me! I also want to thank my dear dad, Dr. Thomas Wright Jr., for our weekly talks and rants about interesting *Wall Street Journal* articles or frustrations with President Barack Obama. New and old friends provided me with encouragement when I wanted to give up blogging. They include James Link, Andrew Lee, Emily Barsh, and Krista Shepard.

A special thanks to Abena Darkeh, who inspired me to start *Conservative Black Chick* in the first place; Richard Ivory, editor of *Hip Hop Republican*, among other things, for seeing something in me early on that I couldn't and encouraging me to write; and David Frum, who published my first blog post, in 2009, and embraced my unique perspective.

Thanks to WMAL Radio in D.C., which gave me fill-in hosting opportunities—Regnery's senior editor Harry Crocker heard me one day on the radio and asked if I'd be interested in writing a book.

Finally, to the people who helped me with the nuts and bolts. Thanks to David Limbaugh, a published author many times over, who gave me invaluable practical advice on getting the words on paper. I also would have been lost without my great researcher David Wilezol, who was adept at finding great sources to back up my arguments. Thanks to my editors at Regnery: Harry for giving me this opportunity and encouraging me to make some changes even when I resisted, and Elizabeth Kantor for her patience and nudging in helping me get the words just right.

NOTES

INTRODUCTION

1. Daniel Patrick Moynihan, "Defining Deviancy Down," *American Scholar* 62, no. 1 (Winter 1993): 21, 25. Available online at http://www.utexas.edu/law/journals/tlr/sources/Volume%2092/Issue%206/Koppelman/Koppelman.fn051.Moynihan.DefiningDeviancy.pdf.

2. Melissa Clyne, "Critics: Baltimore Mayor Gave Protesters 'Permission to Riot,'" Newsmax, April 28, 2015, http://www.newsmax.com/Newsfront/Baltimore-riots-mayor-Stephanie-Rawlings-Blake/2015/04/28/id/641206/.

3. Richard A. Oppel Jr., "West Baltimore's Police Presence Drops, and Murder Soars," *New York Times*, June 12, 2015, http://www.nytimes.com/2015/06/13/us/after-freddie-gray-death-west-baltimores-police-presence-drops-and-murders-soar.html?_r=0/.

4. "Abortion and Race: For Decades, Abortion Has Disproportionately Targeted Minority Babies," Abort73, last updated June 29, 2015, http://www.abort73.com/abortion/abortion_and_race/.

5. Susan W. Enouen, "New Research Shows Planned Parenthood Targets Minority Neighborhoods," Life Issues Institute, October 1, 2012,

http://www.lifeissues.org/2012/10/new-research-shows-planned-parenthood-targets-minority-neighborhoods/.

6.   Tony Lee, "Wendy Davis Raises $1.2 Million in Six Weeks after Abortion Filibuster," Breitbart, August 30, 2013, http://www.breitbart.com/big-government/2013/08/30/wendy-davis-raises-1-2m-in-six-weeks-after-abortion-filibuster/.

7.   Liz Kreutz, "Hillary Clinton Calls Planned Parenthood Videos 'Disturbing,'" ABC News, July 29, 2015, http://abcnews.go.com/Politics/hillary-clinton-calls-planned-parenthood-videos-disturbing/story?id=32757475.

8.   *2013–14 Annual Report: Our Health. Our Decisions. Our Moment* (Planned Parenthood, 2014), http://plannedparenthood.org/files/6714/1996/2641/2013-2014_Annual_Report_FINAL_WEB_VERSION.pdf.

9.   Paul Bedard, "Group Touts 4,000 Abortions in 1 Year with Clinton's Support," *Washington Examiner*, September 26, 2014, http://www.washingtonexaminer.com/group-touts-4000-abortions-in-1-year-with-clintons-support/article/2553999.

10.   "Defining Deviancy Down," 26, quoting from Moynihan's own article in the Jesuit periodical *America*.

11.   Ibid., 26.

12.   Kevin Sack and Megan Thee-Brenan, "Poll Finds Most in U.S. Hold Dim View of Race Relations," *New York Times*, July 23, 2015, http://www.nytimes.com/2015/07/24/us/poll-shows-most-americans-think-race-relations-are-bad.html?_r=1.

13.   "Defining Deviancy Down," 30.

CHAPTER ONE: THE PARTY OF CRIME

1.   D.C. Metropolitan Police Department Twitter account, https://twitter.com/DCPoliceDept.

2.   Erica Goode, "Incarceration Rates for Blacks Have Fallen Sharply, Report Says," *New York Times*, February 27, 2013, http://www.nytimes.com/2013/02/28/us/incarceration-rates-for-blacks-dropped-report-shows.html?_r=0.

3.   Jason L. Riley, "Family Secret: What the Left Won't Tell You about Black Crime," *Washington Times*, July 21, 2014, http://www.

washingtontimes.com/news/2014/jul/21/family-secret-what-the-left-wont-tell-you-about-bl/.

4. Jon Greenberg, "Giuliani: 93% of Black Murders Are Committed by Blacks," Politifact, November 25, 2014, http://www.politifact.com/punditfact/statements/2014/nov/25/rudy-giuliani/giuliani-93-black-murders-committed-blacks/.

5. Juan Williams, "Race and the Gun Debate," *Wall Street Journal*, March 26, 2013, http://www.wsj.com/articles/SB1000142412788732386960457836688248460071 0.

6. Ibid.

7. The Violence Policy Center, "Black Homicide Victimization in the United States," January 2014, http://www.vpc.org/studies/black homicide15.pdf.

8. Daniel Patrick Moynihan, *The Negro Family: The Case for National Action* (Washington, DC: U.S. Department of Labor Office of Policy Planning and Research, March 1965), http://www.blackpast.org/primary/moynihan-report-1965.

9. A transcript of President Obama's remarks can be found at "Remarks by the President on the Nomination of Dr. Jim Kim for World Bank President," WhiteHouse.gov, March 23, 2012, https://www.whitehouse.gov/the-press-office/2012/03/23/remarks-president-nomination-dr-jim-kim-world-bank-president.

10. Crystal Wright, "Zimmerman, the Media and Black Leaders Pimping of Blacks," *Conservative Black Chick* (blog), July 21, 2013, http://conservativeblackchick.com/blog/2013/07/21/zimmerman-the-media-and-black-leaders-pimping-of-blacks/.

11. "Remarks by the President on Trayvon Martin," transcript, White House.gov, July 19, 2013, http://www.whitehouse.gov/the-press-office/2013/07/19/remarks-president-trayvon-martin.

12. William Bratton, *Crime and Enforcement Activity in New York City, January 1–December 31, 2013* (New York: New York Police Department, 2014), 1, http://www.nyc.gov/html/nypd/downloads/pdf/analysis_and_planning/2013_year_end_enforcement_report.pdf.

13. John Woodrow Cox and Michael Smith, "With Two Killed in D.C. Friday Night, Homicide Tally Matches All of 2014's," *Washington Post*, August 29, 2015, http://www.washingtonpost.com/local/crime/gunfire-erupts-all-over-district-friday-night-as-police-step-up-

patrols/2015/08/29/8a623eb8-4e05-11e5-bfb9-9736d04fc8e4_story.
html.

14. Will Greenberg, "Police Chiefs from around the Country Meet in D.C.
to Discuss Violent Summer," *Washington Post*, August 3, 2015, http://
www.washingtonpost.com/local/crime/police-chiefs-from-around-
the-country-meet-in-dc-to-discuss-violent-summer/2015/08/03/
e2ec8a9c-3a06-11e5-8e98-115a3cf7d7ae_story.html.

15. Nick Valencia, "Pistol-Whipped Detective Says He Didn't Shoot
Attacker because of the Headlines," CNN, August 14, 2015, http://
www.cnn.com/2015/08/13/us/alabama-birmingham-police-detective-
pistol-whipped/.

16. Heather Mac Donald, "The New Nationwide Crime Wave," *Wall
Street Journal*, May 29, 2015, http://www.wsj.com/articles/the-new-
nationwide-crime-wave-1432938425.

17. Tracey Leong, "45 Homicides in July Becomes Baltimore's Deadliest
since 1972," CBS Baltimore, July 31, 2015, http://baltimore.cbslocal.
com/2015/07/31/july-is-baltimores-3rd-most-deadliest-month-in-
history/.

18. Williams, "Race and the Gun Debate."

CHAPTER TWO: THE PARTY OF MOB VIOLENCE

1. Holbrook Mohr, David Lieb, and Philip A. Lucas, "Ferguson Grand
Jury Testimony Full of Inconsistencies," Huffington Post, November
27, 2014, http://www.huffingtonpost.com/2014/11/27/ferguson-
grand-jury-testimony_n_6232034.html.

2. Associated Press, "Fact and Fiction from Ferguson Witnesses," CBS
News, November 28, 2014, http://www.cbsnews.com/news/ferguson-
grand-jury-documents-show-inconsistencies-in-witness-testimony/.

3. "Statement by Attorney General Holder on Recent Shooting Incident
in Ferguson, Missouri," press release, Department of Justice, August
11, 2014, http://www.justice.gov/opa/pr/statement-attorney-general-
holder-recent-shooting-incident-ferguson-missouri.

4. "Attorney General Eric Holder Delivers Update on Investigations in
Ferguson, Missouri," transcript, Department of Justice, March 4,
2015, http://www.justice.gov/opa/speech/attorney-general-holder-
delivers-update-investigations-ferguson-missouri.

5. Ibid.

6. Rend Smith, "The Thin Black Line: How D.C.'s Majority Black Police
    Force Helps the City," *Washington City Paper*, May 20, 2011, http://
    www.washingtoncitypaper.com/articles/40853/how-dcs-majority-
    black-police-force-helps-the-city/.
7. Ashley Halsey III, "Report: $55 Million D.C. Tickets Went Unpaid
    Last Year," *Washington Post*, February 2, 2015, http://www.
    washingtonpost.com/local/trafficandcommuting/report-55-million-
    dc-tickets-went-unpaid-last-year/2015/02/02/ff346a9e-aa28-11e4-
    abe8-e1ef60ca26de_story.html.
8. Sari Horwitz, "Justice Department Declines to Prosecute Ferguson
    Officer in Brown Shooting," *Washington Post*, March 3, 2015, http://
    www.washingtonpost.com/world/national-security/justice-dept-
    declines-to-prosecute-ferguson-officer-in-brown-shooting
    /2015/03/04/2c0acbb2-c29d-11e4-9271-610273846239_story.html;
    and Ray Sanchez, "Ferguson's Ugly, Racist Emails Released," CNN,
    April 4, 2015, http://www.cnn.com/2015/04/03/us/ferguson-justice-
    department-report-emails//.
9. Smith, "The Thin Black Line."
10. "Percentage of Local Police Officers Who Were Racial or Ethnic
    Minorities Nearly Doubled between 1987 and 2013," press release,
    Bureau of Justice Statistics, May 14, 2015, http://www.bjs.gov/content/
    pub/press/lpd13ppppr.cfm.
11. Ben Kesling and Cameron McWhirter, "Percentage of African-
    Americans in U.S. Police Departments Remains Flat Since 2007," *Wall
    Street Journal*, May 14, 2015, http://www.wsj.com/articles/percentage-
    of-african-americans-in-u-s-police-departments-remains-flat-
    since-2007-1431628990.
12. Deborah Simmons, "Baltimore Riots over Freddie Gray Spread Al
    Sharpton's Message," *Washington Times*, April 30, 2015, http://www.
    washingtontimes.com/news/2015/apr/30/deborah-simmons-
    baltimore-riots-over-freddie-gray-/?page=all.
13. Mark Levine, "Baltimore Police: DOJ Announces Federal Probe of
    Entire Department," ABC News, May 8, 2015, http://abcnews.go.
    com/US/freddy-gray-doj-announces-federal-probe-entire-baltimore/
    story?id=30899279.
14. Peter Hermann, John Woodrow Cox, and Ashley Halsey III, "After
    Peaceful Start, Protest of Freddie Gray's Death in Baltimore Turns
    Violent," *Washington Post*, April 25, 2015, http://www.washington

post.com/local/baltimore-readies-for-saturday-protest-of-freddie-grays-death/2015/04/25/8cf990f2-e9f8-11e4-aae1-d642717d8afa_story.html.

15. Jazz Shaw, "CNN Contributor Tags Baltimore Riots as #BaltimoreRising While City Burns," *Hot Air* (blog), April 28, 2015, http://hotair.com/archives/2015/04/28/cnn-contributor-tags-baltimore-riots-as-baltimorerising-while-city-burns/.

16. Evan McMurry, "Rep. Cummings Defends Baltimore Protests: Police Relations 'Civil Rights Cause' of Generation," Mediaite, April 26, 2015, http://www.mediaite.com/tv/rep-cummings-defends-baltimore-protests-police-relations-civil-rights-cause-of-generation/.

17. Peter Hermann, "Baltimore Tries to Recover After Unrest Leads to Damage, Multiple Arrests," *Washington Post*, April 26, 2015, http://www.washingtonpost.com/local/baltimore-police-34-protesters-arrested-saturday-night-early-sunday/2015/04/26/b407c980-ec2c-11e4-8666-a1d756d0218e_story.html.

18. Andrew Desiderio, "Freddie Gray Protesters Attack, Rob Reporter Videotaping Them," Mediaite, April 26, 2015, http://www.mediaite.com/online/freddie-gray-protesters-attack-rob-reporter-videotaping-them/.

19. Emily Shapiro, "National Guard Troops Deployed After Violent Clashes in Baltimore," ABC News, April 27, 2015, http://abcnews.go.com/US/hundreds-people-clash-police-baltimore-mall/story?id=30622868.

20. Shapiro, "National Guard Troops Deployed."

21. Curtis Houck, "CNN's Marc Lamont Hill on Baltimore: 'This Is Not a Riot' but 'Uprisings' against 'Police Terrorism,'" Newsbusters, April 28, 2015, http://newsbusters.org/blogs/curtis-houck/2015/04/28/cnns-marc-lamont-hill-baltimore-not-riot-uprisings-against-police.

22. Julie Zauzmer, Hamil R. Harris, and Lynh Bui, "As Baltimore Mayor Lifts Curfew, National Guard Begins Pullout," *Washington Post*, May 3, 2015, http://www.washingtonpost.com/local/crime/mayor-lifts-curfew-in-baltimore/2015/05/03/fcbffdfc-f1a2-11e4-90bc-afe06f530791_story.html.

23. McMurry, "Rep. Cummings Defends Baltimore Protests."

24. Rich Lowry, "Baltimore, a Great Society Failure," *Politico Magazine*, April 29, 2015, http://www.politico.com/magazine/story/2015/04/baltimore-a-great-society-failure-117493.html#.VvxsOpNVikq.

25. Jordan Malter, "Baltimore's Economy in Black and White," CNNMoney, April 29, 2015, http://money.cnn.com/2015/04/29/news/economy/baltimore-economy/index.html.

26. Peter Hermann, "After Rioters Burned Baltimore, Killings Pile Up Largely under the Radar," *Washington Post*, May 17, 2015, http://www.washingtonpost.com/local/crime/violence-has-become-part-of-life-in-baltimore/2015/05/17/4909264a-f714-11e4-a13c-193b1241d51a_story.html.

27. Malter, "Baltimore's Economy."

28. "Remarks by President Obama and Prime Minister Abe of Japan in Joint Press Conference," transcript, WhiteHouse.gov, April 28, 2015, https://www.whitehouse.gov/the-press-office/2015/04/28/remarks-president-obama-and-prime-minister-abe-japan-joint-press-confere.

29. Elizabeth Harrington, "Baltimore Received $1.8 Billion from Obama's Stimulus Law," Washington Free Beacon, May 4, 2015, http://freebeacon.com/issues/baltimore-received-1-8-billion-from-obamas-stimulus-law/.

30. Hermann, "After Rioters Burned Baltimore."

31. Ibid.

32. Crystal Wright, "Zimmerman, the Media and Black Leaders Pimping of Blacks," *Conservative Black Chick* (blog), July 21, 2013, http://conservativeblackchick.com/blog/2013/07/21/zimmerman-the-media-and-black-leaders-pimping-of-blacks/.

33. Ibid.

34. Erin McClam, "Protests Erupt After St. Louis Officers Fatally Shoot Mansur Ball-Bey," NBC News, August 20, 2015, http://www.nbcnews.com/news/us-news/protests-erupt-after-st-louis-police-fatally-shoot-mansur-ball-n412921.

35. Anthony Christopher, "Stealing from Wal-Mart Is Not a Crime, UW Relations Director Declares," MRCTV, August 20, 2015, http://www.mrctv.org/blog/wisc-director-community-relations-suggests-shoplifting-not-crime#.g1a2zp:Fe3e.

36. John Gibson, "Black Privilege: 'Cops Shouldn't Use Stealing as an Excuse to Arrest Us,'" Fox News Radio, August 25, 2015, http://radio.foxnews.com/2015/08/25/black-privilege-cops-shouldnt-use-stealing-as-an-excuse-to-arrest-us/.

37. Kyle Becker, "Sheriff Clarke Charges President Obama with Starting 'War on Police' after Texas Cop's 'Execution,'" Independent Journal,

August 2015, http://www.ijreview.com/2015/08/407302-sheriff-clarke-charges-president-obama-with-starting-war-on-police-after-texas-cops-execution/?utm_source=Facebook&utm_medium=Owned&utm_term=conservativedaily&utm_campaign=Crime.

38. Bob Price and Lana Shadwick, "Texas Deputy Executed Days After Black Radical Group Calls for Killing Cops," Breitbart, August 28, 2015, http://www.breitbart.com/texas/2015/08/28/texas-deputy-executed-days-after-black-radical-group-calls-for-killing-cops/.

39. Emily Shapiro, "Suspect Allegedly Unloaded His Entire Pistol in Texas Deputy," *Good Morning America*, Yahoo! News, August 31, 2015, https://gma.yahoo.com/suspect-allegedly-unloaded-entire-pistol-texas-deputy-161827999—abc-news-topstories.html#.

40. Shadwick, "Black Activists Call for Lynching and Hanging of White People and Cops," Breitbart, August 28, 2015, http://www.breitbart.com/texas/2015/08/28/black-activists-called-for-lynching-and-hanging-of-white-people-and-cops/.

41. "FukYoFlag," last updated August 2015, http://fukyoflag.blogspot.com/.

42. Thomas Sowell, "'Affirmative Action': A Worldwide Disaster," *Commentary*, December 1, 1989, https://www.commentarymagazine.com/article/affirmative-action-a-worldwide-disaster/; and Kasturi DasGupta, review of *Affirmative Action around the World: An Empirical Study*, by Thomas Sowell, H-Peace, July 2005, https://networks.h-net.org/node/19206/reviews/19337/dasgupta-sowell-affirmative-action-around-world-empirical-study.

43. Jason Silverstein, "Dylann Roof Was Obsessed with Trayvon Martin, Wanted to Save the 'White Race': Friend," *New York Daily News*, June 20, 2015, http://www.nydailynews.com/news/national/dylann-roof-obsessed-trayvon-martin-white-race-article-1.2263647; and Shapiro, "Charleston Shooting: Closer Look at Alleged Gunman Dylann Roof," *Good Morning America*, Yahoo! News, June 18, 2015, https://gma.yahoo.com/charleston-shooting-closer-look-alleged-gunman-dylann-roof-203816813—abc-news-topstories.html.

44. Pierre Thomas, Jack Cloherty, Jack Date, and Mike Levine, "After Shooting, Alleged Gunman Details Grievances in 'Suicide Notes,'" ABC News, August 26, 2015, http://abcnews.go.com/US/shooting-alleged-gunman-details-grievances-suicide-notes/story?id=33336339.

45. Ibid.

CHAPTER THREE: THE PARTY OF HOPELESS SLUMS

1. Nicholas Lenmann, "Four Generations in the Projects," *New York Times Magazine*, January 13, 1991, http://www.nytimes.com/1991/01/13/magazine/four-generations-in-the-projects.html?page wanted=all.

2. Ibid.

3. National Low Income Housing Coalition, "Who Lives in Federally Subsidized Housing?," *Housing Spotlight* 2, no. 2 (November 2012), http://nlihc.org/sites/default/files/HousingSpotlight2-2.pdf.

4. Gene Falk, *Temporary Assistance for Needy Families (TANF): Size and Characteristics of the Case Assistance Caseload* (Washington, DC: Congressional Research Service, August 5, 2014), http://fas.org/sgp/crs/misc/R43187.pdf.

5. Rich Morin, "The Politics and Demographics of Food Stamp Recipients," Pew Research Center, July 12, 2013, http://www.pewresearch.org/fact-tank/2013/07/12/the-politics-and-demographics-of-food-stamp-recipients/.

6. National Low Income Housing Coalition, "Who Lives in Federally Subsidized Housing?," 2.

7. Brooks Jackson, "Blacks and the Democratic Party," FactCheck.org, April 18, 2008, http://www.factcheck.org/2008/04/blacks-and-the-democratic-party/.

8. "Election Polls: Presidential Vote by Groups," Gallup, http://www.gallup.com/poll/139880/election-polls-presidential-vote-groups.aspx.

9. "Subsidized Housing, A Cross-City Comparison," in *State of New York City's Housing and Neighborhoods, 2011* (New York: NYU Furman Center for Real Estate and Urban Policy, May 2012), 42, http://furmancenter.org/files/sotc/SOC_2011.pdf.

10. "National and State Housing Data Fact Sheets," Center on Budget and Policy Priorities, updated May 6, 2015, http://www.cbpp.org/cms/index.cfm?fa=view&id=3586.

11. National Low Income Housing Coalition, "Who Lives in Federally Subsidized Housing?"

12. Will Fischer, "Research Shows Housing Vouchers Reduce Hardship and Provide Platform for Long-Term Gains among Children," Center for Budget and Policy Priorities, March 10, 2014, http://www.cbpp.org/cms/index.cfm?fa=view&id=4098.

13. Ibid.
14. Danny Vinik, "The Alarming Retirement Crisis Facing Minorities in America," *New Republic*, February 18, 2015, http://www. newrepublic.com/article/121084/urban-institute-study-minorities- have-built-less-wealth-whites.
15. Ibid.
16. Marion Barry, "A Needed Conversation on Welfare in D.C.," *Washington Post*, November 19, 2010, http://www.washingtonpost. com/wp-dyn/content/article/2010/11/19/AR2010111907303.html.
17. Ian Shapira, "Longtime D.C. Welfare Residents Prepare for Life off the Rolls," *Washington Post*, December 20, 2010, http://www. washingtonpost.com/wp-dyn/content/article/2010/12/20/ AR2010122005385.html.
18. "Study: Welfare Recipients in D.C., Md. Make More Than Twice Minimum Wage," CBSDC, August 22, 2013, http://washington. cbslocal.com/2013/08/22/study-welfare-recipients-in-md-dc-make- more-than-twice-minimum-wage/.
19. "HUD's Public Housing Program," U.S. Department of Housing and Urban Development, accessed March 6, 2015, http://portal.hud.gov/ hudportal/HUD?src=/topics/rental_assistance/phprog.

CHAPTER FOUR: THE PARTY OF ILLEGAL IMMIGRATION

1.   *Criminal Alien Statistics: Information on Incarcerations, Arrests, and Costs* (Washington, DC: Government Accountability Office, March 2011), http://www.gao.gov/products/GAO-11-187.
2.   Jonathan Capehart, "Donald Trump's 'Mexican Rapists' Rhetoric Will Keep the Republican Party Out of the White House," *PostPartisan* (blog), *Washington Post*, June 17, 2015, http://www.washingtonpost. com/blogs/post-partisan/wp/2015/06/17/trumps-mexican-rapists-will- keep-the-republican-party-out-of-the-white-house/.
3.   Katie Pavlich, "Exclusive: Illegal Border Crossings Double, Border Becomes Less Secure as Beltway Gets Close to Deal on Immigration Reform," Townhall.com, April 1, 2013, http://townhall.com/tipsheet/ katiepavlich/2013/04/01/exclusive-illegal-border-crossings-double-as- beltway-gets-close-to-deal-on-immigration-reform-n1554148.

4. "The U.S. Department of Homeland Security's Response to Chairman
    Grassley and Senator Flake's February 25, 2015 Letter," May 28,
    2015, available on Senator Grassley's website, http://www.grassley.
    senate.gov/sites/default/files/judiciary/upload/2015-05-28%20
    ICE%20to%20CEG%20and%20Flake%20%28Altimirano%29.pdf.

5. "ICE Arrests Ecuadorian National Wanted for Raping a Child in
    Baltimore," press release, U.S. Immigration and Customs Enforcement,
    May 16, 2013, http://www.ice.gov/news/releases/ice-arrests-
    ecuadorian-national-wanted-raping-child-baltimore.

6. "The U.S. Department of Homeland Security's Response to Chairman
    Grassley and Senator Flake's February 25, 2015 Letter."

7. "ICE Arrests Ecuadorian National Wanted for Raping a Child in
    Baltimore"; and Peter B. Gemma, "Illegal Alien Crime and Violence
    by the Numbers: We're All Victims," Constitution Party, accessed
    August 2015, http://cpwp.swehes.com/illegal-alien-crime-and-
    violence-by-the-numbers-were-all-victims/#_ftnref1.

8. Chuck Ross, "Father of Black Teenager Murdered by Illegal Alien Asks
    'Do Black Lives Really Matter?,'" Daily Caller, February 25, 2015,
    http://dailycaller.com/2015/02/25/father-of-black-teenager-murdered-
    by-illegal-alien-asks-do-black-lives-really-matter/.

9. Ian Hanchett, "Obama: 'We've Expanded My Authority' under
    Prosecutorial Discretion," Breitbart, February 25, 2015, http://www.
    breitbart.com/video/2015/02/25/obama-weve-expanded-my-
    authority-under-prosecutorial-discretion/.

10. Devin Dwyer, "President Obama Offers Legal Status to Millions of
    Undocumented Immigrants," ABC News, November 20, 2014, http://
    abcnews.go.com/Politics/president-obama-offer-legal-status-millions-
    undocumented-immigrants/story?id=27063573.

11. Ibid.

12. See the March 2, 2011, ICE memorandum "Civil Immigration
    Enforcement: Priorities for the Apprehension, Detention, and Removal
    of Aliens," available online at http://www.ice.gov/doclib/news/releas
    es/2011/110302washingtondc.pdf.

13. Ibid.

14. "Deferred Action for Childhood Arrivals," U.S. Department of
    Homeland Security, updated July 17, 2015, http://www.dhs.gov/
    deferred-action-childhood-arrivals.

15. Jarrad Saffren, "Unaccompanied Migrant Kids Flocking over Border," *USA Today*, June 12, 2014, http://www.usatoday.com/story/news/nation/2014/06/12/johnson-unaccompanied-minors-immigrants/10393001/.

16. The text of HR 7311, the William Wilberforce Trafficking Victims Protection Reauthorization Act of 2008, is available online at the U.S. Department of State website, http://www.state.gov/j/tip/laws/113178.htm.

17. Todd Starnes, "Medical Staff Warned: Keep Your Mouths Shut about Illegal Immigrants or Face Arrest," FoxNews.com, July 2, 2014, http://www.foxnews.com/opinion/2014/07/02/medical-staff-warned-keep-quiet-about-illegal-immigrants-or-face-arrest.html.

18. Stephen Dinan, "Immigration Debate May Have Increased Illegal Crossings," *Washington Times*, March 1, 2015, http://www.washingtontimes.com/news/2015/mar/1/border-jumpers-enticed-by-legalization-debate-in-u/.

19. *Central America: Information on Migration of Unaccompanied Children from El Salvador, Guatemala, and Honduras* (Washington, DC: Government Accountability Office, 2015), http://www.gao.gov/assets/670/668749.pdf.

20. "Hillary Clinton: I Will Fight for Comprehensive Immigration Reform," HillaryClinton.com, May 6, 2015, https://www.hillaryclinton.com/feed/comprehensive-immigration-reform-roundtable/.

21. Editorial Board, "Donald Trump's Immigration Plan Would Wreak Havoc on U.S. Society," *Washington Post*, August 17, 2015, https://www.washingtonpost.com/opinions/donald-trumps-immigration-plan-would-wreck-havoc-on-us-society/2015/08/17/19703368-451d-11e5-8ab4-c73967a143d3_story.html.

22. Rakesh Kochhar, C. Soledad Espinoza, and Rebecca Hinze-Pifer, "After the Great Recession: Foreign Born Gain Jobs; Native Born Lose Jobs," Pew Research Center Hispanic Trends, October 29, 2010, http://www.pewhispanic.org/2010/10/29/after-the-great-recession-brforeign-born-gain-jobs-native-born-lose-jobs/.

23. George Borjas, Jeffrey Grogger, and Gordon H. Hanson, "Immigration and the Economic Status of African-American Men," January 2009, p. 1, http://gps.ucsd.edu/_files/faculty/hanson/hanson_publication_immigration_men.pdf.

24. Bruce Bartlett, "Donald Trump Doesn't Need Latino Voters to Win," *Washington Post*, September 4, 2015, https://www.washingtonpost.com/opinions/donald-trump-doesnt-need-latino-voters-to-win-the-nomination/2015/09/04/9fd2e40c-524f-11e5-933e-7d06c647a395_story.html.

25. Rudolph Bell, "Trump Dodges Party Pledge Issue during Greenville Stop," Greenville Online, August 28, 2015, http://www.greenvilleonline.com/story/news/politics/2015/08/28/trump-dodges-party-pledge-issue-greenville-stop/71275652/.

26. Tony Lee, "Slate's Jamelle Bouie: 'Not a Bad Play' for Trump to Court Black Voters with Pro-U.S. Worker Immigration Plan," Breitbart, August 28, 2015, http://www.breitbart.com/big-government/2015/08/28/slates-jamelle-bouie-not-a-bad-play-for-trump-to-court-black-voters-with-pro-u-s-worker-immigration-plan/.

27. "Immigration Reform That Will Make America Great Again," DonaldJTrump.com, accessed August 2015, https://www.donaldjtrump.com/positions/immigration-reform.

28. Crystal Wright, "The Problem with Jeb Bush," *Telegraph* (UK), August 25, 2015, http://www.telegraph.co.uk/news/worldnews/us-politics/11822660/The-Problem-with-Jeb-Bush.html.

29. Evan Perez and Corey Dade, "An Immigration Raid Aids Blacks—for a Time," *Wall Street Journal*, January 17, 2007, http://www.wsj.com/article_email/SB116898113191477989-lMyQjAxMDE3Nj E4NzkxODcxWj.html.

30. *Making Immigration Work for American Minorities: Hearing before the Subcommittee on Immigration Policy and Enforcement of the Committee on the Judiciary*, 112th Cong. (2011).

31. David Jackson and Alan Gomez, "Obama Declares 'Lawful Action' to Protect 5M Immigrants," *USA Today*, November 20, 2014, http://www.usatoday.com/story/news/nation/2014/11/20/obama-immigration-josh-earnest/19316835/.

32. Tony Lee, "Civil Rights Commissioner: Timing of Obama's Amnesty 'Could Not Be Worse' for Black Workers," Breitbart, August 7, 2015, http://www.breitbart.com/big-government/2014/08/07/civil-rights-commissioner-timing-of-obama-s-amnesty-could-not-be-worse-for-black-workers/.

33. "Foreign-Born Workers—Labor Force Characteristics, 2014," press release, Bureau of Labor Statistics, May 21, 2015, http://www.bls.gov/news.release/pdf/forbrn.pdf.

34. Ibid.

35. Stephanie Czekalinski, "Deported Illegal Immigrants Return Repeatedly," *Columbus (OH) Dispatch*, August 1, 2011, http://www.dispatch.com/content/stories/local/2010/12/27/deported-illegal-immigrants-return-repeatedly.html.

36. Hunter Walker, "Donald Trump Just Released an Epic Statement Raging against Mexican Immigrants and 'Disease,'" Business Insider, July 6, 2015, http://www.businessinsider.com/donald-trumps-epic-statement-on-mexico-2015-7.

37. Capehart, "Donald Trump's 'Mexican Rapists' Rhetoric."

38. Brian Stelter, "Univision Dumps Trump, Cancels Miss USA over His Comments about Mexicans," CNNMoney, June 25, 2015, http://money.cnn.com/2015/06/25/media/univision-donald-trump-mexicans/index.html.

39. Denise Hassanzade Ajiri, "Is Donald Trump Backtracking on His Criticism of Mexicans?," *Christian Science Monitor*, June 27, 2015, http://www.csmonitor.com/USA/USA-Update/2015/0627/Is-Donald-Trump-backtracking-on-his-criticism-of-Mexicans.

40. Michele Corriston, "Whoopi Goldberg Defends Kelly Osbourne's Comment on Latinos: 'If You've Ever Met a Racist, It's Pretty Clear,'" *People*, August 5, 2015, http://www.people.com/article/whoopi-goldberg-defends-kelly-osbourne-racist-comments-donald-trump?xid=socialflow_twitter_peoplemag.

41. David A. Fahrenthold, Jenna Johnson, and Max Ehrenfreund, "Trump Driving Migrant Debate among GOP Field," *Washington Post*, August 17, 2015, http://www.washingtonpost.com/politics/with-trumps-rise-hard-line-immigration-ideas-take-hold-in-gop/2015/08/17/85dbbf3e-4506-11e5-846d-02792f854297_story.html?hpid=z1.

42. Joshua Partlow, "For Mexicans, Trump's Bid Is Getting Scarier," *Washington Post*, August 18, 2015, https://www.washingtonpost.com/world/the_americas/for-mexicans-the-donald-trump-candidacy-is-getting-scarier/2015/08/18/b603af1b-b06f-4cd9-a3af-82401e85f363_story.html.

CHAPTER FIVE: THE PARTY OF SANCTUARY CITIES

1. "Paraclete," "Santuary Cities, USA," FromtheTrenchesWorldReport. com, August 1, 2014, http://www.fromthetrenchesworldreport.com/ sanctuary-cities-usa/98759.
2. San Francisco Administrative Code, Chapter 15: Immigration Status, available online at http://sfgsa.org/index.aspx?page=1069.
3. Steve Almasy, Pamela Brown, and Augie Martin, "Suspect in Killing of San Francisco Woman Had Been Deported Five Times," CNN, July 4, 2015, http://www.cnn.com/2015/07/03/us/san-francisco-killing-suspect-immigrant-deported/index.html.
4. Chuck Ross, "Father of Black Teenager Murdered by Illegal Alien Asks 'Do Black Lives Really Matter?,'" Daily Caller, February 25, 2015, http://dailycaller.com/2015/02/25/father-of-black-teenager-murdered-by-illegal-alien-asks-do-black-lives-really-matter/.
5. Ibid.
6. Marc A. Thiessen, "Obama's Silence on Kathryn Steinle Killing Is Deafening," *Washington Post*, July 13, 2015, https://www. washingtonpost.com/opinions/obamas-silence-on-kathryn-steinle-killing-is-deafening/2015/07/13/06f5730e-2959-11e5-a5ea-cf74396e59ec_story.html.
7. "Remarks by the President on Trayvon Martin," transcript, WhiteHouse.gov, July 19, 2013, https://www.whitehouse.gov/the-press-office/2013/07/19/remarks-president-trayvon-martin.
8. "Statement by the President," transcript, WhiteHouse.gov, August 14, 2014, https://www.whitehouse.gov/the-press-office/2014/08/14/statement-president.
9. Thiessen, "Obama's Silence on Kathryn Steinle Killing Is Deafening."
10. "Statement by the President," transcript, WhiteHouse.gov, August 14, 2014, https://www.whitehouse.gov/the-press-office/2015/04/28/remarks-president-obama-and-prime-minister-abe-japan-joint-press-confere.
11. Geneva Sands and Ali Weinberg, "Kate Steinle's Father Testifies before Congress about His Daughter's Death, Calls for Immigration Reform," ABC News, July 21, 2015, http://abcnews.go.com/Politics/kate-steinles-father-testifies-congress-daughters-death/story?id=32596569.
12. "Chairman Becerra: Don't Take the Donald Trump Bait to Punish Local Communities," Dems.gov, July 23, 2015, http://www.dems.gov/

chairman-becerra-dont-take-donald-trump-bait-punish-local-communities/.

13. Colby Bermel, "House Passes Anti–Sanctuary Cities Bill," *National Journal*, July 23, 2015, http://www.nationaljournal.com/congress/house-passes-anti-sanctuary-cities-bill-20150723.

14. Bryan Griffith and Marguerite Telford, "Map: Sanctuary Cities, Counties and States," Center for Immigration Studies, July 2015, http://cis.org/Sanctuary-Cities-Map.

15. "Immigration Subcommittee to Examine Dangerous Sanctuary City Policies," press release, U.S. House of Representatives Judiciary Committee, July 16, 2015, http://judiciary.house.gov/index.cfm/press-releases?id=7D028CF2-4147-4C34-B2D3-67E0630E115D.

16. Jerry Markon, "DHS Deportation Program Meets with Resistance," *Washington Post*, August 3, 2015, http://www.washingtonpost.com/politics/dhs-finds-resistance-to-new-program-to-deport-illegal-immigrants/2015/08/03/4af5985c-36d0-11e5-9739-170df8af8eb9_story.html.

17. Michael Matza, "Phila. Acts to Halt Immigrant Deportation over Minor Crimes," Philly.com, April 18, 2014, http://articles.philly.com/2014-04-18/news/49217469_1_detainers-deportation-staff-attorney.

18. Kevin R. Johnson, "In Final Months, Time to Work on Jobs Legacy," Philly.com, July 24, 2015, http://www.philly.com/philly/opinion/20150724_In_final_months__time_to_work_on_jobs_legacy.html#QL0uWqWmUTr8JaWg.99.

19. "Philadelphia's Mayor Michael Nutter on African-American Males," YouTube video, from press conference on September 15, 2011, posted by "FloodTheDrummer," September 16, 2011, https://www.youtube.com/watch?v=CZ0wPQ5lC3E.

20. Markon, "DHS Deportation Program Meets with Resistance."

21. Ed Lazere, "Left Behind: DC's Economy Is Failing Many Residents," East of the River DC News, accessed August 2015, http://www.capitalcommunitynews.com/content/left-behind-dc%E2%80%99s-economy-failing-many-residents-0#sthash.eTVzF2PV.dpuf.

22. Ovetta Wiggins, "Dozens Protest Hogan's Decision to Cooperate with Feds over Detainees," *Washington Post*, August 13, 2015, http://www.washingtonpost.com/local/md-politics/dozens-protest-hogans-

decision-to-cooperate-with-feds-over-detainees/2015/08/13/fd609c20-
41cb-11e5-8ab4-c73967a143d3_story.html.

23. Michael Pearson, "What's a 'Sanctuary City,' and Why Should You
Care?," CNN, July 8, 2015, http://www.cnn.com/2015/07/06/us/san-
francisco-killing-sanctuary-cities/.

24. Cinnamon Stillwell, "San Francisco: Sanctuary City Gone Awry,"
SFGate.com, July 16, 2008, http://www.sfgate.com/politics/article/
San-Francisco-Sanctuary-City-Gone-Awry-2481280.php.

25. Nick Sanchez, "Sanctuary Cities: 200 Places Shield Immigrants in the
US," Newsmax, July 9, 2015, http://www.newsmax.com/TheWire/
sanctuary-cities-shield-immigrants/2015/07/09/id/654155
/#ixzz3hg7v61FO.

26. "Sanctuary Ordinance," City and County of San Francisco, accessed
August 2015, http://sfgsa.org/index.aspx?page=1067.

27. Stillwell, "San Francisco."

28. David Kelly and Maria L. LaGanga, "'Dumping' May Land S.F. in
Court," *Los Angeles Times*, July 4, 2008, http://articles.latimes.
com/2008/jul/04/local/me-immig4.

29. Stillwell, "San Francisco."

30. Ibid.

31. Vivian Ho, "Immigration Debate: Gangster Gets 10 Years in S.F.
Killings," SFGate.com, July 10, 2015, http://www.sfgate.com/crime/
article/Gangster-gets-10-years-in-S-F-killings-that-6377971.php.

32. "U.S. Citizenship," U.S. Citizenship and Immigration Services, last
updated January 17, 2013, http://www.uscis.gov/us-citizenship.

33. Nicole Duran, "DHS Says It Cannot Force Sanctuary City
Compliance," *Washington Examiner*, July 14, 2015, http://www.
washingtonexaminer.com/dhs-says-it-cannot-force-sanctuary-city-
compliance/article/2568280.

34. Byron York, "When Clinton, Obama and Biden Debated Sanctuary
Cities," *Washington Examiner*, July 9, 2015, http://www.
washingtonexaminer.com/when-clinton-obama-and-biden-debated-
sanctuary-cities/article/2567899.

35. "Hearing: Oversight of the United States Department of Homeland
Security," transcript, U.S. House of Representatives Judiciary
Committee, July 14, 2015, http://www.judiciary.house.gov/index.cfm/
hearings?Id=A67DCDA2-A9BD-47D7-A238-977A9920C76B&
Statement_id=5E21674B-B809-41A3-8D89-356DC45EECD3.

36. Ibid.

37. Matthew Boyle, "Mother Whose Son Murdered by DREAMer Illegal Alien Breaks Down in Rally Speech," Breitbart, August 13, 2013, http://www.breitbart.com/big-government/2013/08/13/mother-whose-son-murdered-body-burned-by-dreamer-illegal-alien-emotionally-breaks-down-in-rally-speech/.

38. Julia Hahn and Katie McHugh, "Politicians: 'Your Silence Speaks Volumes,'" Breitbart, July 21, 2015, http://www.breitbart.com/big-government/2015/07/21/mother-of-son-murdered-by-illegal-alien-slams-sanctuary-cities-politicians-your-silence-speaks-volumes/.

39. Ibid.

40. "State Criminal Alien Assistance Program (SCAAP)," Bureau of Justice Assistance, accessed August 2015, https://www.bja.gov/ProgramDetails.aspx?Program_ID=86#horizontalTab6.

41. Jessica Vaughan and Russ Doubleday, "Subsidizing Sanctuaries: The State Criminal Alien Assistance Program," Center for Immigration Studies, November 2010, http://www.cis.org/subsidizing-sanctuaries.

42. *Criminal Alien Statistics: Information on Incarcerations, Arrests, and Costs* (Washington, DC: Government Accountability Office, March 24, 2011), http://www.gao.gov/products/GAO-11-187.

43. Tom Tancredo, "Illegal Alien Crime Accounts for Over 30% of Murders in Many States," Breitbart, August 8, 2015, http://www.breitbart.com/big-journalism/2015/08/08/illegal-alien-crime-accounts-for-over-30-of-murders-in-some-states/.

44. Ibid.

CHAPTER SIX: THE PARTY OF ABORTION PROFITEERS

1. "Abortion," Planned Parenthood, accessed August 2015, http://plannedparenthood.org/learn/abortion/#sthash.Wra2Kz5y.dpuf.

2. "Bill Clinton," *Abortion Info* (blog), accessed August 2015, http://abortion.info/politics/presidents-and-abortion/bill-clinton/.

3. *2013–14 Annual Report: Our Health. Our Decisions. Our Moment* (Planned Parenthood, 2014), http://plannedparenthood.org/files/6714/1996/2641/2013-2014_Annual_Report_FINAL_WEB_VERSION.pdf.

4. "Technician Details Harvesting Fetal Parts for Planned Parenthood in Latest Video," FoxNews.com, July 28, 2015, http://www.foxnews.

com/politics/2015/07/28/new-planned-parenthood-video-focuses-on-payment-for-fetal-tissue/.

5. Jennifer Haberkorn, "Human Tissue Firm Cuts Ties with Planned Parenthood," *Politico*, August 14, 2015, http://www.politico.com/story/2015/08/planned-parenthood-fetal-tissue-company-cuts-ties-videos-121371.

6. "Human Capital—Episode 1: Planned Parenthood's Black Market in Baby Parts," YouTube video, uploaded by "The Center for Medical Progress," July 28, 2015, https://www.youtube.com/watch?v=Xw2xi9mhmuo.

7. "Bill Clinton," *Abortion Info*.

8. "Planned Parenthood: Cecile Richards' Official Video Response," YouTube video, uploaded by "Planned Parenthood," July 16, 2015, https://www.youtube.com/watch?v=dZUjU4e4fUI.

9. "The Power of Partnership," StemExpress, last updated 2015, http://stemexpress.com/partnerships/.

10. Caleb Howe, "Center for Medical Progress Releases Sixth Planned Parenthood Video," Truth Revolt, August 12, 2015, http://www.truthrevolt.org/news/center-medical-progress-releases-sixth-planned-parenthood-video.

11. "Planned Parenthood Baby Parts Buyer StemExpress Wants 'Another 50 Livers/Week,'" YouTube video, uploaded by "The Center for Medical Progress," August 25, 2015, https://www.youtube.com/watch?v=cz1gRNPgMvE.

12. John McCormack, "Planned Parenthood Baby Parts Buyer Laughs about Shipping Severed Heads," *Weekly Standard*, August 25, 2015, http://www.weeklystandard.com/blogs/new-planned-parenthood-video-baby-parts-buyer-jokes-about-shipping-severed-heads_1018420.html.

13. "Human Capital—Episode 3: Planned Parenthood's Custom Abortions for Superior Product," YouTube video, uploaded by "The Center for Medical Progress," August 19, 2015, https://www.youtube.com/watch?v=FzMAycMMXp8.

14. "Planned Parenthood's Harvest," Review and Outlook, *Wall Street Journal*, July 29, 2015, http://www.wsj.com/articles/planned-parenthoods-harvest-1438211973.

15. Michael J. New, "Why the Senate Vote on Defunding Planned Parenthood Provides Cause for Optimism," *The Corner* (blog),

National Review Online, August 4, 2015, http://www.nationalreview. com/corner/422018/why-senate-vote-defunding-planned-parenthood-provides-cause-optimism-michael-j-new.

16. Andrea Cuttler, "Jenny Slate on *Obvious Child,* Which Is like *Sleepless in Seattle,* but with Abortion," *Vanity Fair,* June 6, 2014, http://www. vanityfair.com/hollywood/2014/06/jenny-slate-obvious-child-interview; and *2013–14 Annual Report.*

17. "iTunes Preview: *Obvious Child* (2014)," iTunes, accessed August 2015, https://itunes.apple.com/us/movie/obvious-child-2014/ id885581815?ign-mpt=uo%3D4.

18. Asawin Suebsaeng, "Are the Director and Star of 'Obvious Child' Concerned about Anti-abortion Backlash?," *Mother Jones,* June 12, 2014, http://www.motherjones.com/mixed-media/2014/06/obvious-child-interview-jenny-slate-gillian-robespierre-abortion-conservatives.

19. Fred Lucas, "White House Responds to Latest Graphic Planned Parenthood Video: 'Tactic of Extremists on the Right,'" TheBlaze, July 30, 2015, http://www.theblaze.com/stories/2015/07/30/white-house-responds-to-latest-graphic-planned-parenthood-video-tactic-of-extremists-on-the-right/.

20. Josiah Peterson, "Elizabeth Warren Is Totally Wrong about Planned Parenthood," Federalist, August 26, 2015, http://thefederalist. com/2015/08/26/elizabeth-warren-is-totally-wrong-about-planned-parenthood/.

21. Kirsten Andersen, "Hillary Clinton Tells UN: No Human Progress without Abortion-on-Demand," LifeSiteNews.com, March 13, 2014, https://www.lifesitenews.com/news/hillary-clinton-tells-un-no-human-progress-without-abortion-on-demand.

22. Ibid.

23. Joel Gehrke, "International Planned Parenthood Got $26 Million in U.S. Aid in Clinton's Last Two Years at State," *National Review,* July 30, 2015, http://www.nationalreview.com/article/421823/usaid-sent-26m-international-planned-parenthood-clintons-last-two-years-state-joel.

24. See Hillary Clinton's tweet at https://twitter.com/UriBlago/status /627107144920203264.

25. Jeanne Mancini, "The Racist Views of Planned Parenthood's Founder," Daily Signal, August 13, 2015, http://dailysignal. com/?p=196519.

26. Ibid.

27. Steven Ertelt, "Black Pastors Demand Smithsonian Remove Statue of Planned Parenthood Founder Margaret Sanger," LifeNews.com, August 27, 2015, http://www.lifenews.com/2015/08/27/black-pastors-demand-smithsonian-remove-statue-of-planned-parenthood-founder-margaret-sanger/.

28. Dan Joseph, "Nearly 50 Million Abortions Have Been Performed in U.S. Since Roe v. Wade Decision Legalized Abortion," CNS News, January 25, 2011, http://cnsnews.com/news/article/nearly-50-million-abortions-have-been-performed-us-roe-v-wade-decision-legalized.

29. "Remarks at Planned Parenthood Federation of America Awards Gala," transcript of remarks by Hillary Rodham Clinton, March 27, 2009, available online at http://www.state.gov/secretary/2009 2013clinton/rm/2009a/03/120968.htm.

30. Bradford Thomas, "Planned Parenthood Celebrates Black History Month," Truth Revolt, February 3, 2015, http://www.truthrevolt.org/news/planned-parenthood-celebrates-black-history-while-aborting-millions-black-babies.

31. Miriam Berg, "Announcing Planned Parenthood's 99 Dream Keepers," Planned Parenthood Action Fund, February 2, 2015, http://plannedparenthoodaction.org/elections-politics/blog/announcing-planned-parenthoods-99-dream-keepers/#sthash.zq8ezp8t.dpuf.

32. Michael W. Chapman, "NYC: More Babies Killed by Abortion Than Born," CNS News, February 20, 2014, http://www.cnsnews.com/news/article/michael-w-chapman/nyc-more-black-babies-killed-abortion-born.

33. Planned Parenthood, "About Us," accessed March 5, 2015, http://plannedparenthoodaction.org/about-us/.

34. Ertelt, "79% of Planned Parenthood Abortion Clinics Target Blacks, Hispanics," LifeNews.com, October 16, 2012, http://www.lifenews.com/2012/10/16/79-of-planned-parenthood-abortion-clinics-target-blacks-hispanics/.

35. See the Facebook chat at https://www.facebook.com/hillaryclinton/posts/946945482028648.

36. Dan Merica, "On Women's Health, Clinton Compares Republicans to 'Terrorist Groups,'" CNN, August 28, 2015, http://www.cnn.com/2015/08/27/politics/hillary-clinton-republicans-terrorist-groups/?utm_; and Mark Steyn, "Hillary Is Deleting Herself,"

SteynOnline, August 28, 2015, http://www.steynonline.com/7138/
hillary-is-deleting-herself.

37. Annie Karni and Anna Palmer, "Clinton's Planned Parenthood Ties
Run Deep," *Politico*, July 30, 2015, http://www.politico.com/
story/2015/07/hillary-clinton-planned-parenthood-ties-120794.html.

38. Mark Hemingway, "*Politico* & *NYT* Fail to Mention Report
Exonerating Planned Parenthood Produced by Democratic Opposition
Research Firm," *Weekly Standard*, August 27, 2015, http://www.
weeklystandard.com/blogs/politico-fails-mention-report-exonerating-
planned-parenthood-produced-democratic-opposition-research-
firm_1020250.html.

CHAPTER SEVEN: THE PARTY OF BABY BUTCHERS

1. *Investigation of the Women's Medical Society in Philadelphia: Report
of the Grand Jury* (Darby, PA: Diane Publishing, 2011), 23, available
online at http://www.phila.gov/districtattorney/PDFs/GrandJury
WomensMedical.pdf.

2. Ironically, it was the election of "pro-choice" Republican Tom Ridge
to replace pro-life Democrat Bob Casey as Pennsylvania governor that
ended abortion clinic inspections in Pennsylvania. But, as we have
already seen, the Democrat Party has moved even further into the
pro-abortion camp since the career of the elder Casey, with his
supposedly pro-life son voting not to defund Planned Parenthood in
the wake of the undercover videos. Erin Fuchs, "Horrifying Illegal
Abortion Clinic Wasn't Inspected for 17 Years due to Pro-choice
Policy," Business Insider, April 10, 2013, http://www.businessinsider.
com/kermit-gosnell-clinic-not-inspected-2013-4.

3. "Abortion Doctor Kermit Gosnell Convicted of First-Degree Murder,"
NBC News, May 13, 2013, http://usnews.nbcnews.com/_
news/2013/05/13/18232657-abortion-doctor-kermit-gosnell-
convicted-of-first-degree-murder?lite; and Maryclaire Dale, "Kermit
Gosnell to Get Life Sentence after First-Degree Murder Conviction,"
Associated Press, updated July 14, 2013, available on the Huffington
Post, http://www.huffingtonpost.com/2013/05/14/kermit-gosnell-life-
sentence_n_3275000.html.

4. *Investigation of the Women's Medical Society in Philadelphia.*

5.   David Knowles, "Former Worker Testifies That Dr. Kermit Gosnell Snipped the Spines of Moving Babies Following Abortions at Philadelphia Clinic," *New York Daily News*, April 11, 2013, http://www.nydailynews.com/news/crime/abortion-doc-snipped-moving-babies-spines-witness-article-1.1314193.

6.   "Clinton Vetoes Partial-Birth Abortion Bill," CNN, April 10, 1996, http://www.cnn.com/ALLPOLITICS/1996/news/9604/10/abortion/index.shtml.

7.   "Bill Clinton," *Abortion Info* (blog), accessed August 2015, http://abortion.info/politics/presidents-and-abortion/bill-clinton/.

8.   "Clinton Vetoes Partial-Birth Abortion Bill."

9.   "Clinton Again Vetoes Abortion Ban," CNN, October 10, 1997, http://www.cnn.com/ALLPOLITICS/1997/10/10/lateterm.abortion/.

10. Conor Friedersdorf, "Why Dr. Kermit Gosnell's Trial Should Be a Front-Page Story," *Atlantic*, April 12, 2013, http://www.theatlantic.com/national/archive/2013/04/why-dr-kermit-gosnells-trial-should-be-a-front-page-story/274944/.

11. Jon Hurdle, "Abortion Doctor's Murder Trial Opens," *New York Times*, March 18, 2013, http://www.nytimes.com/2013/03/19/us/philadelphia-abortion-doctors-murder-trial-opens.html?_r=1.

12. "Planned Parenthood Statement on Gosnell Verdict," press release, Planned Parenthood, May 13, 2013, http://plannedparenthood.org/about-us/newsroom/press-releases/planned-parenthood-statement-gosnell-verdict#sthash.ZPNDLCki.dpuf.

13. Steven Ertelt, "Democrats Again Oppose Resolution Condemning Abortionist Kermit Gosnell," LifeNews.com, May 16, 2013, http://www.lifenews.com/2013/05/16/democrats-again-oppose-resolution-condemning-abortionist-kermit-gosnell/.

14. Ertelt, "House Will Vote on Bill to Ban Abortions after 20 Weeks Near Anniversary of Kermit Gosnell Conviction," LifeNews.com, May 8, 2015, http://www.lifenews.com/2015/05/08/house-will-vote-on-bill-to-ban-abortions-after-20-weeks-on-anniversary-of-kermit-gosnell-conviction/.

15. Ertelt, "Gosnell Movie 'America's Biggest Serial Killer' Will Tell Story of Abortionist Who Killed Babies Born Alive," LifeNews.com, March 31, 2014, http://www.lifenews.com/2014/03/31/gosnell-movie-americas-biggest-serial-killer-will-tell-story-of-abortionist-who-killed-babies-born-alive/.

16. "Kermit Gosnell Speaks from Prison," interview between Kathryn Jean Lopez and Ann McElhinney, *National Review*, May 22, 2015, http://www.nationalreview.com/article/418779/interviewing-kermit-gosnell-nr-interview.

17. Ibid.

18. Jim Kiertzner, "Raid on Doctor's Office After Possible Fetuses Found in Car—Was He performing Illegal Abortions?," ABC 7 WXYZ Detroit, updated October 14, 2015, http://www.wxyz.com/news/region/oakland-county/possible-fetuses-human-tissue-found-in-local-doctors-car-was-he-peforming-illegal-abortions; and E. R. Wiebe, K. J. Trouton, and E. Savoy, "Intra-cervical versus I.V. Fentanyl for Abortion," *Human Reproduction* 20, no. 7 (July 2005): http://humrep.oxfordjournals.org/content/20/7/2025.full.

19. The eviction notice is available online at http://abortiondocs.org/wp-content/uploads/2014/12/EVICTION_NOTICE_ROTH1.pdf.

20. Ertelt, "Police Raid Abortionist's Home, Find 14 Plastic Containers of Aborted Babies in His Car," LifeNews.com, October 14, 2015, http://www.lifenews.com/2015/10/14/police-raid-abortionists-home-find-14-plastic-containers-of-aborted-babies-in-his-car/.

21. The consent order for this violation and corresponding fine are available online at http://abortiondocs.org/wp-content/uploads/2013/04/Michael-A.-Roth-License-Discipline-Dec-17-2012.pdf.

22. "Michael Arthur Roth," AbortoinDocs.org, accessed October 2015, http://abortiondocs.org/clinic/abortionist/1021/?doing_wp_cron=1418073417.5054030418395996093750.

23. Ertelt, "Police Raid Abortionist's Home."

CHAPTER EIGHT: THE PARTY OF FAMILY BREAKDOWN

1. Daniel Patrick Moynihan, "The Tangle of Pathology," chapter 4 of *The Negro Family: The Case for National Action* (Washington, DC: U.S. Department of Labor Office of Policy Planning and Research, March 1965), http://www.dol.gov/oasam/programs/history/webid-meynihan.htm.

2. Bill Clinton, "I Still Believe in a Place Called Hope," transcript of 1992 nomination acceptance speech, June 16, 1992, http://www.democraticunderground.com/speeches/clinton.html.

3. Ron Haskins and Isabel Sawhil, *Creating an Opportunity Society* (Washington, DC: Brookings Institution, 2009), 15, http://www. brookings.edu/~/media/Events/2009/10/27%20opportunity%20 society/1027_opportunity_society_presentation.pdf.

4. Lisa Gartner, "For Teen Parents, Day Care Free at Area High Schools," *Washington Examiner*, December 6, 2012, http://www. washingtonexaminer.com/for-teen-parents-day-care-free-at-area-high-schools/article/2515294.

5. Sabrina Tavernise, "Visiting Nurses, Helping Mothers on the Margins," *New York Times*, March 8, 2015, http://www.nytimes. com/2015/03/09/health/program-that-helps-new-mothers-learn-to-be-parents-faces-broader-test.html?_r=0.

6. "Remarks by the President on My Brother's Keeper Initiative," transcript, WhiteHouse.gov, February 27, 2014, http://www. whitehouse.gov/the-press-office/2014/02/27/remarks-president-my-brothers-keeper-initiative.

7. Ibid.

8. Eli Saslow, "A Father's Initiative," *Washington Post*, May 16, 2015, http://www.washingtonpost.com/sf/national/2015/05/16/ a-fathers-initiative/.

9. Ibid.

10. George Will, "A Poverty of Thought," *Washington Post*, September 13, 2005, http://www.washingtonpost.com/wp-dyn/content/ article/2005/09/12/AR2005091201260.html.

11. "Remarks by the President on My Brother's Keeper Initiative."

12. Shelby Steele, *White Guilt: How Blacks and Whites Together Destroyed the Civil Rights Era* (New York: Harper Perennial, 2007), 148.

CHAPTER NINE: THE PARTY OF RACIAL DIVISION

1. Dan Merica, "Martin O'Malley's Criminal Justice Plan: Abolish Death Penalty, Reclassify Marijuana," CNN, July 31, 2015, http:// linkis.com/www.cnn.com/2015/07/KmQKm.

2. Clarence Thomas, *My Grandfather's Son* (New York: HarperCollins, 2008), 99.

3. Ibid., 142.

4. Andrew Kaczynski, "Democratic Congressman Makes Shocking Racial Comments about Republicans, Clarence Thomas, Mitch McConnell," BuzzFeed, April 29, 2014, http://www.buzzfeed.com/andrewkaczynski/democratic-congressman-makes-shocking-racial-comments-about#.yn3xojKk1n.

5. Bob Grant, "Press Approves of Racist Attack on Condoleezza Rice," Newsmax, November 12, 2002, available online at http://www.freerepublic.com/focus/f-news/787453/posts.

6. Ibid.

7. Kaczynski, "Democratic Congressman Makes Shocking Racial Comments about Republicans."

8. Ibid.

9. "Presidential Vote by Groups," Gallup, accessed February 17, 2015, http://www.gallup.com/poll/139880/election-polls-presidential-vote-groups.aspx.

10. "Mia Love's Interview with CNN, 05-01-2012," YouTube video, uploaded by "mialoveinterviews," May 7, 2012, https://www.youtube.com/watch?v=ZORxRGGhp_U.

11. "Voter Identification Laws," video of Congressional Black Caucus Panel Discussion, C-SPAN, September 20, 2012, http://www.c-span.org/video/?308294-1/voter-identification-laws.

12. Danielle Belton, "About Last Night: Live Tweeting the State of the Union," NBCBLK, NBC News, January 20, 2015, http://www.nbcnews.com/news/nbcblk/about-last-night-live-tweeting-state-union-n290111.

13. Ashley Killough, "NAACP Leader Compares Tim Scott to 'Dummy' for Tea Party 'Ventriloquist,'" CNN, January 21, 2014, http://politicalticker.blogs.cnn.com/2014/01/21/naacp-leader-compares-tim-scott-to-dummy-for-tea-party-ventriloquist/.

14. Ben Terris, "The Undercover Senator: Tim Scott Goes Anecdote Shopping in South Carolina," Washington Post, May 7, 2014, http://www.washingtonpost.com/lifestyle/style/the-undercover-senator-sen-tim-scott-goes-anecdote-shopping-in-south-carolina/2014/05/06/98e534b0-cbb9-11e3-93eb-6c0037dde2ad_story.html.

15. Rich Morin, "The Politics and Demographics of Food Stamp Recipients," Pew Research Center, July 12, 2013, http://www.pewresearch.org/fact-tank/2013/07/12/the-politics-and-demographics-of-food-stamp-recipients/; and Michael W. Chapman, "White

Unemployment 5.3%—Black Unemployment 11.4%," CNS News, September 5, 2014, http://cnsnews.com/news/article/michael-w-chapman/white-unemployment-53-black-unemployment-114.

16. Terris, "The Undercover Senator."

17. Crystal Wright, "Barack Obama Has Done Zero for Black People," *Telegraph* (UK), August 3, 2015, http://www.telegraph.co.uk/news/worldnews/barackobama/11779946/Barack-Obama-has-done-zero-for-black-people.html.

18. Hal Boedeker, "Trump: Jeb Has Weak Tone," *Orlando Sentinel*, August 2, 2015, http://www.orlandosentinel.com/entertainment/tv/tv-guy/os-trump-jeb-has-weak-tone-20150802-post.html.

19. "#CBC114 Butterfield Speech Text," *Crew of 42* (blog), January 7, 2015, http://www.crewof42.com/news/cbc114-butterfield-speech-text/#sthash.7IYOLTS9.hDV763by.dpuf.

20. Ibid.

21. Keli Goff, "Could Gay Marriage Spur Black Voter Drop?," *Blogging the Beltway* (blog), The Root, September 17, 2012, http://www.theroot.com/blogs/blogging_the_beltway/2012/09/emanuel_cleaver_on_why_gay_marriage_could_cost_obama_black_votes.html?wpisrc=root_lightbox.

22. Ibid.

23. "Who Lives in Federally Assisted Housing?," *Housing Spotlight* 2, no. 2 (November 2012): http://nlihc.org/sites/default/files/HousingSpotlight2-2.pdf.

24. Erica Goode, "Incarceration Rates for Blacks Have Fallen Sharply, Report Says," *New York Times*, February 27, 2013, http://www.nytimes.com/2013/02/28/us/incarceration-rates-for-blacks-dropped-report-shows.html?_r=0.

25. "Wealth Inequality between Blacks and Whites Worsens," CNNMoney, February 27, 2013, http://money.cnn.com/2013/02/27/news/economy/wealth-whites-blacks/index.html.

26. "Blacks and the Democratic Party," FactCheck.org, April 18, 2008, http://www.factcheck.org/2008/04/blacks-and-the-democratic-party/.

27. Bruce Bartlett, *Wrong on Race* (New York: Palgrave Macmillan, 2009), 152.

28. Ibid., 75.

29. Ibid., 157.

30. David Barton, *Setting the Record Straight: American History in Black and White* (Aledo, TX: Wallbuilder, 2004), 79–80.

31. Ibid., 61–67.

32. Ibid.

33. Simeon Booker and Carol McCabe Booker, *Shocking the Conscience: A Reporter's Account of the Civil Rights Movement* (Jackson: University Press of Mississippi, 2013), 236.

34. Bruce Drake, "Incarceration Gap Widens Between Whites and Blacks," Pew Research Center, September 6, 2013, http://www.pewresearch.org/fact-tank/2013/09/06/incarceration-gap-between-whites-and-blacks-widens/.

35. "Percent of High School Dropouts (Status Dropouts) among Persons 16 to 24 Years Old, by Sex and Race/Ethnicity: 1960–2003," Digest of Education Statistics, http://nces.ed.gov/programs/digest/d04/tables/dt04_107.asp.

36. "High School Graduation Rates," Digest of Education Statistics, http://nces.ed.gov/programs/coe/indicator_coi.asp.

37. These statistics come from the U.S. Census. See, for example, "School Enrollment, October 1964," *Population Characteristics*, no. 148, https://www.census.gov/hhes/school/data/cps/1964/p20-148.pdf.

38. Ben Casselman, "Race Gap Narrows in Enrollment, but Not in Graduation," 538, April 30, 2014, http://fivethirtyeight.com/features/race-gap-narrows-in-college-enrollment-but-not-in-graduation/.

39. "Graduation Rates of First-Time, Full-Time Bachelor's Degree-Seeking Students at 4-Year Postsecondary Institutions, by Race/Ethnicity, Time to Completion, Sex, and Control of Institution: Selected Cohort Entry Years, 1996 through 2006," Digest of Education Statistics, http://nces.ed.gov/programs/digest/d13/tables/dt13_326.10.asp.

40. George Akerlof and Janet Yellin, "An Analysis of Out-of-Wedlock Births in the United States," Brookings Institution, August 1996, http://www.brookings.edu/research/papers/1996/08/childrenfamilies-akerlof.

41. Brady Hamilton et al., "Births: Preliminary Data for 2012," *National Vital Statistics Report*, 62, no. 3., (Centers for Disease Control, September 6, 2013): http://www.cdc.gov/nchs/data/nvsr/nvsr62/nvsr62_03.pdf.

42. Shelby Steele, *White Guilt: How Blacks and Whites Together Destroyed the Civil Rights Era* (New York: Harper Perennial, 2007), 124.

43. Jamilah Lemieux, "O'Malley Debuts Criminal Justice Reform Plan (Interview)," Ebony.com, July 31, 2015, http://www.ebony.com/news-views/omalley-debuts-criminal-justice-reform-plan-interview-503#ixzz3hrrlmpzi.

CHAPTER TEN: THE PARTY OF IDENTITY POLITICS

1. See http://www.democrats.org/.

2. A. J. Delgado, "Democrats Throw Black Voters under the Bus," *National Review*, July 9, 2014, http://www.nationalreview.com/article/382338/black-americans-true-casualties-amnesty-j-delgado.

3. "About theGrio," theGrio, accessed March 4, 2015, http://thegrio.com/about/.

4. "About Us," Root, accessed March 4, 2015, http://www.theroot.com/articles/politics/2012/11/about_us.html.

5. "About Us," Politic365, accessed March 4, 2015, http://politic365.com/about/.

6. Isabel Wilkerson, "'African-American' Favored by Many of America's Blacks," *New York Times*, January 31, 1989, http://www.nytimes.com/1989/01/31/us/african-american-favored-by-many-of-america-s-blacks.html.

7. Ibid.

8. Library of Congress, "African-American History Month," updated July 31, 2015, http://www.loc.gov/law/help/commemorative-observations/african-american.php.

9. Carter G. Woodson, *The Mis-Education of the Negro*, first published in 1933, available online at http://historyisaweapon.com/defcon1/misedne.html.

10. "Nike 2015 BHM Collection," Nike.com, http://www.nike.com/us/en_us/launch/c/2015-01/nike-2015-bhm-collection.

11. "Frito-Lay Celebrates Black History Month By 'Calling All Artists' for a Chance to Win a Grand Prize of $10,000," press release, PR Newswire, February 4, 2015, http://www.prnewswire.com/news-releases/frito-lay-celebrates-black-history-month-by-calling-all-artists-for-a-chance-to-win-a-grand-prize-of-10000-300030436.html;

"American Airlines Proudly Celebrates Black History Month," press
release, PR Newswire, February 2, 2015, http://hub.aa.com/en/nr/
pressrelease/american-airlines-proudly-celebrates-black-history-
month; "Macy's Salutes the Culture-Defining Soul Era of Black Style
in Celebration of Black History Month 2015," press release, Business
Wire, January 29, 2015, http://www.businesswire.com/news/
home/20150129005179/en/Macy%E2%80%99s-Salutes-Culture-
Defining-Soul-Era-Black-Style#.Vh6MuBNViko; "Colgate-Palmolive
and Family Dollar Partner to Celebrate Black History Month," press
release, PR Newswire, February 4, 2015, http://www.prnewswire.
com/news-releases/colgate-palmolive-and-family-dollar-partner-to-
celebrate-black-history-month-300029832.html; and "Sony Movie
Channel Celebrates Black History Month with a Special Programming
Block Mondays at 10 P.M. ET in February," press release, PR
Newswire, January 30, 2015, http://www.prnewswire.com/news-
releases/sony-movie-channel-celebrates-black-history-month-with-a-
special-programming-block-mondays-at-10-pm-et-in-february-
300028668.html.

12.   Chris Isidore, "African-American CEOs Still Rare," CNNMoney,
      March 22, 2012, http://money.cnn.com/2012/03/22/news/companies/
      black-ceo/.

13.   Ibid.

14.   Gregory Wallace, "Only 5 Black CEOs at America's 500 Biggest
      Companies," CNNMoney, January 29, 2015, http://money.cnn.
      com/2015/01/29/news/economy/mcdonalds-ceo-diversity/index.html.

15.   Crystal Wright, "Black History Has Become a Commodity Traded by
      Republicans and Corporations," *Guardian* (UK), February 10, 2014,
      http://www.theguardian.com/commentisfree/2014/feb/10/republicans-
      jump-on-black-history-month.

16.   Valerie Jarrett, "Kicking Off Black History Month at the White
      House: #BlackHistoryMonth," *White House Blog*, February 3, 2015,
      http://www.whitehouse.gov/blog/2015/02/03/kicking-black-history-
      month-white-house-blackhistorymonth.

17.   Seung Min Kim, "Senate Confirms Loretta Lynch as Attorney
      General," *Politico*, April 23, 2015, http://www.politico.com/
      story/2015/04/loretta-lynch-confirmation-soon-117278.
      html#ixzz3YAUQxbIG.

18. Valerie Jarrett, "Meeting with African American Leaders at the White House," *White House Blog*, November 10, 2011, https://www. whitehouse.gov/blog/2011/11/10/african-american-policy-conference.

19. "Readout of the President's Meeting with African-American Faith Leaders," press release, WhiteHouse.gov, August 26, 2013, https:// www.whitehouse.gov/the-press-office/2013/08/26/readout-president-s-meeting-african-american-faith-leaders.

20. "Readout of the President's Meeting with African American Civil Rights and Faith Leaders," press release, WhiteHouse.gov, February 26, 2015, https://www.whitehouse.gov/the-press-office/2015/02/26/readout-presidents-meeting-african-american-civil-rights-and-faith-leade.

21. "Panel Examines Zimmerman Trial Outcome," clip of the July 14, 2013, episode of *Meet the Press*, NBC News, http://www.nbcnews. com/video/meet-the-press/52472656#52472656.

22. Kevin Sheehan and Carl Campanile, "Garner's Kid on Sharpton: He's All about the Money," *New York Post*, February 24, 2015, http:// nypost.com/2015/02/24/eric-garners-daughter-on-al-sharpton-hes-all-about-the-money/.

23. Ibid.

24. "About," National Action Network, http://nationalactionnetwork. net/about/.

25. "Eric Garner and Trayvon Martin Families, Michael Brown's Lawyer, and Others Accuse Al Sharpton of Exploiting Their Tragedies in New James O'Keefe Video," Project Veritas, February 23, 2015, http:// projectveritas.com/posts/news-blog-media-video/eric-garner-and-trayvon-martin-families-michael-brown%E2%80%99s-lawyer-and.

26. Joseph P. Fried, "Hoping Brawley Thinks of 'Damage She Caused,'" *New York Times*, March 2, 2003, http://www.nytimes. com/2003/03/02/nyregion/following-up.html.

27. Sho Wills, "Tawana Brawley Starts Paying Man She Falsely Accused of Rape in 1987," CNN, August 5, 2013, http://www.cnn. com/2013/08/04/justice/new-york-brawley-settlement/index.html.

28. Wright, "Racism Today Is All in the Hustle," *Conservative Black Chick* (blog), February 28, 2014, http://conservativeblackchick.com/ blog/2014/02/18/racism-today-is-all-in-the-hustle/.

29. Russ Buettner, "As Sharpton Rose, So Did His Unpaid Taxes," *New York Times*, November 18, 2014, http://www.nytimes.com/2014

/11/19/nyregion/questions-about-al-sharptons-finances-accompany-his-rise-in-influence.html?_r=2.

30. Michelle Ye Hee Lee, "Giuliani's Claim the White House Invited Al Sharpton Up to 85 Times," *Fact Checker* (blog), *Washington Post*, December 30, 2014, http://www.washingtonpost.com/blogs/fact-checker/wp/2014/12/30/giulianis-claim-the-white-house-invited-al-sharpton-up-to-85-times/.

31. Dionne Buxton, "Michael Eric Dyson on Jay-Z Georgetown University Course," MTV Rap Fix, October 10, 2011, http://rapfix.mtv.com/2011/10/10/michael-eric-dyson-on-jay-z-georgetown-university-course/.

32. Chris Richards, "Hoyas and Hova—Georgetown Sociology Course Focuses on Rap Star Jay-Z," *Washington Post*, November 2, 2011, http://www.washingtonpost.com/lifestyle/style/hoyas-and-hova--georgetown-sociology-course-focuses-on-rap-star-jay-z/2011/11/01/gIQA0KLkgM_story.html.

33. Shelby Steele, *White Guilt: How Blacks and Whites Together Destroyed the Civil Rights Era* (New York: Harper Perennial, 2007), 60.

34. Ibid., 57.

35. Dinesh D'Souza, *Letters to a Young Conservative* (New York: Basic Books, 2002), 114–15.

36. Sam Stein, "Ivy League Faculty Giving Democratic, More Heavily than Ever," Huffington Post, March 28, 2008, http://www.huffingtonpost.com/2007/11/12/ivy-league-faculty-giving_n_72300.html.

37. "Courses for Spring 2015," Brown University Africana Studies Department, accessed March 5, 2015, http://www.brown.edu/academics/africana-studies/courses.

38. "Spring 2015," Dartmouth University African and African-American Studies Department, accessed March 5, 2015, http://aaas.dartmouth.edu/undergraduate/courses/spring-2015.

39. Ibid.

40. "Spring 2015 Courses," Columbia University Institute for Research in African American Studies, accessed March 5, 2015, http://www.iraas.com/node/383.

41. "Courses," Cornell University Africana Studies and Research Center, accessed March 5, 2015, http://www.asrc.cornell.edu/courses/index. cfm.

42. "Spring 2015 Courses," Princeton University Center for African-American Studies, accessed March 5, 2015, http://www.princeton. edu/africanamericanstudies/undergraduate/courses/.

43. Ibid.

44. "The Undergraduate Major in African-American Studies," Yale University Department of African-American Studies, accessed March 5, 2015, http://afamstudies.yale.edu/academics/undergraduate-major-african-american-studies.

45. Wright, "DC Mayor Bowser Appoints Black Director to Help Her Address Black Concerns," *Conservative Black Chick* (blog), February 6, 2015, http://conservativeblackchick.com/blog/2015/02/06/dcs-mayor-bowser-appoints-black-director-to-help-her-address-black-concerns/.

CHAPTER ELEVEN: THE PARTY OF BIGOTRY AND LOW EXPECTATIONS

1. Simeon Booker, *Shocking the Conscience* (Oxford: University Press of Mississippi, 2013), 252.

2. Ibid.

3. "Inaccurate, Costly, and Inefficient: Evidence That America's Voter Registration System Needs an Upgrade," Pew Charitable Trusts, February 14, 2012, http://www.pewtrusts.org/en/research-and-analysis/reports/2012/02/14/inaccurate-costly-and-inefficient-evidence-that-americas-voter-registration-system-needs-an-upgrade.

4. Robert D. Popper, "Political Fraud about Voter Fraud," *Wall Street Journal*, April 27, 2014, http://www.wsj.com/articles/SB1000142405 2702303380004579521603120225572.

5. Byron York, "When 1,099 Felons Vote in Race Won by 312," *Washington Examiner*, August 6, 2012, http://www.washington examiner.com/york-when-1099-felons-vote-in-race-won-by-312-ballots/article/2504163.

6. Jesse Richman and David Earnest, "Could Non-Citizens Decide the November Election?," *Washington Post*, October 24, 2014, http://

www.washingtonpost.com/blogs/monkey-cage/wp/2014/10/24/could-non-citizens-decide-the-november-election/.

7. Ed Meese and Ken Blackwell, "Holder's Legacy of Racial Politics," *Wall Street Journal*, September 28, 2014, http://www.wsj.com/articles/ed-meese-and-j-kenneth-blackwell-holders-legacy-of-racial-politics-1411945138.

8. Oral argument, *Shelby County v. Holder*, Washington, DC, February 27, 2013, http://www.supremecourt.gov/oral_arguments/argument_transcripts/12-96.pdf.

9. Kerry Picket, "Flashback: Obama Claims Voter ID Laws Do Not Stop 'Our Folks' from Voting," Daily Caller, March 7, 2015, http://dailycaller.com/2015/03/07/flashback-obama-claims-voter-id-laws-do-not-stop-our-folks-from-voting/?utm_campaign=true.

10. Dan Merica, "Hillary Clinton Speech Fans 2016 Speculation," CNN, August 13, 2013, http://www.cnn.com/2013/08/13/politics/clinton-2016-speculation/.

11. "Amid Lawsuits and Controversy, States Prepare for Voter ID," *Richmond Times-Dispatch*, September 3, 2012, http://www.richmond.com/news/article_06195415-7823-5284-bce8-104e5b1fc4e6.html.

12. "The Diversifying Electorate—Voting Rates by Race and Hispanic Origin in 2012 (and Other Recent Elections)," *Population Characteristics Current Population Survey* (Washington, DC: U.S. Census Bureau, May 2013), 3, http://www.census.gov/prod/2013pubs/p20-568.pdf.

13. Meese and Blackwell, "Holder's Legacy of Racial Politics."

14. "Holder's Racial Incitement," Review and Outlook, *Wall Street Journal*, May 31, 2012, http://www.wsj.com/articles/SB10001424052702303552104577438421678904222.

15. "Remarks by the President at the National Action Network's 16th Annual Convention," transcript, WhiteHouse.gov, April 11, 2014, http://www.whitehouse.gov/the-press-office/2014/04/11/remarks-president-national-action-networks-16th-annual-convention.

16. Popper, "Political Fraud about Voter Fraud."

17. John F. Harris, "U.S. Bilingual Education Funds Ruled Out for Ebonics Speakers," *Washington Post*, December 25, 1996, http://www.washingtonpost.com/wp-srv/politics/govt/admin/stories/riley122596.htm.

18. Nanette Asimov, "Jackson Calls for Ebonics Funds," *San Francisco Chronicle*, December 31, 1996, http://www.sfgate.com/news/article/PAGE-ONE-Jackson-Calls-for-Ebonics-Funds-He-2954256.php.

19. Jack Sidnell, "African American Vernacular English," University of Hawaii, accessed March 14, 2015, http://www.hawaii.edu/satocenter/langnet/definitions/aave.html#vocab-hce.

20. Ibid.

21. Ibid.

22. "Stanford University, Fall 1996, Prof. John R. Rickford; Linguistics 73: African American Vernacular English (AAVE)," Stanford University, accessed March 14, 2015, http://web.stanford.edu/~rickford/AAVE.html.

23. John R. Rickford, "The Oakland Ebonics Decision: Commendable Attack on the Problem," *San Jose Mercury News*, December 26, 1996, http://web.stanford.edu/~rickford/ebonics/SJMN-OpEd.html.

24. Carol Cratty, Ashley Hayes, and Phil Gast, "DEA Wants to Hire Ebonics Translators," CNN, August 24, 2010, http://www.cnn.com/2010/US/08/24/dea.ebonics/index.html.

25. "Justice Department Seeks Ebonics Experts," The Smoking Gun, August 22, 2010, http://www.thesmokinggun.com/documents/bizarre/justice-department-seeks-ebonics-experts.

26. Shelby Steele, *A Dream Deferred* (New York: HarperCollins, 1999), 108.

27. Ibid.

CHAPTER TWELVE: THE PARTY OF CORRUPTION AND NEVER-ENDING EXCUSES

1. "Butterfield Takes Helm of the Congressional Black Caucus," press release and transcript of January 6, 2015, remarks, Congressman G. K. Butterfield official website, http://butterfield.house.gov/media-center/press-releases/butterfield-takes-helm-of-the-congressional-black-caucus.

2. Richard Spiropoulos, "10 Richest African Americans in Congress," *Black Enterprise*, September 16, 2014, http://www.blackenterprise.com/money/wealth-management-money/the-richest-african-americans-in-congress/4/.

3. Daniel Greenfield, "1/3 of Congressional Black Caucus Members Were Named in Ethics Probes," FrontPage Magazine, February 21, 2013, http://www.frontpagemag.com/2013/dgreenfield/13-of-congressional-black-caucus-members-were-named-in-ethics-probes/.

4. Shane Goldmacher, "Disparate Impact: Black Lawmakers and Ethics Investigations," *Atlantic*, March 3, 2012, http://www.theatlantic.com/politics/archive/2012/03/disparate-impact-black-lawmakers-and-ethics-investigations/253931/.

5. John Bresnahan, "Racial Disparity: All Active Ethics Probes Focus on Black Lawmakers," *Politico*, November 4, 2009, http://www.politico.com/story/2009/11/racial-disparity-all-active-ethics-probes-focus-on-black-lawmakers-029055.

6. Susan Crabtree, "Watchdog Comes Back to Bite Democrats," *Hill*, October 13, 2009, http://thehill.com/homenews/house/62729-dems-growl-as-watchdog-comes-back-to-bite-them.

7. Ibid.

8. "Resolution Threatens Power of Office of Congressional Ethics," editorial, *Washington Post*, June 4, 2010, http://www.washingtonpost.com/wp-dyn/content/article/2010/06/03/AR2010060304464.html.

9. Bresnahan, "Racial Disparity."

10. David Weigel, "Black Democrats against the Office of Congressional Ethics," Slate, December 3, 2010, http://www.slate.com/blogs/weigel/2010/12/03/black_democrats_against_the_office_of_congressional_ethics.html.

11. Christopher Lee, "Congressman Seeks Ethics Probe of Fundraising," *Washington Post*, July 18, 2008, http://www.washingtonpost.com/wp-dyn/content/article/2008/07/17/AR2008071701752.html.

12. Thomas Kaplan, "Rangel Fends Off Challenges to Win a Difficult Primary," *New York Times*, June 26, 2012, http://www.nytimes.com/2012/06/27/nyregion/rangel-wins-a-difficult-primary.html?pagewanted=all&_r=1&.

13. Paul Kane and David A. Fahrenthold, "House Votes to Censure Rep. Rangel," *Washington Post*, December 3, 2010, http://www.washingtonpost.com/wp-dyn/content/article/2010/12/02/AR2010120206418.html.

14. "Charles Rangel Censured on House Floor," *Washington Post*, December 2, 2010, http://www.washingtonpost.com/wp-dyn/content/article/2010/12/02/AR2010120204563.html.

15. Michael S. Schmidt, "Jesse Jackson Jr. Pleads Guilty: 'I Lived Off My Campaign,'" *New York Times*, February 20, 2013, http://www. nytimes.com/2013/02/21/us/politics/jesse-l-jackson-jr-pleads-guilty-to-wire-and-mail-fraud.html; Ryan J. Reilly, "Jesse Jackson Jr. Guilty: Former Representative and His Wife Face Prison Time," Huffington Post, February 20, 2013, http://www.huffingtonpost.com/2013/02/20/ jesse-jackson-jr-guilty_n_2724328.html; and Samantha Abernethy, "Fur Capes, Michael Jackson's Fedora, and Jesse Jackson Jr.'s Other Campaign Purchases," Chicagoist, February 16, 2013, http:// chicagoist.com/2013/02/16/fur_capes_and_michael_jacksons_fedo. php.

16. Ashley Southall, "Jesse Jackson Jr. Gets 30 Months, and His Wife 12, to Be Served at Separate Times," *New York Times*, August 14, 2013, http://www.nytimes.com/2013/08/15/us/politics/jesse-jackson-jr-sentenced-to-30-months.html.

17. "Rooting Out Corruption: A Look Back at the Jefferson Case," FBI. gov, April 9, 2013, http://www.fbi.gov/news/stories/2013/ april/a-look-back-at-the-william-j.-jefferson-corruption-case.

18. Jonathan Allen and John Bresnahan, "Ethics Office Details Charges against Maxine Waters," *Politico*, August 8, 2010, http://www. politico.com/news/stories/0810/40551.html.

19. Bresnahan, "Racial Disparity."

20. Ben Pershing, "House Ethics Panel Finds Richardson Broke Law, Obstructed Probe," *Washington Post*, August 1, 2012, http://www. washingtonpost.com/politics/rep-laura-richardson-broke-federal-law-obstructed-probe-house-ethics-panel-finds/2012/08/01/ gJQAWmmuPX_story.html.

21. "Our History," Congressional Black Caucus Foundation, accessed March 11, 2015, www.cbcfinc.org/learn-about-us/history/.

22. "What Is the Annual Legislative Conference (ALC)?," Congressional Black Caucus Foundation, accessed March 11, 2015, http://www. cbcfinc.org/annual-legislative-conference/.

23. Associated Press, "Rep. Johnson Admits to Awarding Relatives CBC Scholarships," theGrio, August 30, 2012, http://thegrio. com/2010/08/30/rep-eddie-johnson-admits-to-awarding-relatives-cbc-scholarships/.

24. Peter Flaherty, "Ethics Committee Nails Rangel on NLPC-Exposed Caribbean Junket," National Legal Policy Center, February 25, 2010,

http://nlpc.org/stories/2010/02/25/ethics-committee-nails-charles-rangel-nlpc-exposed-caribbean-junket.

25. Javier David, "Congressional Black Caucus Bogged Down by New Ethics Scandal," theGrio, August 31, 2010, http://thegrio.com/2010/08/31/congressional-black-caucus-bogged-down-by-another-ethics-scandal/.

26. Lauren French and John Bresnahan, "Black Caucus Pledges Support for Seniority," *Politico*, November 13, 2014, http://www.politico.com/story/2014/11/congressional-black-caucus-seniority-democrats-112887.html#ixzz3R0nfJzUO.

27. Ibid.

28. "Marcia Fudge (D-OH-11) US Congress Voted for Amnesty for Illegal Aliens," forum, Americans for Legal Immigration PAC, October 1, 2014, http://www.alipac.us/f34/marcia-fudge-d-oh-11-us-congress-voted-amnesty-illegal-aliens-312003/.

29. Joyce Jones, "Is Immigration Reform Bad for African-Americans?," BET, April 24, 2013, http://www.bet.com/news/politics/2013/04/24/is-immigration-reform-bad-for-african-americans.html.

30. Sheila Jackson Lee, "Selfish for Obama to Deny Illegals Amnesty, Work Permits," Breitbart, November 18, 2014, http://www.breitbart.com/big-government/2014/11/18/sheila-jackson-lee-selfish-for-america-to-deny-illegals-amnesty-work-permits/.

31. Charles Edwards, "Congressional Black Caucus Holds Jobs Tour," NPR, August 19, 2011, http://www.npr.org/2011/08/19/139799440/congressional-black-caucus-holds-jobs-tour.

32. Mike Lillis, "Top Black Dems to Skip Netanyahu Speech," *Hill*, February 5, 2015, http://thehill.com/homenews/house/231915-top-black-dems-to-skip-netanyahu-speech.

33. Ibid.

APPENDIX: A PERSONAL STORY

1. Cited as evidence in *Wright vs. Salisbury Club, LTD*, U.S. District Court for the Eastern District of Virginia, Richmond Division, Judgment Order issued October 18, 1979, p. 21.

2. U.S. District Court Eastern District of Virginia Plaintiffs' Motion for Summary Judgment, July 17, 1979.

3.   *Wright vs. Salisbury Country Club, LTD*, Appeals Brief, January 1980.
4.   *Richmond Afro-American*, July 16, 1977.
5.   Ibid.
6.   Ibid.
7.   Ibid.
8.   *New York Times*, July 12, 1977.
9.   Unknown publication, "Some Salisbury Members Launch Protest," 1977.
10. Ibid.
11. Ibid.
12. Ibid.
13. "Obenshain Also Objects, Troy in Salisbury Protest," *Richmond Times-Dispatch*, September 30, 1977.
14. "Some Salisbury Members Launch Protest."
15. *Richmond Afro-American*, July 16, 1977.
16. *Richmond Times-Dispatch*, July 16, 1977.
17. Ray McAllister, "Club Fight Tires Black Dentist," *Richmond Times-Dispatch*, June 5, 1980.
18. Ibid.
19. Ibid.
20. Ibid.
21. Ibid.

INDEX

J

K

L

O

Y

Z